# Experience India's Golden Triangle 2018

Len Rutledge

**Experience India's Golden Triangle**

**Len Rutledge**

Experience Guide Series

Copyright Len Rutledge 2015, 2016, 2017, 2018

**4th Edition**

**January 2018**

Published by Northpress

17 Saltwater Drive, Toomulla Beach, Australia 4816

ISBN-10: 1983793221
ISBN-13:978-1983793226

# CONTENTS

All Photographs by Phensri Rutledge

23 Maps

32 Pictures

## Introduction

Experience Travel Guides, the Guides the Travel Industry trust, are unique in that they are designed to be read in the same way as a novel. They are a valuable resource for those planning to visit a destination, a source of information for those just interested in finding out more about a country or city, and a pleasure for those armchair travellers who just enjoy a good read.

**Experience India's Golden Triangle** highlights the more rewarding parts of the area so that those planning a visit can quickly and efficiently plan an itinerary. We locate and detail the best places to see and the top experiences to enjoy, and recommend accommodation options in all areas. All are based on the personal experience of the author.

We capture the personality and the underlying cultural and historical significance of the region. We explore the wonderful temples, mosques, forts and museums, and recommend things to buy, eat, and experience. In the process we meet friendly, helpful people, buy fascinating handicrafts, try tantalizing cuisine, and enjoy charming hospitality.

As more people travel to new destinations, guidebooks grow in importance. Hard-copy books, however, are often out of date before they are printed and users are frustrated by experiences contrary to what is described. This book has no such problem as it was completely updated in December 2017 and can be updated as often as necessary to keep it right up to date. In addition, we post regular updates on the authors' web page.

Some people believe the internet has all the answers these days but be aware that many internet sites provide out of date or inaccurate information and many are extremely biased. We have done everything possible to ensure our information is up to date and we will continue to update the book as necessary. We also accept no advertising or sponsorship so can give an honest opinion about everything we see.

Please realise, however, that no guidebook can substitute for common sense. The Golden Triangle is a very diverse area and to see it properly requires considerable travel. This can be done by air, rail, or road and the best is probably a combination of all three. Be aware that summer can be very hot while in winter it can get very cold at night.

While many people speak English, India is very different from other English-speaking countries. It is very much an Asian country so you should be aware of the customs and traditions associated with the culture and the various religions, particularly when visiting temples and mosques.

We believe that every place in the world provides unique experiences which make a visit worthwhile. The Golden Triangle has great experiences at every turn. We encourage you to explore, meet the locals, and grab each new opportunity as it arises. Traveling is fun but always do it with care and compassion. In that way your Golden Triangle experience can provide lifetime memories.

# 1 THE GOLDEN TRIANGLE

India is a country of enormous contrasts where poverty sits beside wealth, beauty intermingles with filth, and structure and chaos compete for supremacy. It will dazzle all your senses and cause you heartache at the same time. It can be challenging and charming, overwhelming and stunningly beautiful. The eager friendliness of the people is endearing, and the food is unforgettable but there is likely to be unexpected glitches no matter how much you plan.

India is a large country and the one with the second-largest population in the world. It really is many countries all rolled into one. If you lay a map of India over a map of Europe you will see that it covers the area from Scandinavia to North Africa and from Spain to Russia. It is one of the world's oldest living civilizations yet the present nation-state is just 70 years old.

The country is perhaps the most diverse in the world. I remember reading somewhere that India has over 4000 separate ethnic groups who speak over 300 different languages and practice more than seven religions. A visitor will only slowly become aware of this.

You first notice the things that are different from your home country, then you see the differences in dress, language and food as you move to different areas, and finally, you become aware of the things that distinguish people of different castes and social classes.

India has become a popular tourist destination in recent years yet few tourists actually experience all of India in one trip. Maharashtra has traditionally been the most popular state for foreign tourists while domestic tourists visit the states of Uttar Pradesh, Andhra Pradesh, and Tamil Nadu most frequently. Chennai (formerly Madras), Delhi, Mumbai (formerly Bombay), and Agra have been the four most visited cities of India by foreign tourists.

This visitation has been responsible for the development of India's famous Golden Triangle tourist route of Delhi, Agra, and Jaipur. This is now very popular as it hosts many of India's great cultural gems, and provides a good range of landscapes and cultures. The circuit is about 1000 km by road and it is traditionally done in 6-8 days, starting from and returning to Delhi.

In fact, this route has become so popular that variations are now appearing. For those with a few extra days, it is possible to include visits to Pushkar, Jodhpur, and Udaipur as well. The most practical way to do this is to fly from Delhi to Udaipur, then travel by road back to Delhi. This involves a flight of around one hour and a little over 1000 kilometres by road.

It is equally practical doing this if you enter India at Mumbai. Simply substitute a Mumbai to Udaipur flight for the Delhi-Udaipur flight in the previous paragraph. You will end your trip in Delhi and can then travel on to another Indian destination, fly back to Mumbai, or leave the country from Delhi.

This **extended Golden Triangle** trip will take 11-13 days and is highly recommended. I have used this trip as a format for this book. **Delhi** is scattered with mosques, forts, and monuments from the Mughal period but there are also some more modern temples and other buildings. There is great contrast between rambling Old Delhi and well planned New Delhi, and it's interesting to spend time exploring both.

**Udaipur**, in Rajasthan, is sometimes called the most romantic city in India because of its famed lakes and palaces. The City Palace complex, the architecturally splendid Bagore Ki Haveli, and Lake Pichola with its beautiful Lake Palace Hotel are just some of the highlights.

**Jodhpur** is famous for its blue buildings and for the unusual pants worn by a polo team when visiting England in 1897. The impregnable Mehrangarh Fort, which rises above the city, is one of the largest forts in India. The magnificent Umaid Bhawan Palace was one of the last great palaces to be built in the country. The royal family of Jodhpur still occupies a section of it but most has been converted into a luxury hotel. Nearby Mandore was the capital of the Marwar region before Jodhpur was founded.

**Pushkar** is a sleepy little holy town that attracts a lot of backpackers and hippie types and is one of the most visited pilgrimage places in India.

Surrounding by hills on three sides, Pushkar abounds in temples and is centred on the lake which has mythological importance. Pushkar Camel Fair, Rajasthan's most famous festival, is held here late October or early November depending on the moon.

India's desert capital of **Jaipur**, known as the Pink City because of the pink walls and buildings of the old city, lures visitors with its stunning ancient palaces and forts. Nearby Amber Fort is set on a hill top overlooking Maota Lake. This was the home of Rajput royalty until Jaipur city was constructed and is now a much-enjoyed attraction. Jaipur is an excellent place to shop for gemstones, silver jewelry, bangles, clothes, blue pottery, and textiles.

There are quite a few worthwhile places to visit in **Agra** and around, apart from India's most famous monument -- the Tāj Mahal. The many interesting remnants of the Mughal era will surprise you and the crazy, congested bazaars of the Old City will fascinate you. Don't miss a visit to majestic Agra Fort, Mehtab Bagh known as the Moonlight Garden, and the tomb of Itimād-ud-Daula or 'Little Tāj'.

To fully enjoy the Golden Triangle you must know a little about the history and culture of this area. The north-west of India has seen traders and invaders entering the area through the mountains to the north for millennia. There has been a pattern of marauding armies arriving in autumn, looting the cities in winter then retreating when summer allowed access again through mountain passes.

At times some of these invaders stayed to found empires which lasted briefly or for centuries. In time, there was some absorption into the general Indian community but even today it is fascinating to see the continued survival of communities of differing racial origins.

A major change in the people who were invading came around 1000AD when Muslims arrived. Previous invaders had been at least partially absorbed into the Hindu order but the Muslims remained apart. For the next 700 years, they effectively ruled over a population that was of a different religion.

They were not the first religion to challenge Hinduism. In the 6th century BC, both Jainism and Buddhism had emerged. Both attacked some aspects of Hindu belief and for awhile Buddhism became a powerful force. But it did not last here and it is only because of adherents in other countries that Buddhism remains a force in the world.

Hinduism is an extremely complex philosophy and religion and most visitors only understand a smattering of its beliefs. One of the problems is that new ideas have generally not replaced the old; they have just been added.

So after several thousand years, there is a sprawling set of beliefs and practices that vary between areas and temples and it is difficult to pin down a neatly-arranged religion as there are hundreds of different sects and millions of major and minor deities. You can believe a variety of things about God, the universe, and the path to liberation and still be considered a Hindu.

Most visitors know that India has cows walking its streets and roads. Many believe that this is because Hindus worship cows or consider them as gods. In ancient India, oxen and bulls were sacrificed to the gods and their meat was eaten. Later, in the period that produced strictly vegetarian Jainism and highly influential Buddhism, Hindus stopped eating beef.

By the early centuries AD, the cow was designated as the appropriate gift to the Brahmans (high-caste priests) and it was soon said that to kill a cow is equal to killing a Brahman. So it is more accurate to say the cow is taboo in the Hindu religion, rather than sacred.

Another Indian feature known by many visitors is the caste system. Caste involves the division of society into groups based on a number of factors. People are born into their caste and find it difficult to escape from it during their life. The rank and caste were important in the context of Hinduism because ideas of purity were involved.

It is common to say that there are five castes; Brahmins who are priests, Kshatriyas who are soldiers and administrators, Vaishyas who are traders and merchants, Shudras who are agricultural peasants, and the Untouchables who are really outside the system altogether. In practice, however, there are thousands of castes, known as *jati*, that exist.

When I first went to India 45 years ago, the caste system was fairly obvious. Today, particularly in the cities, it is much less so. Governments have enacted laws to try to stop discrimination against people on grounds of caste. This has not entirely wiped out the system and the Untouchables are still effectively stuck at the bottom partly because of their lack of education and the traditions in the villages.

Short-term visitors are unlikely to be aware of most areas of discrimination but a notice at a Delhi Golf Club shows how some Indians still act. "Members Domestic Employees are not permitted in the club house, lounges, annexe, golf course etc. Ayahs are only allowed to sit in the demarcated area near the swings. If a member wishes to give the Ayah food, the member has to pick the food from the counter as ayahs are not allowed to do so."

Many visitors are oppressed by the poverty they see. You cannot avoid this but on the tourist route you probably don't see the worst situations. Some people react badly to this while others try to put it out of their mind. It is difficult to know what to do. You will encounter beggars in most places but visitors often give their money to professional beggars rather than those in genuine need.

Your attitude will be a very personal one but be aware that in public places giving to one will encourage a host of others to appear. Fortunately, the practice of tugging at your arm or shirt sleeve as you walk down the street has gone from most places.

One thing that I find off-putting is the filth that is found in many areas. It seems that there is no education program aimed at stopping littering so roadsides, parks, and even many tourist sites are covered in rubbish. There are papers, plastics, cans, old clothes, and much worse everywhere. It becomes more obvious when you visit the affluent suburbs of Delhi, the Taj Mahal, and some other sites which are litter free.

Another thing that grates is the way an obscenely rich minority flaunt their wealth and flout the rules while the impoverished minority seem to have an unhealthy trust in fate and hardly seem to notice.

While I dislike these things, I am prepared to tolerate them in return for the numerous sites and experiences that I find fascinating throughout this whole area. I hope this is your experience as well.

**Some words to help your visit**

Hotel – when you see this along a road between towns it means a restaurant.

Military hotel – non-vegetarian restaurant

Guru – teacher

Mandir – Hindu temple

Gurdwara – Sikh temple

Masjid – mosque

Pol – gate

Sanctum sanctorum – innermost part of temple

Aarti or arati – Hindu worship service

Ayahs – Household helper

## Costs in this book

Most costs are given in Indian rupees designated as Rs. Here is a link to a popular conversion site. http://www.xe.com/currency/inr-indian-rupee

## Maps

Maps are provided throughout the book detailing places of interest. In addition Google maps are always useful so here is the appropriate link. https://www.google.com./maps/

# 2 DELHI SIGHTSEEING

Delhi is the capital of India and the largest city by area and population. It has a population of around 18 million and is a vibrant, growing metropolis. The Delhi area has seen continuous habitation since the 6th century BC and has been a capital of various kingdoms and empires for much of that time. What you see today is mainly a combination of building over 400 years but there are some reminders of earlier occupation.

Unfortunately, there are no reliable records of the early civilizations but it is believed the earliest city was known as Indraprastha and was centred near the present day Purana Qila. According to Indian folklore, this was a magnificent and opulent city and the capital of the Pandavas Empire. Records improve by the 10th century AD and it is known that the city of Qila Rai Pithora was created by Prithviraj Chauhan in the area around Qutb Minar.

These cities were followed by Siri, Tughlakabad (now mainly washed away), Jahanpanah near Qutb Minar, Firozabad in present day New Delhi, the city around Purana Qila, and then Shahjahanabad. Each of these cities grew around the palace-fortress of a particular dynasty and every dynasty wished to have a new headquarters.

Old Delhi is basically the remains of a city called Shahjahanabad which was built in 1639 by the Mughal Emperor Shah Jahan. This was the capital of the Mughal Empire from 1649 until 1857. Much of Old Delhi is still confined within the area of the walls of this old city, and several gates still remain.

New Delhi, on the other hand, is comparatively new as it was built to the south of the old city during the 1920s. It became the national capital of India in 1947. It is here that you see young jean-clad men and women striding alongside *purdah*-clad women and smart business men in white shirts and ties. Such is the contrast in modern Delhi.

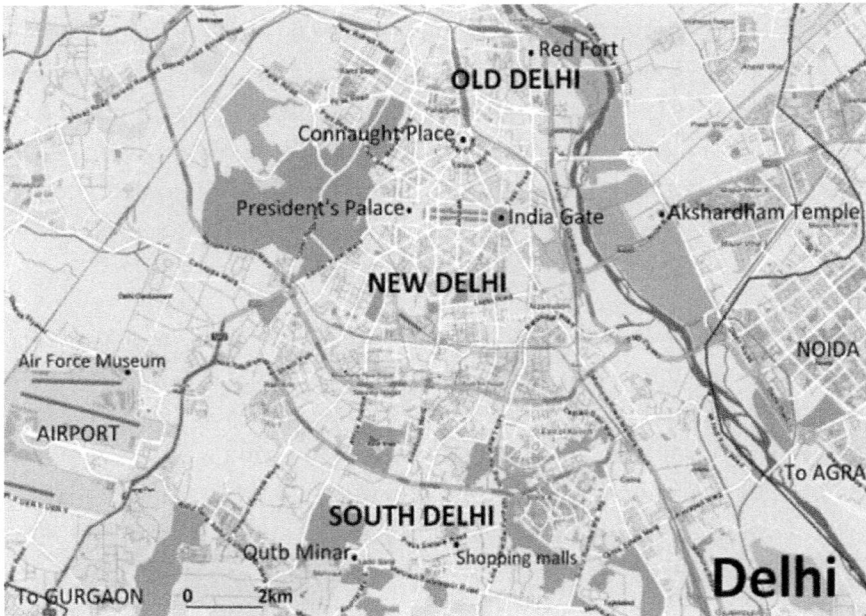

Its magnificent history and remains of lost empires place the city on a par with places like Istanbul, London, and Rome and draw an estimated 15 million visitors each year. Delhi today is a financial, medical, and education hub.

Visitors to Delhi will notice two prominent geographic features: the Yamuna River flood plain and the Delhi Ridge. The river runs to the east of Old Delhi and its flood plains are prone to recurrent floods. The Delhi

Ridge encircles the west, north-west, and north-east parts of the city providing protection from the hot westerly winds and some green lungs for the city.

Delhi has three World Heritage Sites – the Red Fort, Qutb Minar, and Humayun's Tomb–but these are only three of a long list of attractions to see. Some of the other monuments that are not to be missed are the Jama Masjid; India Gate; the Jantar Mantar, an 18th-century astronomical observatory; and the Purana Qila, a 16th-century fortress.

Several temples, office towers and government buildings are examples of modern architecture. Raj Ghat and other memorials along the river pay tribute to Mahatma Gandhi and other notable personalities.

Delhi is served by Indira Gandhi Airport to the west of the central city. This handles both international and domestic flights from two terminals that are quite some distance apart. International visitors arrive at terminal T3 and there are metro, taxi and bus connections to the city. (See chapter 10).

There are three main railway stations in the city but most trains of interest to visitors leave from the busy New Delhi Station. There are also three interstate bus terminals but the most important for the Golden Triangle area is the one north of the Old Delhi railway station near Kashmere Gate.

Once in Delhi, you can navigate the vast sprawl by metro, bus, taxi, rental car with driver, and auto-rickshaw. Local travel can also be undertaken by cycle rickshaw or by walking.

The appropriate place to start sightseeing is in Old Delhi at the **Red Fort** (http://whc.unesco.org/en/list/231).

This massive sandstone fort is a very popular sightseeing place for both foreign and local visitors. Ticket costs Rs500 for foreigners and Rs35 for locals (December 2017). Much of what was within the walls was destroyed during British rule but what is left is very interesting and well worth seeing. It was the centre of Mughal India, functioning as both a military fort and palace, and it is still used for important speeches on special occasions.

The Red Fort dates from the very peak of Mughal power when the emperors would ride out into the streets of Old Delhi on elephants in a magnificent display of pomp and power. It is still easy to picture this on a visit today.

Red Fort is protected by a massive 18 m-high wall and inside there is some outstanding architecture, shaded pathways, decent toilets, and beautiful gardens. The history behind the place is just astounding and the bazaar inside is something I did not expect. It appears that the authorities let the place go for a while and are now playing catch-up on some much-deferred maintenance.

*The Walls of Red Fort*

The major architectural features of Red Fort are in a mixed condition and all the water features around it are dried up. There are a few buildings which are still in a fair condition as their decorative elements are left undisturbed, but others are in a bad state with the old decoration being removed by looters.

A visit here will last several hours if you want to see all areas. I recommend you get the audio guide - there's a lot of information in it which makes the experience more interesting. The fort is closed Mondays.

Lahori Gate is the main entrance. The three-storey gateway in the western wall of the fort is decorated with panels and is flanked by semi-octagonal towers crowned by two open octagonal pavilions. The gate is built in red sandstone but the pavilion roofs are white. Every year since 1947, the national flag has been raised here on Indian Independence Day and the Prime Minister has made a speech from the ramparts at the gate.

Immediately beyond the gate, is the Chatta Chowk (covered bazaar) selling various souvenirs. This once sold fancy silks, jewellery, and gold that the royal household might fancy but today it is mainly down-market tourist souvenirs.

This in turn, leads to Naubat Khana, the drum house that stands at the entrance to the inner court. Musicians would announce the arrival of dignitaries here. Everyone except princes had to dismount from their elephants at this point, before entering further into the inner fort complex.

It is a three-storied rectangular structure built in red sandstone which is covered in white plaster. The carved floral designs on the walls are attractive and the interior was colourfully painted as you can see in the entrance chamber. The Indian War Memorial Museum is currently located in the first and second stories. It opens 8 a.m. to 5 p.m. Tuesday to Sunday.

Going further east, you reach the imposing Diwan-i-Am (Hall of

Audiences) where the Mughal emperor received members of the general public and heard their grievances. It consists of an open front hall backed by a set of rooms faced in red sandstone. The royal stone canopy was for the emperor while the low bench was for the prime minister.

The hall is divided into 27 square bays by columns which support the impressive façade of nine engraved arch openings. The hall was ornamented with gilded and white plaster work and its ceiling and columns were painted with gold.

Further east again, the Khas Mahal was the emperor's private residence. It consists of three parts: the Chamber of Telling Beads, the sleeping chamber, and the wardrobe or sitting room. The interior is decorated with carved white marble painted with colourful floral decorations and the ceiling was also partially gilded. A highlight is a marble screen carved with the scales of justice. Unfortunately, all this area is out of bounds to visitors at the moment.

The Mumtaz Mahal is off to the south. This is one of the six main palaces that were situated facing the Yamuna River. All six palaces were connected by the Stream of Paradise, a waterway which ran through them. It was built for Shar Jahan's favourite queen. The building consists of six apartments divided by arched piers and the interior was originally painted with floral decorations.

When the British occupied the fort, it was used as a prison camp. The building currently houses the Red Fort Archaeological Museum, consisting largely of exhibits of the Mughal period. The objects are displayed thematically in six galleries. The most interesting section is probably the gallery on Mughal miniature art and calligraphy. Photography inside is not allowed.

The Diwan-i-Khas, or Hall of Private Audiences, served a similar purpose to the Hall of Audiences except here was where the emperor received courtiers and state guests. In the past, it was more extensive but today it consists of a rectangular central chamber, surrounded by a series of arches rising from marble piers.

The original silver and gold ceiling is long gone. The current ceiling was installed in 1911. The spectacular solid gold Peacock throne which sat here was taken by Nadir Shah of Persia in 1739 although the marble pedestal on which it sat remains. The hall today is, therefore, only a shell of what it used to be.

Immediately to the north-west is the Moti Masjid (Pearl Mosque) a white marble mosque built by Emperor Aurangzeb in 1659. The prayer hall is roofed with three bulbous domes, which were originally covered in copper. The white outer walls align with the walls of the fort, while the inner walls align with the location of Mecca. As with most mosques, there is an ablution fountain in the courtyard. The floor of the prayer-hall is inlaid with outlines of small carpets for prayers.

The Fort's nightly **Sound and Light show** (except Mondays) provides a chance to relive the history of Delhi and the Mughal Empire. You can watch the recreation of 300 years of India's history as the Fort is illuminated with special light effects and animated with accompanying music and narration. The 60-minute show is popular with visitors.

You hear how a king's daughter was reduced to a maid in the town of Hastinapur and how King Prithviraj Chauhan elopes with a beautiful woman. We also heard of the legendary rule of Razia Sultana - the only woman ruler of both the Sultanate and the Mughal periods. Entry is Rs80 for adults and Rs30 for children.

On leaving the fort, we enter **Chandni Chowk** one of the oldest and busiest markets in Old Delhi, Built in the 17th century by Shāh Jahān, and supposedly designed by his daughter, Jahan Ara, the market was originally built in a half-moon shaped pattern. It was once famous for its silver merchants and some can still be found here now.

The street called Chandni Chowk runs through the middle of Old Delhi, from the Lahori (Lahore) Gate to the Fatehpuri Masjid. A canal once ran down its middle as a part of the water supply scheme. Even though Chandni Chowk is choked with congestion today, it retains its historical character. In fact, it offers a full medieval bazaar experience complete with bullock and hand carts, and a cacophony of noise. It is bustling with activity as everybody goes about their business.

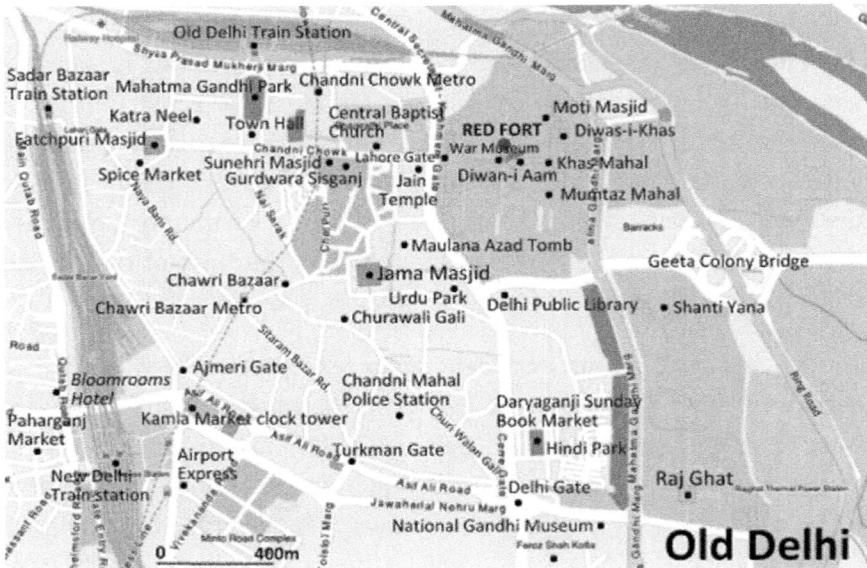

Overhead, a thousand electricity cables are strung haphazardly above the myriad garbage-littered alleyways. Passing cycle rickshaws are tightly packed with pint-size children in uniform on the way to school or wide-hipped matrons on a shopping expedition. Motorcycles mix with labourers carrying huge loads on their shoulders. There is really something special about this place but those put off by crowds should visit before 8 a.m.

The street is home to several famous restaurants/confectioners. It's a crowded street and you have to be careful about your wallet and other valuables. The roads off here are crowded, dirty, and many are rough.

Different streets and areas specialise in different things. If you plunge into the many narrow lanes you will find shops selling books, clothing, shoes, leather goods, electronic and consumer goods, and more.

Dariba Kalan is the place to look for pearls, gold and silver jewellery, and natural perfumes. Khari Baoli is a paradise for the spice-lover while Chawri Bazaar will meet all your paper needs. Nearby Churiwali Gali is the lane of bangle sellers.

Kinari Bazaar is the best place to look for tinsel trimmings. The cloth bazaar of Katra Neel offers all kinds of fabrics while Bhagirath Palace is Asia's largest market for electrical goods. Moti Bazaar has thousands of shawls and is another place to look for pearls.

This whole area is either awful or great depending on your point of view. It is certainly not for the faint-hearted but for those who persist, there is never a dull moment! A rickshaw ride is great if pressed for time but make it clear to the driver that you want "no shops" from the start. The Spice Market is amazing - climb the stairs all the way to the roof for some interesting photos.

Chandni Chowk has several religious shrines, belonging to coexisting religions which should give you some insight into the complications of India. Starting from the Red Fort, you first see the **Sri Digambar Jain Lai Mandir**, established in 1656, which has a bird hospital to further the principle of preserving all life.

Next is the Christian **Central Baptist Church** built in 1814 and probably the oldest Christian mission in the whole of the northern Indian region. It is a fine example of European architecture of that time.

The Sikh **Gurdwara Sis Ganj Sahib** marks the spot where the 9th Sikh Guru was executed by the Mughals in 1675 A.D. The *Gurdwaras* in the form of memorials were built in 1783 after Delhi was captured by the Khalsa.

The Muslim **Sunehri Masjid** built in 1721 is barely visible from the street but it has a bloody history. This is where the Persian invader Nadir Shar spent several hours on the top of the mosque observing the killing that he had ordered which resulted in 30,000 deaths. Its signature gilded copper domes are today overshadowed by the surrounding buildings. The mosque stands on a 2 m-high platform with a narrow staircase leading to the first of three marble courtyards.

Finally, we reach the Muslim **Fatehpuri Masjid** which was built by Fatehpuri Begum in 1650, one of the queens of Shah Jahan. Immediately north of here, on Khari Baoli, are the **spice markets**. This is the largest such market in Asia and it is fascinating. The market started in the 17th century and it might appear shabby and disorganized, but, you will soon realize that this place is highly organized. It is crowded with traders, and shoppers looking for the cheapest deals and bargains.

There are hundreds of shops dealing in refined, local and exotic spices on the main road and down tiny, narrow alleys. The market area is rich in colour and photographic opportunities but don't leave before you get up onto the roof of one of the buildings. From here you get a good view of the wider market area and back towards the Red Fort.

Some readers will be interested in searching out the **Mirza Ghalib Haveli** where the poet Mirza Ghalib lived and worked during the decline of the Mughal Empire. To reach it, you take Charkhiwalan Gali south from Chandni Chowk then find Gali Qasim Jan to the right. The former home's ground floor is now restored as a Ghalib Memorial and is open to visitors from 11 am to 6 pm on all days except Monday.

The restoration which was carried out about 20 years ago included using Mughal Lakhori bricks, sandstone, and a wooden entrance gate and this has created something of the late 19th century. It's not outstanding but makes an interesting visit in this amazingly crowded area.

South of all this jumble, is the **Tomb of Maulana Azad** and the Jama Masjid. Azad was a freedom fighter who chose not to migrate to

Pakistan following the Indian partition. The first education minister of a free India, he died in 1958. The tomb is marked by a white marble canopy which is said to be derived from the central arch of the Jama Masjid. Unfortunately, it is not well cared for.

The **Jama** **Masjid** (http://www.archive.india.gov.in/knowindia/culture_heritage.php?id=4 6) is the largest mosque in India, with a huge courtyard. It was begun in 1644 and ended up being the final architectural extravagance of Shāh Jahān, the Mughal emperor who built the Tāj Mahal and the Red Fort.

*Jama Masjid*

This is a highly decorative mosque with three gates, four towers, and two 40 m-high minarets with distinctive strips of red sandstone and white marble. Three black and white marble domes surmount the prayer hall.

Three flights of red sandstone steps lead to the courtyard of the mosque. Each of the covered colonnades has a lofty gateway in the centre. A hall with seven arched entrances is under the striking domes and beyond this is a prayer hall with eleven arched entrances. The floor of the mosque has imitation Moslem prayer mats outlined in black on the white marble.

The mosque is closed to non-Muslim visitors during prayer times. Cameras are allowed, with a supposedly ridiculous charge of Rs300 for foreign tourists (even for your mobile phone camera). One of the main attractions is to climb one of its minarets to the highest level and get a great 360 degrees aerial view of the mosque and the city. The view is worth the climb.

There seems to be much confusion with visitors regarding the entry fee, shoe fee, and camera fee, and tourists, particularly foreigners, are harassed on these counts. In fact, the whole thing looks like a highly organised con which is participated in by many guides. Entry to the mosque is supposed to be free and there is no official shoe fee. It costs Rs100 to climb the minaret.

Foreign women will probably be forced to wear a robe for which you will be charged a fee. This is unnecessary unless you are in shorts or have bare shoulders and you will see locals wearing less than some foreigners. This whole hassle with costs leaves a bad impression with many visitors and it needs to be eliminated.

There is a more recent historic spot close by that is rarely visited by visitors. A temple-like pavilion in Ramlila Maidan was built by Prime Minister Jawaharlal Nehru in 1961 for Queen Elizabeth II. It was here, in 2011, that activist Anna Hazare fasted for 12 days, forcing Parliament to endorse his demand for strong anti-corruption legislation.

In 1975, socialist leader Jayaprakash Narayan opposed various orders of Prime Minister Indira Gandhi, prompting her to impose 'Emergency' the same night. In early 2014, this same rostrum hosted yoga guru Baba Ramdev, who sat alongside Narendra Modi, the present Prime Minister.

After visiting the mosque and park we walk east beside the southern wall of the Red Fort to the large parkland beside the Yamuna River. This is where there are several memorials to important recent Indian leaders. The first one we come to is to Jawaharlal Nehru, the first Prime Minister of independent India, and then we see the one to Indira Ghandi, who was assassinated. Further south is the one considered most important of all.

**Raj                                                              Ghat**
(http://www.delhitourism.gov.in/delhitourism/tourist_place/memorial_delhi.jsp) is a black marble platform that marks the spot of Mahatma Gandhi's cremation, in 1948, a day after his assassination. It has an eternal flame which burns perpetually at one end. You need to remove your footwear before entering the Raj Ghat walls. There are both free and paid areas for shoes. In general, locals use the free area while foreigners are steered towards the paid area.

Gandhi is known as the Father of India for his tireless and pacifist work to obtain India's independence from Britain. Every Friday, the day of his death, a memorial ceremony is held. The structure is surrounded by a beautiful park with labelled trees planted by various world leaders. Two museums dedicated to Gandhi are nearby.

The **Gandhi Smriti** (http://gandhismriti.gov.in/indexb.asp), housed in the Old Birla House is the place where Mahatma Gandhi died on 30 January 1948 and where he lived for the last 144 days of his life. It is across the road from Raj Ghat. There are four pavilions, a film auditorium, a children's corner and a library.

At the main entrance is a statue of Gandhi, with a boy and a girl holding a dove in their hands, emerging out of the globe, symbolises his universal concern for the poor and the deprived.

The museum in the building houses a number of articles associated with Gandhi's life and death. Visitors can tour the building and grounds, viewing the preserved room where Gandhi lived and the place on the grounds where he was shot while taking his nightly public walk. It is open 10 a.m. to 5 p.m. but is closed Mondays. A multi-media show is held between 1 p.m. and 1:30 p.m.

The **National Gandhi Museum** (http://gandhimuseum.org/site/) is a block or so to the west showcasing his life and principles. The imposing two storey museum which was formally inaugurated in 1961 has a large number of paintings and personal items of his.

A short way to the south is **Feroz Shah Kotla**. In 1354, Sultan Feroz Shah Tughlaq established the city of Firozabad and Feroz Shah Kotla is the core of that extensive development. The walls of the citadel are up to 15 metres high and have a slight slope on the outside. The top parapets have now disappeared but the arrow slits can still be seen.

A highlight is the Pyramidaal Structure, a three-storey building which was specially commissioned by Feroz Shah to support the 13m-high Ashoka pillar set up by the great Mauryan Emperor Ashoka and containing several edicts regarding Ashoka's principles of government inscribed on it. Many classical concerts have been held here in the past. You may see believers praying, lighting candles, and writing letters to supernatural creatures of Islamic mythology in the alcoves of its stone walls.

The citadel is next to a famous cricket ground with the same name established in 1883 which is the second oldest international cricket stadium still functional in India. If you attend a game here you will get the flavour of the real India. Tickets are cheap, and you'll find yourself next to a range of locals who will likely invite you to share their food and their lives!

Continuing to the west we come to **Delhi Gate**, the most southern and largest gate in the historic walled city of Shahjahanabad. The gate now links New Delhi city with the old walled city. The impressive sandstone structure stands in the middle of the road and was built by Emperor Shah Jahan in 1638.

Here too is **Shri Shiv Mandir**, perhaps the most simple and beautiful

Hindu temple in Delhi. It is so small that you can walk around it in two minutes but it is true to the Hindu idea that you can find God in a pebble. It has no stately flight of stairs, no imposing tower of stone but the principal praying room is quiet, dark, and has a cluster of gods, and a giant *peepal* tree stretches upwards through the roof. A small staircase lets you climb onto the roof to watch the surrounding city life.

Old Delhi's greatly diminished boundary wall once had 14 gateways but now only four survive. Further west again is **Turkman Gate**, named after Hazrat Shah Turkman Bayabani. His tomb, dated to 1240, is located to the east of the gate. The gate is flanked by a police post and the multi-storeyed Delhi Stock Exchange. In 1905, a beautiful Byzantine church with a succession of white domes, topped with lantern-like structures, was built here.

Finally, we come to **Ajmeri Gate**, built in 1644 and now surrounded by a lovely park. Diagonally opposite is Ghazi-ud-Din's Tomb and Madrassa. The 17th century imposing red sandstone madrassa was at one time Delhi's most important, and there is a mosque on its western side. Close by is the maniacally busy **New Delhi Railway Station**.

If we cross under the railway we reach **Paharganj**, Delhi's backpacker ghetto. It has become the area of choice for low-budget foreign tourists in Delhi, though, with rising congestion, the proliferation of illegal bars and illegal activities, Paharganj has also become a hotspot for crime and a criminal hideout. There are lots of scam artists and touts along Main Bazar Road.

The narrow alleys can be intimidating, but if you stick mostly to the main thoroughfares you will have a feast for the senses - wonderful shops and restaurants (all cheap), and an exciting vibe. You can easily experience the daily life of a very typical Indian neighbourhood if you keep your wits about you. There are a number of rooftop cafes that provide some relief from the chaos below.

The fourth surviving Old Delhi gateway is in the north of the old city.

During the siege of Delhi in 1857, the British mounted the final assault at **Kashmere Gate**. A plaque on the western side commemorates those who died. The once gracious shops fronting the arch are now shabby and dilapidated. The nearby Kashmere Gate Metro station with an infrastructure of five floors and links with three Metro lines is one of the biggest Delhi Metro stations.

Just to the south is the delightful **St. James's Church** one of the oldest churches in Delhi. It is built in the shape of a Greek cross surmounted by an imposing dome. Unlike a few other Delhi churches, the church is modest and the surroundings here are intimate but nevertheless, the design is elaborate. Immediately below the communion table is the tombstone of Colonel James Skinner, the military adventurer who gave his name to the church. Anglican morning prayers & supper are held every Sunday.

To the south is the old Delhi general post office while just to the north is the imposing former residence of the British Commissioner William Fraser now the Northern Railways Office.

North of the gate is one of Delhi's oldest British cemeteries, guarded by a cross-shaped gateway. The grassy landscape is dotted with tombstones, the most prominent being that of Brigadier General John Nicholson who was nicknamed "the lion of Punjab". This and many other graves date from the 1857 uprising. The gate is often closed but if you knock, the attendant will open it for you.

It's worth going a kilometre or so further north to see **Majnu ka Tila**, a Tibetan refugee colony famous for its food and market. The best way to reach here is by rickshaw. When you reach MKT as it is frequently known, you find winding alleys, faint echoes of the Daalai Lama's message, graceful Tibetan ladies in their traditional attire selling momos, vibrant colours, unusual smells, and the serene soft music made by the temple prayer bells. You may find yourself frantically clicking away to store memories of yet another unique pocket of the city.

There is a small monastery and Buddhist temple, curio shops selling Tibetan handicrafts, and numerous restaurants specialising in Tibetan cuisine. The hotels and lodges have decent accommodation at very reasonable price. The neighbourhood is popular among foreign and domestic tourists as well as among students from the nearby Delhi University. Note the interesting signs and messages on the walls, many of which offer good advice for healthy living.

That takes care of our Old Delhi excursion so we now travel further south.

**Another day**

Today's trip is best done by vehicle rather than by foot although there are some sections where walking is very attractive. We start at **Connaught Place** a little south of Old Delhi. This is the colonial heart of New Delhi and is one of the largest financial, commercial and business centres in the city. It was named after a British Field Marshal and was built in 1929-1933. It contains shops, offices and hotels.

It is believed that Connaught Place's Georgian architecture is modelled after the Royal Crescent in Bath, England even though there are some significant differences. The Royal Crescent is semi-circular and is three-storied; Connaught Place is two-storied in almost a complete circle.

Connaught Place is very easy to find on a map because eight roads radiate from a circular central park. This park, built over a Metro station, has long been a venue for cultural events and the largest known Indian flag, which is larger than a badminton court, flies at its centre.

Once, this Central Park was a sanctuary for *hijras* (eunuchs), homosexuals and prostitutes. They have now migrated to the nearby park above Palika Bazaar. Unfortunately, today pickpockets, touts and scam artists also frequent here and parts have become quite grungy.

Plenty of modern history has been created in this area. The nearby Imperial Hotel opened in 1931 and it was here that Nehru, Gandhi, Ali-Jinnah, and Lord Mountbatten met to discuss the birth of Pakistan.

After major protests, Connaught Place became a traffic free zone on weekends in 2017 so the public can once more actually enjoy it and you see many people taking the opportunity to walk and play on roads which are normally choked with cars. The future of this, however, is still uncertain. The metro station under here is one of the major stations on the city system.

Out to the west on Mandir Marg, we find the three-storey **Laxmi Narayan Temple** built in northern Hindu style adorned with carvings depicting scenes from Hindu mythology. The temple is dedicated to Laxminarayan the goddess of prosperity and good fortune, and there are side temples dedicated to Shiva, Krishna and Buddha. The temple spreads over three hectares and has many shrines, fountains, and a large garden.

It is also known as Birla Mandir, because it was built by members of the Birla family in 1933-1939. The temple was inaugurated by Mahatma Gandhi on the condition that people of all castes will be allowed to enter. Entry is free but photography and mobile telephones are not allowed inside the temple. It is one of the most popular Hindu temples in the city. It opens 7 a.m. to noon and 2 p.m. to 9 p.m.

Back to the south of Connaught Place, there are five places worth searching out. The first we come to is the **Sacred Heart Cathedral** (http://sacredheartcathedraldelhi.org/) (1 Ashok Place, New Delhi), Delhi's largest Catholic Church. Completed in 1934, it is the headquarters of the Delhi Archdiocese.

The red brick church has a massive vaulted ceiling, polished stone floors and broad arches. The marble altar is domed and there is a fresco of Jesus and his 12 disciples. Four masses are held each Sunday.

The second is the **Metro Museum** (http://www.delhimetrorail.com/DMRC-Museum/) at Patel Chowk, the only museum about a Metro Railway in the entire South Asian region and possibly the only museum in the world in an operational Metro station.

The Museum has working models of trains, tunnel boring machines, and a giant LED Screen that shows informative films on the Delhi Metro. Since it is located within the Patel Chowk Metro station, visitors can see the museum until 11 p.m. Souvenir items are available.

Just outside, attached to the Sansad Marg post office, is the **National Philatelic Museum** (Dak Bhawan, Sardar Patel Chowk, Sansad Marg.) (http://www.delhitourism.gov.in/delhitourism/entertainment/national_ philately_museum.jsp). This is a small and simple place which is very well organized. It showcases a huge collection of Indian stamps of different decades.

The museum has a small staff, and they maintain the place nicely. A highlight is getting your personalized stamps, 12 for Rs300, in just 20 minutes. The museum is free and there is no photography allowed inside. It opens Monday to Friday.

The fourth is **Jantar Mantar** (http://www.jantarmantar.org/) (Sansad Marg, Connaught Place), a wonderful observatory built in 1724 by Maharaja Jai Singh of Jaipur. It is said that Jai Singh found the astronomical instruments used at the time too small so he built these larger ones to take more accurate measurements.

Jai Singh used the observatory to compile astronomical tables and to predict the times and movements of the sun, moon and planets. Built with brick rubble and plastered with lime, the instruments have been repaired and restored repeatedly, but without any large scale alteration.

Our guide explained that the Samrat Yantra is basically a sundial. It is around 22 m high, 35 m long, and 3 m thick. You can see a quadrant with graduations indicating times.

The Jayaprakash consists of hollowed out spheres with markings on their concave surfaces. By using crosswires an observer could align the position of a star with various markings.

Other instruments had different uses. The Misra Yantra was an instrument to determine the shortest and longest days of the year. The Ram Yantra, which consists of two large buildings open to the sky, was used for measuring the altitude of stars.

Citizens of India and visitors from SAARC countries (Bangladesh, Nepal, Bhutan, Sri Lanka, Pakistan, Maldives and Afghanistan) and BIMSTEC countries (Bangladesh, Nepal, Bhutan, Sri Lanka, Thailand and Myanmar) gain access for Rs5 per head. Others pay Rs100 per head. The complex is open to the public from 9 a.m. to 7 p.m. and is well worth seeing particularly if you are not going to Jaipur where there is a better-preserved version of the same thing.

The fifth place to visit is further east. **Agrasen ki Baoli** (http://agrasenkibaoli.com/) (Hailey Lane off Hailey Rd, Connaught

Place) is a 60 metre long and 15 metre wide historical step well; a 14th-century structure nestled between multi-storey buildings. It is believed that this was originally built by the legendary King Agrasen and later rebuilt by the Agrawal community in the 14th century.

The stone walls of the Baoli, with its arched structure, are grim and desolate but still beautiful. It is a cool and silent place in the heart of the capital. The silence deepens as you move to the bottom of the stairs but you are then faced with litter and possible pests. The monument remains open from 7 a.m. to 6 p.m. and the entry is free. It featured in 2015 in the Bollywood movie *PK*.

South of here on Copernicus Marg is **Kamani Auditorium** (http://www.kamaniauditorium.org/about.html), a unit of the Bharatiya Kala Kendra Trust, and one of the most prestigious Theatre Halls of Delhi. The 632 seat Auditorium hosts national and international theatrical, dance and musical performances. Check out what is on and try to make a visit.

A few blocks to the east is the **Supreme Court Museum** (http://supremecourtofindia.nic.in/museum.htm) (Tilak Marg.). It is a small, circular and single pillared building housing an assortment of calligraphies, manuscripts and inscriptions, souvenirs, and old furniture and paintings from the Supreme Court & Federal Court of New Delhi. You can witness the case-files of Indira and Mahatma Gandhi's assassinations, Indian postal stamps, judges' wigs, silver coins and much more.

Those interested in dolls may like to go a few blocks north to the Shankar's International Dolls Museum (Nehru House, 4, Bahadurshah Zafar Marg). 6000 dolls from 85 countries are on display. Entry is Rs15.

It is now time to travel south to the centre of New Delhi's administration area. **Vijay Chowk** (Victory Square) is a spacious plaza and the site of the Beating the Retreat ceremony, which takes place on 29 January each year, marking the end of Republic Day celebrations.

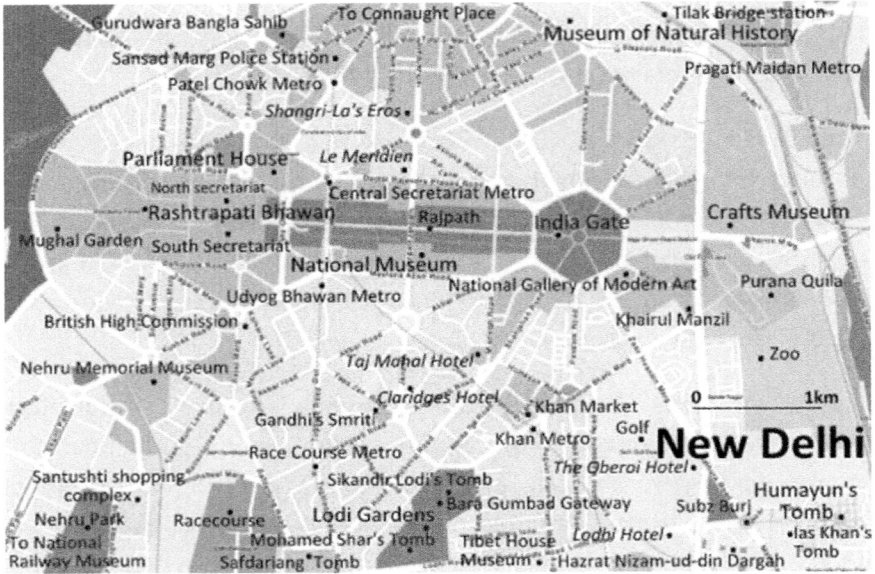

**India Gate** (http://www.cwgc.org/foreverindia/memorials/delhi-memorial.php) in the centre of the square is India's war memorial in honour of those who died in the 19th century Second Anglo-Afghan War, and the First World War. The names of 85,000 Indian army soldiers are inscribed on the monument and it is also India's memorial to the Unknown Soldier. It is dramatically floodlit at night while the fountains nearby make a lovely display with coloured lights. Surrounding the imposing structure is a large expanse of lush green lawns, which is a popular picnic spot.

Here you find one of many almost unknown attractions which are scattered around the city. **MTR 1** is a little steam engine which looks like a toy. It is installed in a tiny landscaped garden outside the gates of the butterfly-shaped Baroda House on Copernicus Marg, and guards the headquarters of the Northern Railway.

**Rajpath** is the ceremonial boulevard that runs from the Rashtrapati

Bhavan (Presidents Palace) through Vijay Chowk and India Gate to the National Stadium. It was designed by British architect Sir Edwin Lutyens who was also responsible for India Gate. The very wide avenue is lined on both sides by huge lawns, canals and rows of trees that are floodlit at night.

This is considered to be one of the most important roads in India and it is where the annual Republic Day Parade takes place. You can have a nice evening walk from the Parliament towards India Gate and absorb the wide spaces around you.

There are several important buildings along here. The **National Museum** (http://www.nationalmuseumindia.gov.in/) is one of the largest museums in India. Established in 1949, it holds a variety of articles ranging from the pre-historic era to modern works of art. The Indus Valley gallery has a collection of artefacts of that civilisation including huge grain jars, seals, pottery, and statuary. The building has 3 floors and is built around a rotunda.

There are many galleries, some cover periods in India's past while others concentrate on one aspect such as miniature paintings. The collections are impressive, but the labels are either non-existent or scruffy, and the whole place seems to lack maintenance. It opens from 10 a.m. to 5 p.m. daily except Monday at a cost of Rs20 for Indians and Rs650 for others. The Rs650 fee includes an audio guide.

**Parliament                                                        House**
(http://www.parliamentofindia.nic.in/ls/intro/p2.htm), called Sansad Bhawan, is an impressive circular building. There were three separate chambers which were built for the three bodies which existed until the end of the British rule; the Chamber of Princes, the State Council, and the Central Legislative Assembly. Today Parliament consists of two houses called Lok Sabha and Rajya Sabha (Upper House) with the President acting as their head.

The building is surrounded by large gardens and the perimeter is fenced off. Permission is necessary before you can go inside. The Parliament Museum stands next to Parliament House and opens 11 a.m. to 5 p.m. Tuesday to Saturday. A large fountain is across Rajpath from here.

The **Secretariat Building** is a huge government office building that we come to next. It actually consists of two parts, North Block and South Block on either side of Rajpath and both house various government departments. Much of the building is in British classical architectural style said to be derived from Christopher Wren's Royal Naval College at Greenwich, England, but it incorporates some Mughal and Rajasthani architectural styles and motifs.

In the Great Court between the two buildings are four Dominion Columns topped with a bronze ship which were presented by Australia, Canada, New Zealand and South Africa.

The huge **Rashtrapati Bhawan** (http://presidentofindia.nic.in/pirb.htm) is the official residence of the President of India. The building consists of four floors and 340 rooms. The front of the palace, on the east side, has twelve unevenly spaced massive columns and a colossal dome which reflects both Indian and British styles.

The entire 130 hectare President Estate that includes the Mughal Gardens has residences for bodyguards and staff, stables, other offices, utilities and large open spaces.

You now have the opportunity to do a museum tour inside Rashtrapati Bhavan. This allows visitors to get an inside view of the palace, its art, architecture, and to learn about the lives and activities of past presidents. Tours need to be booked on-line several days prior to the proposed visit at https://presidentofindia.gov.in/rbvisit/rbvisit.aspx.

**The Cathedral Church of the Redemption** (1 Church Road, North Avenue) is west of Parliament House. This is the former Viceroy's Church and it was only built in 1931. The design is said to be inspired by the 16th-century church of Il Redentore in Venice. Inside there is a dazzling interplay of arches which is enhanced by beams of sunlight through small openings in the side walls. A highlight of the church is the magnificent teakwood pipe organ.

**Gurdwara Bangla Sahib** (http://www.dsgmc.in/) is to the north of Parliament House. This is the most prominent Sikh *gurdwara* (house of worship) in Delhi. It was first built as a small temple by Sikh General, Sardar Baghel Singh in 1783. The grounds now include the temple, a huge kitchen, a large holy pond, a school and an art gallery.

*Entrance to Gurdwara Bangla Sahib*

Visitors must cover their hair and remove shoes to enter and there are guides, head scarves, and a shoe-minding service available free of charge at a special foreigners room. All the people you see working in the kitchen and elsewhere are volunteers. The complex also houses the Baba Baghel Singh Museum, a library and a hospital. The museum is open Tuesday to Sunday from 9 a.m. to 7.30 p.m. Entry is free.

While in this area you may like to see the iconic **Akshara Theatre** (11-B. Baba Kharak Singh Marg) (http://www.aksharatheatre.com/). It has four performance spaces for live performance, and a whole range of facilities for shooting and editing, set design, metal work and stone sculpture, and graphics design. There are classrooms where the performing arts are taught to children and young people.

There are some other attractions back near India Gate. The first is the **National Gallery of Modern Art** (http://ngmaindia.gov.in/) housed in a building known as Jaipur House because it was the former palace of the Maharaja of Jaipur. The butterfly-shaped building with a central dome was built in 1936. An area has been developed into sculpture gardens with works by modern artists from all over the world.

In 2009, a new wing was inaugurated adding almost six times the space to the existing gallery, plus an auditorium, theatre, laboratory, library, academic section, cafeteria and museum shop. It opens daily from 10 a.m. to 5 p.m. except on Mondays. Entry charges are Indian: Rs20, Foreign national: Rs500.

The **Khairul Manzil Masjid** (Mathura Road) is located opposite the Purana Qila (see below) and was built in 1561. It is constructed using rubble which has been coated with white plaster. There are five high arches which lead to the main prayer hall which is topped with a dome. The most impressive feature of the mosque to me is the massive gateway which has been constructed using red sandstone.

A little to the north of here, facing the Purana Quila complex, is the government-run **Crafts Museum** (Bhairon Marg, Pragati Maidan) (http://nationalcraftsmuseum.nic.in/). Today, the museum holds an amazing collection of rare and distinctive craft pieces covering painting, embroidery, textiles, and various crafts of clay, stone and wood.

The museum also houses a village complex spread over two hectares, with 15 structures representing village dwellings, courtyards and shrines from different states of India, with items of day-to-day life displayed.

The village complex is a remnant of a temporary exhibition held in 1972. Several traditional craftsmen can be seen working here and they also sell the crafts they create. There is a shop and a very popular cafe.

Across the road is the massive gateway and walls of **Purana Quila** (Mathura Road) (http://www.delhitourism.gov.in/delhitourism/tourist_place/purana_quila.jsp). These were built by Humayun, the second Mughal Emperor, in about 1533 as part of a new capital city called Dinpanah. It is thought to be built on the site of the most ancient of the numerous cities of Delhi, Indraprastha. Excavations show the area was inhabited in five preceding cities, and maybe even back to 300 BC.

The founder of the Shar Suri Dynasty, Sher Shah Suri, defeated Humayun in 1540, named the fort Shergarh and extended it with more buildings. Purana Quila is roughly rectangular in shape with a perimeter of nearly two kilometres. He named his city Shergarh.

The other two attractions at the fort site are Qila-i-Kuna Masjid and Sher Mandaal. The single-domed Qila-i-Kuna Mosque is an excellent example of a pre-Mughal design. Today, it is the best-preserved building in Purana Qila. The Sher Mandaal is now an observatory, but the structure and style of the building suggest that it was built for entertainment purposes. The moat is a spot for boating and zorbing.

Purana Quila is the venue for a spectacular sound and light show held every evening. Entry is Rs80 for a one hour show. You should take mosquito repellent, water, a hand held fan, and snacks if you attend.

While in this area, you should visit the **National Science Centre** (Near Gate No.1, Bhairon Road, Pragati Maidan) (http://www.nscdelhi.org/). This museum houses working science exhibitions as well as exhibits on the history of architecture. It is spread over several floors and covers a large area but it appears to have not been upgraded recently. Nevertheless, it is a great place for children and has some interest to most adults. Entry is Rs50 and you need to buy tickets for some activities inside.

Across the road from Purana Quila is the tranquil **Khair ul Manzil Masjid** (Mathura Road). The gateway of the mosque is of red sandstone, the courtyard is ornamented with a pool for ablutions and there is also a stone well. Some blue, green, and yellow tiles can still be seen but the whole area is rather dilapidated and has become a permanent home to many pigeons. During the mandated prayer times you will see locals in the building and courtyard.

The **National Zoological Park** (Mathura Road) (http://nzpnewdelhi.gov.in/) is a 71 ha zoo housing around 1350 animals, immediately to the south. The zoo can be seen on foot or by using a battery-operated vehicle which can be rented here. You can see the Asiatic and white lions, a rare breed of fast vanishing white tigers, and a host of other animals, reptiles and birds.

The zoo covers a vast area and you are not allowed to take food inside so fortunately there are places to sit and rest, stalls to purchase cold drinks, and a reasonable cafeteria. Do not carry any bags as these are not allowed inside. Admission for foreigners is Rs200 for adults and Rs100 for children while locals pay Rs40/20. There is a camera charge of Rs50 and video charge of Rs200. It is closed on Fridays.

To the south-west are the Delhi Golf Club, the grand Oberoi Hotel, the Lodhi Hotel, and the **Subz Burj**. This latter structure, a 15th-century building with a blue dome is an unsolved mystery. Who built it and for whom? We don't know. It could have been a mausoleum, or a pleasure pavilion, or even served a functional purpose, but not a fragment of its history is known.

Originally, it possessed vibrant green tiles covering its dome and drum, but during a restoration fiasco it ending up with brilliant blue tiles. For a few years, it was used as a funky police station in British times.

Further to the south is the **tomb of the Mughal Emperor Humayun** (http://www.humayunstomb.com/) (Mathura Road), built in 1569-70.

The tomb is a UNESCO World Heritage Site and has undergone extensive restoration in recent years and was spotlessly clean on my last visit. It is a delightful spot. The pathway from the western entrance passes several smaller structures including Isa Khan's tomb that even pre-dates the main tomb itself.

The tomb was commissioned by Humayun's first wife Bega Begum and was designed by a Persian architect. It was ground-breaking by using red sandstone on such a large scale. The tomb's architecture and the attached garden are the best examples in Delhi of the early Mughal style of tomb and it set a precedent for subsequent monumental Mughal buildings.

*Humayun's Tomb*

The symmetrical and simple exterior is in sharp contrast with the complex interior floor plan of many chambers. Humayun's wife is also buried here.

Other tombs in the garden include that of Humayun's barber and the Isa

Khan Tomb complex, a walled area and the resting place of Isa Khan Niyazi, an influential noble in the court of Sher Shan Suri. There is also a mosque and an octagonal tomb built in the Sur style within Isa Khan's walled complex.

The enclosed garden is divided into four squares by paved walkways and two central water channels. Each square is then further divided into smaller squares with pathways, a design typical of later Mughal gardens. The tomb and the garden are enclosed by high walls on three sides. It opens daily from sunrise to sunset. The entry fee is Rs10 for Indians and US$5 for foreigners.

Also here is Nila Gumbad, or blue dome, Delhi's oldest Mughal-era ruin. Its beauty lies in its tiled dome, rare in Delhi. Built in 1625 by Abdur Rahim Khan-i-Khana, a noble in Akbar's court, the walls of rubble masonry are showing signs of cracks and the chamber is locked by a grilled door.

There is currently a new museum-cum-interpretation centre under construction here which is scheduled to open sometime in 2018. It will display a mix of artefacts that have been locked up in the reserve collections of several of Delhi's museums. It is also proposed to have live demonstrations of building crafts such as stonework, tile work and other Prominent Mughal crafts.

Across the road to the west, but hidden away in a narrow street, is **Hazrat Nizam-ud-din Dargah**, the mausoleum of a famous Sufi saint, Nizamuddin Auliya. He died in 1325 aged 92. The Sufi`s are a mystical sect that believe in a deep emotional attachment to God.

The dargah is visited by thousands of Muslims every week, and also by Hindus, Christians and people of other religions. *Kawallis* are sung at sunset daily but Thursdays and Sundays are special (and crowded) and food is served on those occasions.

The tomb of the saint is in a small main shrine which only men are allowed to enter. The tombs of Sufi musician and poet Amir Khusrow and Mughal princess Jehan Ara Begum are also crowded in within the Nizamuddin Dargah complex. Jehan was the daughter of Emperor Shar Jahan and she stayed with her father during his imprisonment in Agra's Red Fort. A man at the gate will look after your shoes for Rs20.

A little further south is the **tomb of Atgah Khan**, a Mughal-era noble who was murdered by a rival. The mausoleum's 16th-century aesthetics contrast sharply with the shoddily-built modern-day brick structures that crowd in on it.

The huge red sandstone edifice has floral patterns and marble inlays of Islamic calligraphy and a marble dome. Inside the dark chamber, there are three graves; each inlaid with calligraphies and floral patterns. The tomb is surrounded by a wall and the entrance is a bit hard to find but there is no entrance fee.

Travelling west along Lodhi Road brings us to the **Tibet House Museum** (1, Institutional Area, Lodhi Road) (http://www.tibethouse.in/). This serves as a resource centre on Tibet and its history. The collection of the museum includes those items that the Daalai Lama brought from Tibet when he escaped from there.

One of the major attractions of the museum is a collection of painted scrolls illustrating the life of Buddha, dating back to as early as the 15th century. There is a shop selling Tibetan clothes, jewellery, medicines, incense, curios and a range of handicrafts.

Further west is the **India Habitat Centre** (http://www.indiahabitat.org/page?view=aboutihc). This covers nine acres and is an area of architectural excellence. The elegantly designed campus hosts various institutions, supporting infrastructure, and extensive facilities. It also has one of the finest convention centres in the country that is equipped with state-of-the-art facilities. There are also several restaurants, a fitness centre, gym, spa, and roof-top swimming pool.

Close by are the **Lodi Gardens**

(http://www.delhitourism.gov.in/delhitourism/entertainment/lodhi_gar den.jsp). Delhi's lesser known Sayyid (1414-1451) and Lodi (1451-1526) dynasties built several little architectural gems here. Spread over 36 hectares it contains Mohammed Shah's Tomb (the third Sayyid ruler) built in 1444 and this is the earliest structure in the gardens. The octagonal chamber has striking stone overhanging eaves and lotus patterns on the ceiling. It is a good example of a combination of the Hindu and Islamic styles of architecture.

Also here is the elaborate double domed tomb of Sikander Lodi, the most successful ruler of the Lodi dynasty. It was built by his son in 1517 and is also an octagonal structure with Hindu motifs.

Nearby is the seven arched Athpula Bridge, the last of the buildings in Delhi, built during the reign of Mughal Emperor Akbar. It crosses a nice pond containing many fish. You see the Bara Gumbad (Big Dome) in the centre of the garden, a gateway to an attached three-domed mosque, both built in 1494. The other significant structure is the Sheesh Gumbad (Glass Dome) which was once decorated by glazed blue tiles and painted floral designs.

This is a lovely green space in the middle of this chaotic city! Delhi can be very full-on so at times you will want a break and Lodi Gardens is perfect for that. It is particularly attractive in the early evening as it is wonderfully floodlit and safe but it closes at 7 p.m. Note the creatively decorated garbage cans scattered around the park. Heritage walks are organised within the park area, which has become a favourite with morning walkers and yoga enthusiasts.

**International Centre of Gandhian Studies and Research** (http://gandhismriti.gov.in/index.asp?langid=2) is an institution dedicated to Mahatma Gandhi. At present, the Centre provides a comprehensive exhibition on Gandhi, conference halls, camping facilities, a library, children's corner, photo unit and a publications division.

Another place worth visiting for history buffs is the **Nehru Memorial Museum and Library** (Teen Murti Bhawan) (http://nehrumemorial.nic.in/en/) which aims to preserve and reconstruct the history of the Indian independence movement. It is situated about a kilometre almost due west from Gandhi Smriti in what was originally called Flagstaff House. This was built in 1930 as the residence of the Commander in Chief of the British Indian Army.

Later, Jawaharlal Nehru, the first Prime Minister of India, lived here until his death in 1964. The museum was founded after his death and is open 10 a.m. to 5 p.m. daily except Mondays. Also contained within the complex are the Centre for Contemporary Studies and the Nehru Planetarium.

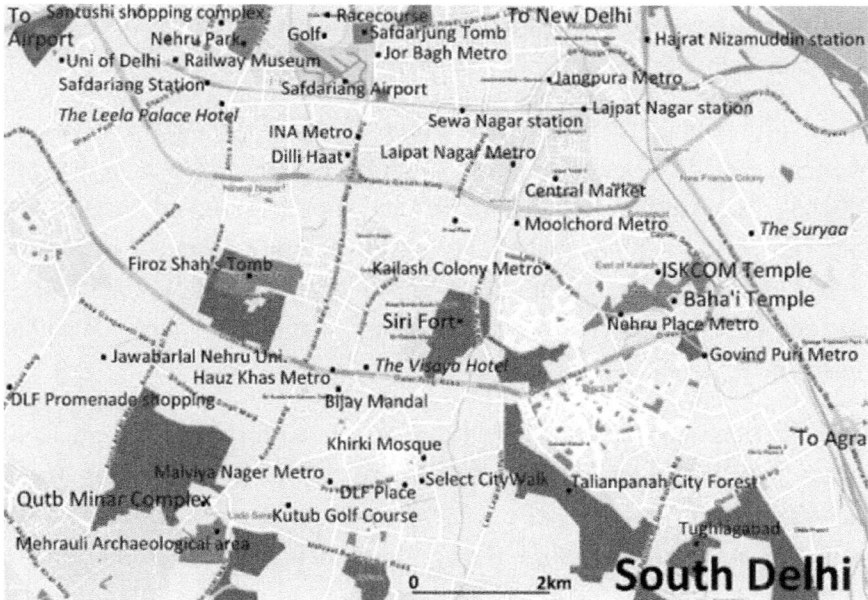

I enjoy the **National Railway Museum** (http://www.delhitourism.gov.in/delhitourism/entertainment/national_rail_museum.jsp). There is a fascinating collection of over 100 Indian Railways exhibits. Static and working models, signalling equipment, antique furniture, historical photographs and related literature etc. are displayed but it's the old engines and carriages that most appeal to me.

The line-up of old coaches includes the handsome Prince of Wales Saloon, built in 1875. Not to be outdone is the Maharaja of Mysore's Saloon built in 1899. The star attraction, however, is the Fairy Queen, built in 1855 and considered to be one of the best-preserved steam locomotives of her age. A ride in the unusual mono rail (PSMT) will be exciting to some.

Nearby **Nehru Park**, is one of city's leading green areas and is a regular venue for art events, concerts, and morning yoga classes. It houses an ancient Shiv Temple, a cafe, and a statue of Vladimir Lenin, the leader of the Russian revolution. He has stood frozen in a three-piece suit, one arm tucked into a trouser pocket, and the other holding a cap since the statue was unveiled by Russian General Secretary Gorbachev and Prime Minister Rajiv Gandhi in 1987.

It is interesting to note that other Russian dignitaries are also remembered in Delhi with statues. With his arms crossed and beard flowing, Leo Tolstoy gazes towards the Janpath outlet of McDonalds, adjacent to Connaught Place. The author of Anna Karenina is not the only Russian giant in Delhi's cultural boulevards. Walk a few minutes further east to Mandi House, and there stands the poet Alexander Pushkin.

East of Nehru Park is the small Safdarjung airport and the adjacent racecourse and Air Force Golf Club. Here too is the **Safdarjung Tomb** built by his son Nawab. Built in 1754, it is one of the last examples of Mughal architecture before the final remnants of the great empire collapsed.

The large double-storeyed gateway has a library and a veranda upstairs while the small mosque to the right has three onion domes. A palm-lined pathway leads to the red and buff sandstone tomb which stands on a high terrace in an extensive garden and is unmistakably in the tradition of the Taj Mahal, onion dome and all.

There is a gap in our sightseeing now as we travel further into southern New Delhi. Hauz Khas is one of the more affluent neighbourhoods around here and at its heart is the ancient **Hauz Khas Complex**. This has a reservoir, an Islamic seminary, a mosque, a tomb and pavilions. It was part of Siri, Delhi's second medieval city.

Established in 1352, the madrassa was one of the leading institutions of Islamic learning in the Delhi Sultanate. At that time, Delhi was the most important place in the world for Islamic education. It was built in an L-Shape on the southern and eastern edges of the reservoir. The madrassa is flanked by a garden on its southern side which houses six impressive pavilions. The northern end of the madrassa is attached to a small mosque.

The austere, domed tomb at the intersection of the two arms of the madrassa is for Firuz Shah. The square chamber is made of local quartzite and has a white plaster finish. The door, pillars and lintels are made of grey quartzite while red sandstone was used for carvings of the battlements.

The fusion of Indo-Islamic architecture is exceptionally photogenic. The area is always filled with gossiping village women, cricket playing boys, camera-carrying tourists, picnicking school children, young lovers, gangs of guitarists, and loners. Classical music concerts and a sound and light show are held some evenings.

The complex is in fairly good condition after recent restoration but plastic litter is a problem. It is open for visitors all days of the week from 10 a.m. to 6 p.m. and there is no entry fee.

East of here on Chor Minar Road off Sri Aurobindo Marg, is the **Chor Minar** (the tower of the thief), which was used to display the severed heads of alleged criminals. Its thick rubble wall has circular holes where the heads were put up on display. The structure sits in a road roundabout surrounded by a small circular garden. The entry to the tower's spiral staircase is locked but it's still worth seeing from the garden or across the street.

We now get into one of the most ancient areas of Delhi. South-east of here is **Siri Fort** built by Ala-ud-Din Khaliji in about 1303 to defend the city of Siri from the onslaught of the Mongols. Siri was the second of the seven cities of medieval Delhi. Targhi, a Mongol ruler, besieged the Fort but could not penetrate the fortifications.

The Mongols later tried to attack again but their army of 50,000 men was annihilated. Subsequent ruthless attacks by Ala-ud Din's army, deep into Mongol territory ensured that Mongols would never attack India again.

Little remains of this old city apart from the south-eastern gate. The destruction of the Fort is probably due to later rulers who removed the fort's stones, bricks and other artefacts for their own buildings.

Eccentric ruler, Mohammed bin Tughlaq, constructed a new city called Jahanpanah between 1326 and 1327 by encircling the earlier cities of Siri and Lalkot (see below) with 13 gates. Little remains of this but one of the structures which has partially survived is **Bijay Mandaal**. This is a typical Toghlaqi structure with an octagonal plan built in rubble masonry.

Historians guess it was the site of the famous thousand-pillared hall with its exquisitely carved roof but nothing of this remains. There are two treasure pits from which pearls, porcelain, gold and rubies were excavated during the last century. Why more of Jahanpanah doesn't exist today is somewhat of a mystery but a possible contributing reason was the idiosyncratic rule of Tughlaq who, amongst other things, inexplicably shifted the capital and Jahanpanah's entire population 1100 km south to the Deccan.

**Another day**

Still further south, the **Qutb complex** (http://asi.nic.in/asi_monu_whs_qutbminar.asp) (Aurobindo Marg, Mehrauli), is even older and it contains many ancient monuments and buildings. It is the said to be the second most visited place in India. This is located in Lalkot, later called Qila Rai Pithora, the first of the seven cities of Delhi, established by a Tomar Rajput ruler.

The original complex contained many ancient Hindu and Jain temples but most were destroyed for material during the construction of the **Qubbat-ul-Islam Mosque**. This was the first mosque built in Delhi after the Islamic conquest of India and it is now known as the Quwwat-ul-Islam mosque. The mosque consists of a courtyard, cloisters, and a prayer hall.

Building of the mosque was begun in 1192 by Qutbu'd-Din Aibak and completed in 1198. The high arched screen facing the prayer hall was added in the 14th century. The mosque is in ruins today and interestingly, various ancient Hindu decorations can still be seen in the structure.

The prominent iron pillar that you see has an interesting history. The pillar, 7.2 m-high and weighing more than six tonnes, was originally erected in front of a Vishnu Temple complex at Udayagiri around 402 AD, and was later shifted to its present location when a Vishnu temple was built here. It was incorporated into the mosque during its construction and has remained rust-free for over 1600 years.

The best-known structure in the complex is the **Qutb Minar** (http://whc.unesco.org/en/list/233), built over many years from 1202. This is claimed to be the tallest brick minaret in the world and is an example of early Afghan architecture. It may have been inspired by the iron "Pillar of the Law" that stands on the site.

The tapered Qutb Minar is 72.5 metres high and has five distinct storeys. The first three storeys are made of red sandstone while the fourth and fifth storeys are made of marble and sandstone. There are

379 steps to the top but there is no access to the public. It is listed as a UNESCO World Heritage Site.

*Qutb Minar*

The domed Alai Darwaza is the main gateway from the southern side of the mosque. It was built in 1311 by Turkish artisans. There are inscriptions in the calligraphic style Naskh Script and latticed stone screens.

At about the same time Ala ud din Khilji, the second ruler of the Khilji dynasty, started building the **Alai Minar**, which was conceived to be twice as high as the Qutb Minar. The construction was abandoned, however, after the completion of the 24.5 meter high first storey, soon after his death. The huge base seen today shows what an ambitious plan this was.

Most people miss it, but take a look at the Mughal Masjid, a small beautiful mosque with three onion-shaped domes just by the entrance to the complex. The original gateway to the mosque is closed and the present entrance is through an opening in the east wall but it's worth searching out because the white-walled prayer chamber and the surrounding garden remain amazingly quiet considering the number of people who pass by.

The complex is open from 6 a.m. to 6 p.m. every day. Tickets are Rs10 for Indians and Rs250 for foreigners. There is a Rs20 charge for a video camera and Rs100 for an audio guide.

The **Mehrauli Archaeological area** spreads over 80 ha adjacent to the Qutb complex. It consists of over 100 historically significant monuments and is the only area in Delhi known for 1,000 years of continuous occupation. It includes the ruins of Lalkot, the first of the Delhi cities, thought to be founded by the Tomar dynasty in 736.

Over the years about 40 monuments have been restored in the Park and signage, heritage trails, and sandstone trail-markers have been installed. Tourists, however, mostly visit the more known Qutb Minar and neglect this site.

The most impressive structure is the Sufi poet Jamali Khamali's mosque. Nearby is the Rajaon ki Baoli an amazing 16th-century step well. Also worth seeing is the serene Hijron Ka Khanquah, a pre-Mughal, Lodi period monument where some eunuchs were buried in the 15th century. The courtyard contains some 50 whitewashed tombs.

Lack of drinking water and public washrooms make it difficult to spend a long time here and the ever-present litter distracts from the experience.

**Gandhak ki Baoli**, Delhi's oldest surviving stepwell, is situated in the Mehrauli Village complex. The sulphur-rich water which are said to have healing properties for skin ailments, explain why this baoli was used as a spa. It is believed to have been built by Sultan Iltutmish in the 13th century.

Baolis were generally very ornately built with very impressive architecture, and they served a very useful social purpose of providing water and a cool shelter. Now, unfortunately, this baoli is often dry but you can still visit and appreciate the intricate design and there is no entry fee or photographic charges.

**Jahaz Mahal**, built during the Lodhi period (1452-1526), was a mosque, the residence of a holy man, or a serai (inn) that took in visiting pilgrims. It depends on which expert you like. It could also have been a pleasure palace, a harem, or a summer refuge for the Delhi royalty. Whatever it was, the ruins today are quite impressive although the structure is in poor shape.

The palace is the venue for the annual Phool Walon Ki Sair Festival in October which includes a colourful procession led by fire dancers, and a three-day cultural program which includes dance, drama and music.

About 1.5 kilometres to the east, is the **Garden of Five Senses** which is designed to stimulate our five senses with its beauty and attractions and give us a chance to touch, smell, hear, see, and even taste our natural surroundings.

The garden contains a section similar to Mughal Gardens, pools of water lilies, bamboo courts, herb gardens, a solar energy park, and a replica of the Labna Arch in Mexico which was originally built by the Mayan civilization nearly 1200 years ago. Entry is Rs35 adult and Rs15 child/senior.

In 2017, a soft adventure park opened here on a trial basis. This has a rock climbing wall, zipline, Burma bridge, and commando net, while activities include sumo wrestling, zorbing, air rifle shooting, paintball, and archery. It looks as if it will become permanent.

Some distance south-west of the garden, you will find the Sanskriti Kendra (Mehrauli-Gurgaon Road, Anand Gram) where there are three museums: the **Museum of Everyday Art**, the **Museum of Indian Terracotta**, and the **Textile Museum**. The museums are open from 10 a.m. to 5 p.m. on all days except Mondays and Public Holidays, and entry if free.

The displays are quite good (certainly better than some other museums) and the grounds would be perfect for a picnic. The Sanskriti Foundation which operates these museums is a non-profit culture and arts promotion organisation.

One of Delhi's most romantic ruins is **Khirki Mosque** in Saket. It is almost opposite the modern Select City Walk shopping centre but it comes from an era 600 years before our modern shrines. One of the seven mosques built in the 1370s by Prime Minister Khan-i-Jahan Junan Shah, the double-storeyed structure now has blackened walls, collapsed domes, tapering minarets and a covered hall. It is a jumble of arches and domes that somehow have great appeal. I hope that this old building can be conserved and preserved.

You might be tempted to stop in this area for **shopping** and there is certainly plenty of choice. The Select City Walk, DLF Place, Metropolitan Mall and Square One mall are close together and they provide everything that the old city markets do not – international brands, air-conditioning, and high prices.

To the east is the **Jahanpanah City Forest**, 250 hectares of green. This vast tract of city forest has several gates and several trails for walking or running, and it is an ideal place for yoga, and bird watching. Entry is free.

As you go deeper into the forest, there are few people and you will be impressed by the beauty of the flora & fauna that surrounds you. There are many rare species of trees and plants dotted around and a number of peacocks too.

*Modern shopping centre*

Just to the east of the forest is **Tughlakabad Fort** (http://asi.nic.in/asi_monu_tktd_delhi_tughlaqfort.asp) which stretches over 6 km. It was built by Ghiyas-ud-din-Tughlak, the founder of the Tughlak dynasty, in 1321, as he established the third historic city of Delhi, which was later abandoned in 1327. The Tughlakabad fort served the twin purpose of a defensive structure as well as the imperial capital.

On the southern side of the fort is the tomb of Ghiyas-ud-din Tughlak, which was built by the ruler himself. The tomb is enclosed in a courtyard with fortified walls and is a fine example of Indo-Islamic architecture.

The ruins of Tughlakabad still consist of remarkable, massive stone fortifications between 10 and 15 metres high, topped by parapets and strengthened by circular bastions. The city is supposed to once have had as many as 52 gates of which only 13 remain today.

Our sightseeing continues with three remarkable modern temple complexes. The **International Society for Krishna Consciousness (ISKCON) Temple** (Hare Krishna Hill, Raja Dhirsain Marg, Sant Nagar) (http://www.iskcondelhi.com/) is one of the largest temple complexes in India. This is a well maintained, properly managed temple.

The walls of the temple have been decorated with the works of artists from Russia. The paintings portray different scenes from the lives of deities like Lord Krishna and Radha, and Lord Ram and Sita. The Vedic cultural museum shows various aspects of the Vedic philosophical and cultural heritage, both through simple exhibits and dioramas and through sophisticated robotic shows.

Govinda's is a pure vegetarian restaurant which serves wholesome and hearty vegetarian meals from noon to 3:30 p.m. and from 7 p.m. to 10 p.m. The temple opens every day but the main hall is closed between 1 p.m. and 4 p.m. Six *aartis* are offered each day. The first is at 4.30 a.m. and the last at 8.30 p.m.

The nearby **Bahá'í Lotus temple** (Lotus Temple Rd, Shambhu Dayal Bagh, Bahapur) (http://www.bahaihouseofworship.in/) was completed in 1986. It is set among lush green landscaped gardens and has won numerous architectural awards. Its unusual lotus shape has made it a major attraction. It was named "The most visited religious building in the world" by Guinness World Records in 2001 and is said to receive more visitors than the Taj Mahal.

The Bahá'í Faith is a world religion whose purpose is to unite all races and peoples in one universal cause and one common faith. Bahá'is are the followers of Bahá'u'lláh, who they believe is the Promised One of all Ages. The temple is open to all, and you can read or chant from Holy

Scriptures belonging to any religion, but nobody is allowed to play musical instruments, give sermons or hold religious ceremonies inside the hall.

*Bahá'í Lotus temple*

The lotus has always enjoyed unparalleled popularity throughout India from the earliest times down to the present day. The temple has 27 free-standing marble clad "petals" arranged in clusters of three to form nine sides. The nine doors of the Lotus Temple open onto a central hall that is capable of holding up to 2,500 people. Light and water are used for decoration in place of the thousands of statues and carvings to be found in other temples.

At sunset it is a dramatic sight as the white marble is stunning. The temple is usually busy but inside it is surprisingly calm. It opens in winter from 9 a.m. to 5:30 p.m. and summer from 9 a.m. to 7 p.m. Tuesday through Sunday. There is no charge for admission.

The **Akshardham Temple** (N. H. 24, Near Noida Mor) (http://www.akshardham.com/), across the river in East Delhi, brilliantly showcases the essence of India's ancient architecture, traditions and spiritual messages as understood by Swaminarayan, who developed this relatively modern sect of Hinduism about 200 years ago. The complex was built in only five years by 11,000 artisans and volunteers and was inaugurated in 2005.

In addition to the large central temple, the complex features lifelike robotics and dioramas from the life of Swaminarayan in the Hall of Values, an IMAX film on the early life of Swaminarayan, a 12-minute boat ride, a musical fountain, and large landscaped gardens. It is sometimes called a spiritual Disneyland.

The central monument in pink sandstone and white marble is perfectly symmetrical resting on a plinth surrounded by 148 elephants. Carvings of deities, dancers, musicians and flora and fauna cover the walls. It has 234 ornately carved pillars, nine domes, and 20,000 statues.

The *Guinness Book of Records* has called this the largest Hindu temple in the world but this is disputed by at least three other temples. This doesn't matter to the visitor and most find this an absolutely amazing place. The big downside, however, is the fact that photographs are prohibited once you enter the grounds. This appears to be nothing more than a money making exercise as several commercial photographers offer to take your picture at various points within the complex.

The temple opens 9.30 a.m. to 6.30 p.m. every day except Monday. There is a 25-minute evening water show which costs Rs80, a restaurant, many food stalls and a large souvenir shop. Admission to the complex is free. Tickets to view the exhibitions are Rs170 for adults, Rs125 for seniors, and Rs100 for children. There is a personal screening process to go through and no food, cameras, video cameras, mobile phones, any electronic items, tobacco, alcohol, and drugs are allowed in the complex.

Although they are on the other side of the city, I'll include two further museums here. The **Indian Air Force Museum** (http://indianairforce.nic.in/) located near the airport, gives an overview of India's aviation history since its inception in 1932. It displays 15 aircraft, historic photos, uniforms & personal weapons, war trophies, electronic equipment, and captured enemy vehicles.

There is also a full-size model of the United States Apollo Lunar Module which carried American Astronauts Neil Armstrong and Edwin Aldrin to the moon's surface in 1969. You can also see a model of the Russian SOYUZ-launch vehicle in which Squadron Leader Rakesh Sharma of the Indian Air Force travelled into space in 1984.

The **Sulabh International Museum of Toilets** (http://www.sulabhtoiletmuseum.org/), which is also near the airport, was established with the objectives of educating and exploring historical trends in the development of toilets across the world. The Museum has a rare collection of facts, pictures and objects detailing the historic evolution of toilets from 2500 BC to the present. *Time* magazine has rated this amongst the world's weirdest museums. It is open every day except national holidays with free admission.

# 3 DELHI – FOR ALL THINGS INDIAN

## Activities

New Delhi has a heap of **spiritual-cleansing options** for those seeking redemption. At the Prerna School of Inspiration (C-211-B,Chattarpur Enclave) (http://www.prernaschoolofinspiration.com/) you can regress to your previous lives.

There are numerous Yoga centres offering classes in English at various levels in and around Delhi. If you're just looking for some simple aura cleansing, sign up for the chakra cleansing at the MCKS Yoga Vidya Pranic Healing Trust (http://delhipranichealing.com/). They have free, monthly healing camps at the Lodi Gardens.

The Yoga Studio (www.theyogastudio.info) in the Hauz Khas neighbourhood is a good spot for a drop-in class. There are 90-minute classes in English every day except Sunday at 8 a.m. and then again at 9:30 a.m. There are evening classes, too.

People either love or loath **Paintball**, which some say encourages trigger-happy, aggressive behaviour. Devotees should head to the new paintball field at the Select Citywalk Mall in Saket to compete on a field with large yellow plastic pods. Games can run for up to an hour, and the pricing depends entirely on the number of pellets you're willing to pay for.

The Delhi **Golf** Club (http://www.delhigolfclub.org/), situated next to the Oberoi Hotel, is the traditional golfing club in Delhi. There is a championship 18-hole Lodhi Course, and the shorter 9-hole Peacock Course. The Delhi Club opens all days 5 a.m. to 7 p.m.

Three others with good reputations are the army golf club, the air force golf club, and the Noida golf course. However, in the last few years, new golf courses have been created around Delhi, offering a completely new experience. There are at least 15 golf courses in the Delhi area.

Newer courses are available at the Classic Golf and Country Club, Golden Greens, and the Jaypee Greens Golf Resort. The Siri Fort Complex (Siri Fort Road) has a driving range and pitch and putt plus a putting green which opens 6 a.m. to 9 p.m. and is floodlit. It is closed on Monday.

The Qutab Golf Course (Press Enclave Road) (http://www.dda.org.in/sports/qutab_golf_course.htm) was the first public golf course in India. As well as the 18-hole course there is a 220 metre, state of the art driving range. It is situated about 5 km off the Ring Road, on the way to Qutb Minar.

**Rock Climbing** enthusiasts, or those just wanting to try the sport, should head to the Indian Mountaineering Foundation, (6, Benito Juarez Road) (https://www.indmount.org/IMF/welcome), where there is an International Standard Artificial Climbing Wall. State Level and National level competitions are frequently organized at the wall.

**Tours**

Delhi has untold tour operators catering to international visitors. I have had experience with only a fraction of them but have never been disappointed in the day tours they operate around the city. Apart from travelling by mini-coach or private car, there are bicycle tours, walking tours, and cycle rickshaw tours.

An alternative is the **Hop-on Hop-off (HoHo) bus** service

(http://hohodelhi.com/) which does a circular run past many of the major sites every 40 minutes or so. There are special air-conditioned buses for these tours and passengers can hop on and hop off as they like at any of the designated pick up and drop off points. There are one-day (Rs540) and two-day routes (Rs640) and one evening route.

Audio guides are also available as you tour and tourists have the option of booking tickets to attractions online, saving them the hassle of lining up endlessly outside ticketing offices. You can also purchase tickets onboard the buses.

**Delhi** **Tourism**
(http://www.delhitourism.gov.in/delhitourism/tour_packages/city_sigh t.jsp) operates two sightseeing tours each day. The morning tour covers the Laxmi Narayan Temple, Qutub Minar, Baha'i Temple, and Gandhi Smiriti, and you drive past India Gate, Parliament House, and the embassies area.

The afternoon tour visits Red Fort, Rajghat, and Humayun's Tomb and you drive past Feroz Shah Kotla, Indira Gandhi Stadium, Shakti Sthal, and Purana Qila. Each costs Rs290. The two tours can be combined for a full day (Rs475).

**Walking tours**

**The Salaam Baalak Trust** (http://www.salaambaalaktrust.com/city-walks.html), a charity caring for the poor and homeless, operates a walking tour. Former street children give guided tours showing aspects of the life of the city's kids and orphans. The tours take you around the old walled city, give you a rickshaw ride, then follow hidden alleys and eventually up on to the city's rooftops. This can be an inspiring experience.

Delhi Magic operates the **Heritage Walk through Nizamuddin** (http://www.delhimagic.com/heritage-walk-nizamuddin.html), a settlement which contains medieval era tombs, shrines, mausoleums and step-wells. You visit Chaunsath Khamba (The 64-Pillars), a beautiful

Mughal-era monument Ghalib's Academy, the busy local bazaar, the dargah of a 20th-century Sufi musician which is now a social centre, and Atgah Khan's Tomb. The highlight is the Nizamuddin dargah complex with its mosque, historical tombs and its miraculous step-well.

## Cycling tours

**DelhiByCycle** (http://www.delhibycycle.com/) offers 5 tours which give a unique focus on the hidden aspects of the city. Surprisingly, these tours are still largely unknown. The usual meeting points of these tours are in the car park opposite the famous Delite Cinema on Asaf Ali Road, Old Delhi (except for the Nizamuddin tour). The bright orange bikes and t-shirts of your tour guides will be difficult to miss.

**Delhi By Bike** (http://www.delhibybike.com/) operates two tours through Old Delhi and one through New Delhi. Tours leave from the Hotel Broadway which is near India Gate.

## Food Tours

Urban Adventures has a range of tours. One that I like is **Home Cooked Delhi** (http://www.urbanadventures.com/delhi-tour-home-cooked-delhi) where you experience an authentic meal in a local home, discover the joyful cultural meanings of Indian cuisine, and learn about traditional spices and cooking techniques.

Another one to consider is **Delhi Food Walk** (http://www.urbanadventures.com/delhi-tour-delhi-food-walk) where you explore the busy streets of Delhi and their famous street food stalls, experience traditional local transportation on a cycle rickshaw ride, indulge in some of Delhi's best local food, and tantalise your tastebuds with some non-alcoholic fruit beer.

**Food Tour in Delhi** (http://foodtourindelhi.com/) offers customized Indian food tours and cooking classes for adventurous foodies who want to explore the tastes of Delhi. You will visit some very interesting places serving good quality and hygienic street food. Many have been in business for 3 generations now.

## Visit a Pottery Village

If you are in Delhi and want to see a traditional side of India, without venturing out far from the capital city, you should definitely visit Kumhar Gram. Located in the western outskirts of Delhi, this is a village that houses about 700 potter families who mould clay for a living. You can find flower pots, wall hangings, bird-feeders, and all kinds of beautiful pottery items to buy here.

Stroll around the village and you will be amazed by the artistic skills of the villagers. You can also try your hand at pottery, with the help of one of the pottery artists. And when hunger strikes, you can easily grab a quick bite to eat from the refreshment counter. For visitors to Delhi, the easiest way to reach here is to take the half-day Indomania Pottery Village Tour which will give you a guided tour from beginning to end. Recent advice is that this tour is not operating at present (December 2017).

## Learn to Dance

The Delhi Dance Academy (http://www.delhidanceacademy.in/) offers one and two-hour workshops aimed at visitors, with the emphasis on fun. You'll learn Bollywood, Bhangra, belly dance and Garba. The instructors are excellent and you get a video of your class as a souvenir.

## Visit Kingdom of Dreams (http://www.kingdomofdreams.in/the-kingdom.html)

This is an entertainment complex with various shows, and exhibitions featuring Indian art and culture. Most of the live shows are filled with great Bollywood songs, performed by a troupe of dancers and singers but there are some jokes and general talk. I recommend the English-language headphones if you want to understand all the Hindi jokes.

## Ancient ceremony

On Thursday evenings at the Nizam-ud-din dargah you can see and hear mystic *sufi* singing, one of Delhi's finest and most unusual cultural experiences. This is the mausoleum of a famous Sufi saint, Auliya, who lived in the 13th century. This is the embodiment of a centuries-old Delhi, whose spirit endures in this area, notwithstanding the modern trappings that now surround it. Muslims still visit to offer prayers.

## Shopping

Markets still dominate the Delhi shopping scene but there are some modern malls and some government-run emporiums. Surprisingly, Delhi has only one mall in the ten largest malls in India despite being the capital and largest city. This is Select Citywalk in Saket.

Most visitors will use a taxi or rickshaw to take them shopping. Taxi and rickshaw drivers receive a commission from many shops, which means you end up paying more if you go there. They will naturally direct you to shops that pay them.

Many visitors find the government-run **Central Cottage Industries Emporium** on Janpath, south of Connaught Place, to be a good place to benchmark prices. This is a showcase of Indian craftsmen, weavers and folk artists with a huge selection of products. It opens every day from 10 a.m. to 7 p.m.

What to buy will depend on the individual but textiles, Indian silks and cottons are popular buys. A cheap silk wraparound skirt will cost a few dollars in Paharganj or you can pay thousands for a designer silk sari in specialist shops. The choice is yours but you need to know where to go. It can be quite confusing.

The villages of South Delhi offer some of the more interesting shopping experiences. Hauz Khas is an eclectic creative urban centre, with artist studios, cafés, restaurants, stores and bookshops. Two blocks away, Shahpur Jat village is a fashion and design destination, being home to dozens of boutiques featuring trendy clothes, fashion accessories, and home decor items. Five minutes' walk further south, Khirki village stands opposite a row of shopping malls in the Saket area.

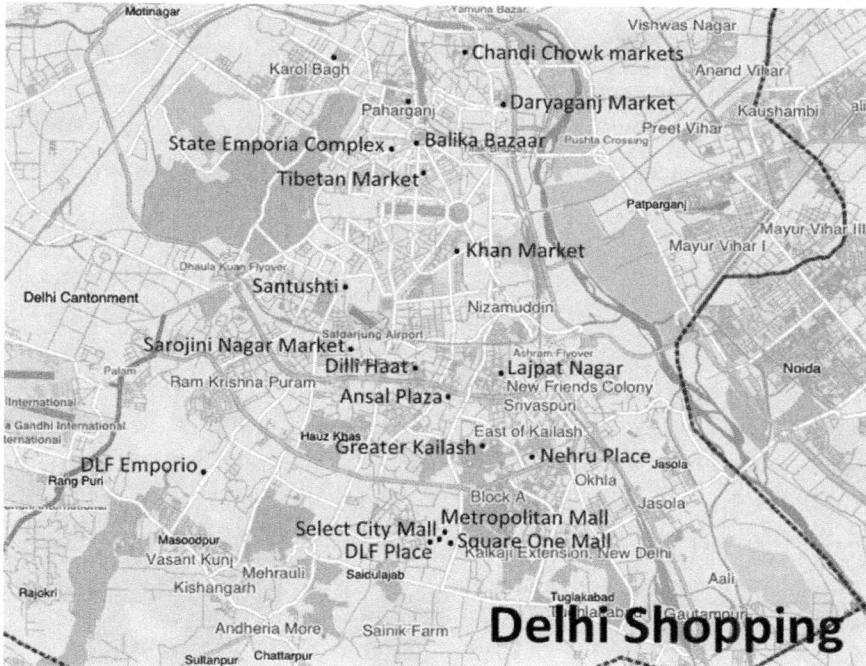

Shopping is not my favourite activity but I have to admit that I find some enjoyment in discovering hidden fabric warehouses where quilts and cushions are stacked to the rafters like colourful skyscrapers. I'm less impressed while sitting watching tireless workers unfurl dusty bolts of fabric for my wife as we sit sipping small cups of sweet tea.

The following are some of the more interesting shopping spots defined by areas of Delhi.

## Old Delhi

**Chandni Chowk** has existed for hundreds of years and most visitors enjoy an exploration of its winding, narrow alleyways. It is certainly an adventure which can be ruined by pickpockets but is great fun when toured on a pedal rickshaw. The area is divided into bazaars for different products. Katra Neel is for fabrics; the Bhagirath Palace area, for a huge range of electronics; and Dariba Kalan for silver jewellery.

Khari Baoli is the spice market and Chawri the stationery market. Nai Sarak, which connects Chandni Chowk Road with Chawri Bazaar, has numerous shops selling textbooks. Food is not forgotten with vendors serving up delicious street food. The market operates daily except Sundays.

**Daryaganj Book Market**, just north of Delhi Gate, is where locals go for cheap books. Stretching for more than a kilometre, the Daryaganj Old Book Market is perhaps the world's largest weekly book market. It operates every Sunday.

**Paharganj** offers some of the best bargain shopping in Delhi opposite the New Delhi railway station. Many shops also deal in wholesale and export so foreign importers come to hunt for unique and inexpensive goods. It is chaotic, noisy and dirty, and is only for shoppers who are good at bargaining.

Textile shops offer bags, bed spreads, cushion covers, wall hangings, and so on. Jewellery shops sell handmade beaded necklaces and bangles in every shape, size and colour. Handicraft places sell carved wooden statues, brass wares and decorations.

Good buys for foreigners are leather sandals, cotton clothing and printed T-shirts. Check the quality carefully before you buy but the prices are some of the best in Delhi. It operates daily until around 9 p.m.

**Karol Bagh** is a few kilometres to the west of here and is said to be Delhi's biggest market. It is a middle-class one-stop for clothes, spices, electronic goods, and just about anything else. Ajmal Khan Road has long been famous for inexpensive ready-made clothes and embroidered garments. Now international labels are also found here.

Bank Street has a row of shops displaying gold jewellery. At Arya Samaj Road to the south, you can buy second-hand books. Ghaffar Market to the west is famous for imported goods.

## Connaught Place

**Palika Bazaar** is an underground, air-conditioned market located below Connaught Place. It is especially famous for cheap electronic goods and clothes but you will also find footwear, perfumes, DVDs and CDs, and a whole lot more. There are hundreds of shops in Palika Bazaar but also many pocket pickers so make use of the bank ATMs when you want to buy something rather than carry cash. Most stall holders and products are down-market.

The **State Emporia Complex**, south-west on Baba Kharak Singh Marg, is something completely different. Most Indian states have outlets here showcasing their local products. Some of the better buys seem to be shawls at Zoon, the Kashmir emporium, and bronze lamps and icons at Poompuhar, the Tamil Nadu emporium. Cauvery, the Karnataka emporium, has exquisite silks.

Amrapali, the Bihar emporium, is famous for Madhubani paintings, while Rajasthali, and Gurjari, are popular destinations for printed cottons, miniature paintings and jewellery. You get tea, silk and cotton saris at Manjusha, the West Bengal emporium, and wood carvings at Mrignayani, the Madhya Pradesh emporium.

**Janpath**, just south of Connaught Place has good street shopping. Small kiosks sell all kinds of cheap cotton clothes which are generally export-surplus garments. There's lots of silver and artificial jewellery with semi-precious stones available here but you need to know the fake from the genuine because you will get no help from the vendors.

The very popular and lively **Tibetan Market** along here has goods from everywhere in India and Tibet, however, you'll need to bargain hard to get a really decent price. The starting price is usually pitched high so go in hard if you want chunky silver jewellery and Tibetan paraphernalia.

### New Delhi

The **Santushti shopping complex**, where you can find some wonderful Indian fashion designers, was started by a welfare organization formed by Air Force Officers' Wives. It is in the diplomatic enclave of Chanakyapuri and in contrast to many Indian shopping precincts, it has a calm, exclusive, and tasteful air about it.

The simple shops, in terracotta-roofed bungalows, mainly sell contemporary Indian clothing, jewellery and home décor. In the evening its manicured lawns are visited by peacocks while a largely expatriate crowd sits around watching them.

**Khan Market**, not far from India Gate, is a small, well established up-market place. Branded outlets sell at fixed prices. There are some interesting book shops and some excellent tailors specialising in fast work. There are also some hidden lounges where you can relax on balconies overlooking the street. It opens daily except Sundays.

**People Tree** (http://peopletreeonline.com/home.html) (8 Regal Building, Parliament St) started life as a studio space for alternative artists; now, it is primarily a bookshop crammed with progressive reads, handmade jewellery and independently designed clothing. You will be browsing alongside Delhi's intellectuals, hippies and hipsters.

### South Delhi

**Hauz Khas** was called "the national capital of ethnic chic" by a New York journalist and it has increased its reputation ever since. Most roads are narrow muddy lanes with sagging electrical cables, potholes and cattle, and boutiques and shops are established in converted old homes. Despite this, it is extremely popular. Most shops sell handicrafts, curios, old carpets and designer clothing.

The Village is home to chic restaurants as well. Flipside and Kunzum are coffee places, Elma's Bakery is good for tea and scones, and The Living Room has music and food.

Saket is host to a collection of modern malls. The malls offer top of the line international and national brands of fashion, accessories and luxury goods. Cinemas show both Indian and International movies and there are outlets of the most loved food chains.

**Select Citywalk Mall** (http://www.selectcitywalk.com/) is the largest and it combines luxury and high-street shopping together with cafes, bistros, restaurants and bars. It is extremely clean and pleasant and provides a great opportunity for visitors to see how upper-middle class India shops. It opens from 10 a.m. to 11 p.m. daily.

**DLF Place** (http://dlfplace.in/), which is attached to Citywalk, has a Marks & Spencers as an anchor store, a retail arcade with many major Indian and international brands of clothes and apparel, a six-screen cinema multiplex and diner, a food court, Hard Rock Cafe, gourmet outlets, office complex and Hilton hotel.

**Square One Mall** provides a complete entertainment and shopping package with a multiplex, a food court and shops like Bandhej, Bella and Kothari Art Jewellers. **MGF Metropolitan Mall** has the Shoppers Stop store as an anchor tenant, a food court, restaurants and bars, a Bose store, spa, and motor vehicle dealerships. The large, up-market **Ambience Mall** and **DLF Promenade Mall** are both in Nelson Mandela Marg near the Jawaharial Nehru University. **Pacific Mall** is a popular place in West Delhi.

**Ansal Plaza** (http://ansalplaza.in/delhi/index.aspx?mid=7) was the first mall to be built in South Delhi and it was an immediate success. It is situated near South Extension and is built in a circular fashion around an amphitheatre with a stage at the centre. Cultural events are held here from time to time and there are many major international brands.

**DLF Emporio** (http://www.dlfemporio.com/) in Vasant Kunj would like to think of itself as 'India's Most Luxurious Shopping Destination'. Some of the brands available here include Giorgio Armani, Salvatore Ferragamo, Louis Vuitton, Cartier, Dior, and Hugo Boss.

Don't think that South Delhi is all malls, however. **Nehru Place** is a sprawling shopping and business centre with a massive bus terminal. Nehru Place Market is the place to go if you are looking for computers and computer parts. Also available are cheap CDs and VCDs of computer games, movies and software. Second-hand books are another attraction. Don't forget to bargain.

**Greater Kailash** is one of the more affluent neighbourhoods in the city. The shopping centres in M and N Block are some of the most popular in Delhi. They are home to a wide range of up-market retail stores with international brands such as Puma, Nike, Adidas and Lacoste, and there are also several restaurants and coffee houses.

**Lajpat Nagar** is the liveliest market of South Delhi. It offers a wide choice of up-market accessories, clothing and home essentials. This market is located between two popular suburbs- Greater Kailash and South Extension. There are branded showrooms and small local retailers, so there is good choice.

It's one of the most popular places with middle class Indian shoppers. One of the market's attractions is having beautiful henna designs applied to your hands. You'll also find reasonably priced Indian tops and suits here. It opens daily except Mondays.

The **Dilli Haat** (Sri Aurobindo Marg, West Kidwai Nagar) (http://www.dillihaat.net.in/) is an open air craft bazaar cum food plaza run by the Delhi Tourism and Transportation Development Corporation (DTTDC). There are two similar bazaars in Delhi; one is opposite the INA Market on Sri Aurbindo Marg; the second is in North Delhi.

Dilli Haat has food stalls representing all Indian states and it offers dishes from throughout the country. Small thatched cottages and kiosks give the plaza a village atmosphere. Only registered craftsmen are eligible to place their stalls here. There are 62 stalls selling handicrafts and the craftsmen come from all over India. The best time to visit is evenings when it glitters with lights. It opens daily from 11 a.m. to 10 p.m. Admission is Rs20 for adults and Rs5 for children.

**Sarojini Nagar** is most famous for its shops and stalls which sell cheap export-reject clothes. There's also a sweet market (Babu Market) and vegetable market (Subzi Mundi) in the area. It is located near Safdarjung Airport and opens daily except Mondays.


**Eating and drinking**

You are in India so naturally you want to eat Indian food but Delhi also offers much more than this.

Chinese food is available in just about every five star hotel in India while many restaurants in Delhi also serve this cuisine. Chinese food is very popular among Delhi locals, so a wide range of Chinese cuisines is available in the city, as well as road-side Chinese fast food.

Continental cuisine can be had at many five star hotels with La Rochelle (The Oberoi), the Orient Express (Taj Palace) and Rick's (Taj Man Singh) being some of the standouts. There are also various multi-cuisine restaurants within the city offering this fare.

*Desi* Junk Food is available all over the city. Among the most popular and widely available are *chaat, gol guppe, paranthe, bhelpuri*, and *chaat papri*.

Delhi Haat has food stalls with menu items from almost every state in India, offering cheap and quality food. The food is coupled with a swanky market showcasing the arts and crafts culture of India. Elsewhere there is a great variety of offerings from Rs50 roadside food stalls to Rs5000 swanky restaurants.

Italian food is very popular in Delhi. Many hotel restaurants offer Italian food and some specific Italian restaurant like Little Italy at the Defence Colony Market, Diva at Greater Kailash Pt.2, and OliveBar and Kitchen near the Qutb Minar serve quality cuisine.

I lay no claim to being a Delhi food expert but I have had some excellent meals in the Indian capital and have found some of the following to be generally reliable.

Delhi Dining & Nightlife

## Top restaurants

All these places have good food, excellent service and nice ambiance but prices are very high when compared to more normal restaurants. For many visitors they will be a one-time treat.

New York-based French restaurant, **Le Cirque**, (Top floor of The Leela Palace; Tel: 011 3933 1234), does excellent comfort food for people who don't mind paying a lot of money for a memorable meal. It is famous for its mix of French and Italian cuisine, and is also known for great people watching. Signature dishes here are black cod, foie gras, lobster risotto and chocolate soufflé. Children under the age of 12 are not permitted. Le Cirque serves dinner only, 7 p.m.-midnight.

The **Royal China** (16th floor, Eros Corporate Towers, Nehru Place; Tel: 011 4981 8000) India's Cantonese cuisine leader, is a favourite with lunching locals. The dim sum lunches are good value.

**Yeti** (M-20, Main Market, 110048 New Delhi; Tel: +91 11 4067 8649), a meaty "Himalayan kitchen," serves one of the city's best Bhutanese and Nepalese thalis. The ambiance is laid-back and friendly.

The Mediterranean-themed **Olive Bar and Kitchen** (One Style Mile, Mehrauli; Tel: 011 2957 4444), at the Qutb, is a good place for lunch. Their truffle risotto and lobster is deservedly popular. Housed in a converted Mughal mansion, the Italian-French-Mediterranean menu caters to vegetarians, with creative dishes such as asparagus and fennel risotto while a wood-fired oven churns out thin-crust pizzas. The Sunday brunch is extremely popular.

**Bukhara** (ITC Maurya, Diplomatic Enclave, Sardar Patel Marg; Tel: 011 2611 2233) has the richest north-western Indian food this side of the Pakistani border. This is where Bill Clinton and Vladimir Putin enjoyed a meal. Food is grilled behind a glass partition. You can watch the chefs while you sip a chilled beer.

Good choices include the *murg tandoori* (a whole chicken marinated in yoghurt, malt vinegar, ginger, and a whole lot more), and the *tandoori pomfret*, a whole flatfish roasted with spices. The *raan*, a slow-cooked shoulder of lamb, is a specialty with a cult following. Some will not like the Flintstones-style décor and the absence of both cutlery and finger bowls. Various platters encourage communal sharing and vegetarians are certainly catered for as well.

Also here is **Dum Pukht** which serves food from the kitchens of 18th-century Awadh. The regal decor and sublime flavours blended by the traditional method of slow cooking in a clay pot takes one back to past eras. Judicious use of aromatic herbs and spices adds another level of sophistication to the dishes. The service, courtesy, and attention are excellent. No children below the age of 10 are permitted. It opens 7 p.m. - 11:45 p.m. nightly and for Sunday lunch.

At **Indian Accent**, (The Lodhi, New Delhi) they experiment by reviving old recipes and combine them with contemporary style cooking. Using seasonal and organic ingredients from across the world, it raises a toast to the Indian food of the 21st century. It has been awarded the best restaurant in India by *Timeout* magazine.

Some of the favourite dishes on the menu include *foie gras stuffed galawat, potato sphere chaat, white pea ragda*, warm *doda burfi* treacle tart, and homemade vanilla bean ice cream. The five wines paired with chef Manish's tasting menu (11 dishes) are the pièce de résistance here.

**Chor Bizarre** (Hotel Broadway, 4/15A Asaf Ali Road; Tel: 011 2327 3821) provides a truly northern Indian experience. The *bhel puri* is excellent, but the real highlight here is the *Kashmiri thali*, a set menu that changes daily depending on what produce is available from the market.

**Karim's** (Gali Kababian, near the Jama Masjid in Old Delhi; Tel: 011 2326 9880) was started by the cook at the Mughal emperors' royal court. It is hidden away down a narrow passage and although it is a renowned institution which has been trading since 1913, it appears that the service and food quality has deteriorated recently. There are two other branches but this one has the history. The *chicken tikka* is a particular favourite.

The **Spice Route** (The Imperial Hotel, Janpath; Tel: 011 2334 1234) is an unusually decorated restaurant within the neo-classical building. The Kerala-inspired Irachi stew of lamb and potato in coconut milk served with *appams* (rice-flour pancakes) is one of the favourites.

**360** (The Oberoi Hotel, Dr. Zakir Hussain Marg; Tel: 011 2436 3030) has five-star Sushi brunches served to New Delhi's political and social power brokers. Its feisty menu is a tribute to old world charm and dishes are nothing less than a piece of art.

## Street food

The Old City streets of Chandni Chowk are a hub for the city's best street food. The choice is vast so the following are just a few local favourites.

Natraj Dahi Bhalle Walle (1396 Main Road, Chandni Chowk; Tel: 98111 67400) sells *dahi bhalla* (a spiced yoghurt snack) while Pandit Baburam Devidayal (9074 Gali Paranthe Wale, Chandni Chowk), has fried, crisp *parantha* breads stuffed with potato, *paneer*, banana or *rabdi*, a creamy Indian dessert). They also have thin *papad paranthas*.

Nearby in Chawri Bazaar, Hira Lal Chaat Corner (Hauz Qazi Chowk and Nai Sadak, near the entrance of Gali Lohe Wali) has interesting variations of fruit *chaat* while Ashok Chatt Corner (3488 Chowk Hauz Qazi, Chawri Bazaar; Tel: 98114 67258) have *gol guppas* and crispy *papri chaat*, thin fried pastry circles, fried chickpea and potato pieces drenched in yoghurt, tamarind and coriander.

I recommend the *sohan halwa* from the 200-year-old Ghantewala (1862-A Chandni Chowk; Tel: 011 2328 0490) Chandni Chowk's oldest sweet shop. Anil Kumar Jain (Jain Coffee House, Raghu Ganj, Chawri Bazaar; Tel: 011 2391 8925), in a grain store where you can sit on a bag of rice, has an interesting seasonal fruit-filled sandwich and *cheeku* fruit shakes.

If plunging into the mad-house of Chandni Chowk seems too much, you can find some street food in other places. South Delhi's Bengali Sweets

(G-19, South Extension Part 1, New Delhi; Tel: 011 2462 1022) and Evergreen Sweet House (S-29-30, Green Park Market, Green Park; Tel: 011 2652 1615) serve street-food restaurant style. Khan Chacha (50, 1/F, Khan Market, New Delhi; Tel: 98106 71103) probably has the city's best mutton kebab rolls.

## Night time

**Kitty Su** (Barakhamba Avenue, Connaught Place, New Delhi; Tel: 011 4444 7777) has a pseudo-erotic Kamasutra vibe, champagne lounges, and huge bathrooms.

**Shiro's** (Samrat Hotel, Kautilya Marg, Chanakyapuri, New Delhi; Tel: 011 2611 0606) is a place for a hectic night out. The nightclub/restaurant has many regulars every weekend for the cool drinks menu and pan-Asian bites.

**Hype** (Welcome Hotel, Plot 3, Sector 10, District Center, Dwarka,) caters to a younger crowd and is almost always crowded.

The **Blue Bar** (Taj Palace, Sardar Patel Marg, Diplomatic Enclave; Tel: 011 4981 5086) is a nice al fresco bar that affords a great urban reprieve for leisurely drink sessions.

**Polo Lounge** (Hyatt Regency Hotel; Tel: 011-6677-1314) has an English colonial pub look, with an informal ambience from the dark-stained wood accents to the dim lighting and relaxed atmosphere. The clientele lives up to this billing, with Western business-types drinking and dancing alongside the local beautiful people. There is a stunning selection of whiskeys and mixers.

## Family Fun Spots

There are few family fun centres in the city but several are easily reached on the outskirts and if you have access to a car, the possibilities are almost endless. Here are some suggestions.

**Delhi Rides** (Kalindi Kunj Park, Okhlia) is about 15 km from Connaught Place (CP). There are water slides, waterfalls, swimming pools and various rides such as Frisbee, Parachute Tower, and Whirl Ride. Maintenance appears to be an issue. It opens 11 a.m. to 7 p.m. daily. Entry is Rs500 on weekdays, Rs600 on weekends, and Rs1100/1200 for couples. See http://www.delhirides.in

**Fun & Food Village** (Old Delhi Gurgaon Road, Kapshera) (http://www.funnfood.com/delhi.html#) is located south of the international airport. This water park is a great place to be with family and friends, especially for children. There are some adrenaline inducing rides, or you can splash around in the regular or wave pool. Entry is child Rs500, adult Rs1000, couple Rs1600.

**Splash Water Park** (near Palla Moad, main GT Kamal Road, Alipur), about 20 km from CP, has water slides, rain dances and wave pools and numerous adrenaline-inducing rides. The park is very well maintained and spotlessly clean. It opens 10 a.m. to 7 p.m. with admission of Rs 400 child, Rs500 single adult with child, and Rs700 adult on weekdays. It is Rs100 higher on weekends. See http://www.splashwaterpark.in

**Adventure Island** (opposite Rithala Metro Station, Sector 10, Rohini) with upwards of 26 rides and attractions, sprawls over a large area about 25 km from CP. This is one of the better parks and it adheres to the globally accepted European Union Safety Standards. The park opens 11 a.m. to 7 p.m. with admission of Rs250 then rides are extra. See http://www.adventureisland.in/home.html

**Worlds of Wonder** (A-2, Sector, Noida), about 25 km from CP, is one of the largest amusement parks in Asia. The Adventure Park is divided into two zones: Road Show and La Fiesta. There is also a water park, go-karting track, and an adjacent retail area. The park opens 11.30 a.m. to 8 p.m. with admission prices of Rs600 adults and Rs500 for children to each park. See http://www.worldsofwonder.in

**Just Chill Water and Fun Park** (near GTB Memorial, GT Karnal Road), 26 km from CP, is divided into a water park, Edu-Tainment Park, and Adventure Games. The Edu-Tainment Park includes demonstrations of pottery making, spinning, milking and other traditional activities. Some of the rides are breathtaking. The park opens from 10 a.m. until 7 p.m. and tickets are adults Rs700 and children Rs500 on weekdays, and adults Rs800 and children Rs600 on weekends. See http://www.justchillwaterpark.com

**Shikhar Adventure Park** (Wazirpur Village, Pataudi Road, Sector 92, Gurgaon), 40 km from CP, is something different. It has challenging climbing towers, obstacle courses, rope ladders, balance beams and much more but is orientated towards groups. It has an admission price of Rs1500 each for a minimum group size of 30. See http://www.shikharadventurepark.com

**Jarasik Park Inn** (GT-Kamal Road, NH1, Sonipat, Haryana) is about 40 km from CP. The park is divided into a water park, amusement park, go-cart track, zipline, food court, restaurant and resort. The water park is particularly outstanding. There is a high waterfall and long slides to provide memorable moments. The park opens from 10.30 a.m. until 6.30 p.m. with weekday entry of Rs750 single, and Rs500 children, and weekend entry of Rs1000/750 respectively. Check out http://jurasikparkinn.com

## Getting around

### From the airport

There are several ways to get from **Delhi International Airport** (http://www.newdelhiairport.in/) to the city. A fast airport express Metro train service operates to connect the airport with the central part of New Delhi. Running 15.7 km underground and 7 km on an elevated rail, the Airport Express Line connects the airport with some of the most prominent points within New Delhi. Travel time to New Delhi station is 25 minutes.

An alternative is by bus. Buses are owned either by the State-owned Delhi Transport Corporation (DTC) or private contractors. The corporation runs an air-conditioned shuttle service about every 30 minutes connecting the airport to the central parts of Delhi.

From Delhi International Airport Terminal, Carzonrent has chauffeur drive, self drive and limousine services. See www.carzonrent.com Reservations: reserve@carzonrent.com

Most international visitors are more likely to take a taxi. There are three alternative services: Meru Cabs– located at T3 International Airport arrivals; Mega Cabs– located at T3 International Airport arrivals; and Easy Cabs– located at T1C Domestic Arrival Terminal. Each provides taxi services to the city. See www.merucabs.com; www.megacabs.com; or www.easycabs.com

**Around town**

For short distances, walking or a rickshaw can be used but for longer trips you need an auto rickshaw, taxi, bus or Metro. **Auto rickshaws** ("autos", similar to a tuk-tuk) are often the fastest way through Delhi's horrific traffic, however, they are not the most comfortable.

You should insist on using the meter as many drivers will not automatically turn it on when you get in. If he refuses, find another driver or else agree on a price first. To help with this, you can log on to www.taxiautofare.com to figure out your approximate fare beforehand. You can also negotiate a half- or full-day rate.

Far more comfortable are **air-conditioned taxis**. To hail a Black & Yellow Roofed Taxi, you normally just wait on the street or go to a taxi stand. Ask the driver to turn on the meter or negotiate a fare. The standard charge at December 2017 was Rs25 for the first kilometre and thereafter Rs14 per kilometre for non-AC taxis, and Rs16 per kilometre for AC taxis. Night charges, waiting time and luggage fees are extra.

**Radio cabs** (or call taxis) such as Meru Cabs (https://www.merucabs.com/) and Easy Cabs (http://www.easycabs.com/) are safe and reliable and congregate at most major crossings and markets. Call taxis operate by the meter. Most taxi drivers do not speak much English however, so you should know a popular landmark or a well-known hotel near your destination, and they will probably understand this and take you there quite easily.

To avoid misunderstandings with all taxis and auto richshaws, make sure you know a popular landmark near the place you wish to visit. You should also familiarise yourself with a map of the city with the desired destination distinctly marked.

Women's safety is still a problem in Delhi and transport is no exception. Amongst many other measures taken to provide safety for women, one notable one is the facility of a Women Cab Service which is slowly and steadily mushrooming in the city. Sakha Cabs for Women (Tel: 9278 708 888), ForShe Cabs (11 4422 2222) and GCabs (11 3942 3942) are some of the services.

Radio cabs are not always available when you want them; especially in peak traffic hours so it is better to book at least 2-3 hours in advance. They are fitted with meters and printers for issuing a receipt. The billing is done on a per kilometre basis.

The **Delhi metro** is cheap and clean but the multiple exits from some stations can be confusing. This is the best way for getting around the city if there is a Metro stop fairly close to where you want to go. Like all forms of public transport in a strange city, the Metro takes a little getting used to but after using it once the system is quite easy to understand and the service is good except during peak periods when stations and trains can be quite crowded.

The system criss-crosses the city and goes deep into some neighbourhoods but there are still sections of the city where you have to rely on radio cabs and auto rickshaws to move around.

A **Tourist Card** is available for unlimited Metro travel over short periods. There are two kinds of cards - 1 day and 3 day. The one-day card costs Rs100 and the three-day card Rs250 (December 2017). A deposit of Rs50 payable at purchase is refundable on the return of the card. One-off fares are paid by tokens which are Rs8 to Rs30.

Delhi Transport Corporation runs extensive **bus services** that connect almost every part of Delhi. Services operate until approximately 10:30 p.m. Unfortunately, there are no route guides available on paper but there are a few web sites that show some of the routes. Most people just ask around to know the correct bus they need to travel in. Bus fares are Rs5, 10, 15 for non A/C (Green) and Rs10, 15, 20, 25 for the A/C buses (Red) depending on distance.

Delhi Metro Route Map
Schematic

# 4 UDAIPUR – A DELIGHTFUL GEM

This lovely city is a very popular tourist destination in the state of Rajasthan. It is located 400 kilometres south-west of the state capital, Jaipur and about 680 km from Delhi. It is known for its beautiful lake and the Rajput-era palaces, many of which are now luxury hotels. With shimmering Lake Pichola and the wooded Aravalli Hills stretching away in every direction, Udaipur has an unmatched romantic setting.

The huge, cupola-crowned City Palace fronts the eastern shore of the lake and it looks out at Udaipur's other famous landmark, the Lake Palace, which is now a hotel. This fairy-tale building seems to float on the lake and is only accessible if you have a booking. Eastward, away from the lake shore, there are tangled lanes lined with homes, temples, shops, and businesses that are fascinating to explore.

Some of the romance is fading a little in the inner city, however, as Udaipur strains to capture more and more tourist rupees. Near the lake, almost every building caters to the tourist trade. Hotels of dubious construction rise ever higher in a quest for the best view, too many restaurants serve up mediocre food, and noisy traffic clogs some of the narrow streets making them unattractive for walking.

If you take a step back from all this, however, you find that Udaipur still has its magic and some wonderful settings. It is a pretty bougainvillea-draped old town where a bit of wandering is the order of the day. Because of its lovely scenery, many Hollywood and Bollywood movies have used Udaipur as a location. It is my favourite city in the Golden Triangle.

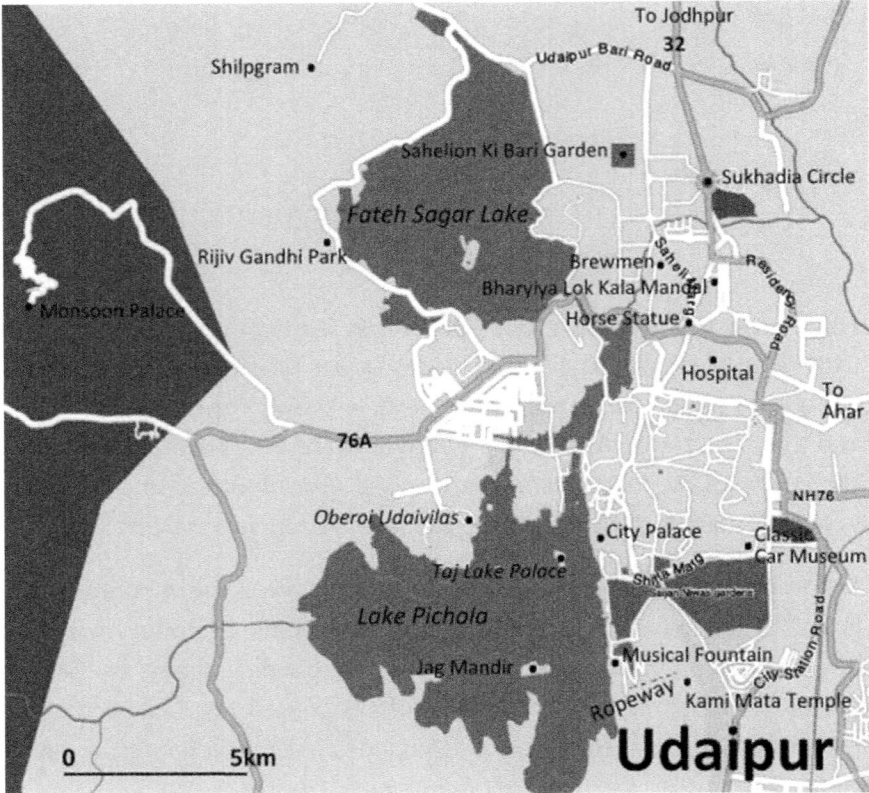

The airport, with regular connections to Delhi and Mumbai, is about 40 minutes east of town. It is served by taxis and a bus. The railway station is a couple of kilometres south-east of the central city and the bus station is about a kilometre further north. Persistent hotel touts will greet you at the railway and bus stations.

Udaipur was founded in 1559 by Maharana Udai Singh II as the final capital of the Mewar kingdom. It was a fortified city with massive gates.

Five of these remain today. It suffered repeated attacks by the Mughals and later the Marathas until the British appeared in the early nineteenth century. They signed a treaty with the Mewar rulers allowing them virtually full control of internal affairs.

The highlight for most visitors today is Lake Pichola, an artificial fresh water lake, created in 1362. It is one of several contiguous lakes that were developed over centuries in and around the city. Dams were built to meet the drinking water and irrigation needs of the city and its neighbourhood and hence the lakes were formed.

There are four islands in Lake Pichola: Jag Niwas with its Lake Palace, Jag Mandir with the palace of the same name, Mohan Mandir, from where the king would watch the annual Gangaur Festival celebration, and Arsi Vilas, a small island where there is a small palace and also a bird sanctuary.

Large palaces, temples, bathing ghats, and elevated hills on all its sides surround the lake. At the southern end, there is a hill that is known as Machhala Magra and you can get a glimpse of Eklinggarh Fort from here. Ornamental arch bridges have been built to span between the banks where the lake narrows.

A boat trip on the lake provides the best views of the impressive buildings. There are two options as explained later in this chapter. The highlight for most people is the closer view of the **Lake Palace** (https://taj.tajhotels.com/en-in/taj-lake-palace-udaipur/) on Jag Niwas Island. This palace, built in marble in 1746 by Maharana Jagat Singh II, spreads across the whole island and some claim it is as impressive as the Taj Mahal.

The James Bond movie *Octopussy* was partially shot inside the Lake Palace and this has added to its fame. It was originally built as a royal summer palace but is now a luxury 5-star hotel, operated by Taj Hotels Resorts and Palaces.

*Lake Palace Hotel*

The Lake Palace has a series of cypress-shaded courtyards, terraces, beautiful fountains, and well laid out gardens. There are several rooms decked out with carved arches, paintings, crystal work, and stained glass work. The elegance, opulence and the truly outstanding setting make this one of the most romantic places in India. The complex was built facing the east so that residents could pray to the sun god at dawn.

This five-star hotel provides world-class amenities with immaculate hospitality to its guests. It is magical to arrive at twilight when the city lights twinkle in the background and the Aravalli Mountains are silhouetted against the evening sky. Unfortunately, only guests staying in the hotel or special guests who are dining at the hotel's restaurants can stop here.

**Jag**                                                         **Mandir**
(http://www.hrhhotels.com/grand_heritage/jagmandir_palace/index.aspx) is a palace built on another island in the lake. It was started in 1551 by Maharana Amar Singh and the royal family initially used it as a summer resort. It is now a small grand luxury adults-only hotel, Jagmandir Island Palace, managed by the HRH Group of Hotels.

Gul Mahal, a small sandstone palace with an imposing dome was the first building and this is now incorporated into the main palace. The entrance pavilion is an impressive white colonnade of cusped arches decorated with large elephants carved in stone.

The large Garden Courtyard is covered with black and white tiles and there are fountains and pools, crisscrossed by walkways. There is special lighting around the rose shrubs and shimmering candlelight reflections from the pool and this brings it alive in the evening. Besides the ornate architecture, there are fountains, water pools, an interesting gallery and a beautiful Ganesh.

On the northern side of the palace is an open-sided terrace with marble columns. This place is now run as a restaurant. A varied a la carte menu is offered for evening dining but the special four-course dinner is highly recommended. Jagriti, a heritage museum on-site, gives an idea of how Jag Mandir Island Palace was built and developed over the centuries.

Back in the city, on the east bank of Lake Pichola is a massive series of palaces called **City Palace** (http://tourism.rajasthan.gov.in/udaipur/17/udaipur-city-palace). From the water, it appears like a fort. The various buildings have been built at different times since 1559 by 22 maharajas and many are in a flamboyant style.

It is considered to be the largest palace in India. There is a general entrance fee of Rs30 for admission to the complex but you really need to buy a museum ticket as this gets you into the most interesting parts of the building. Two hotels occupy other parts of the palace.

The granite and marble exterior of the palace complex, with its balconies, towers and cupolas, is quite dramatic but the interiors have delicate mirror-work, marble-work, murals, wall paintings, silver-work, inlay-work and coloured glass. There is a great view of the lake and Udaipur city from its upper terraces.

*City Palace from the water*

The main entry is through the Bara Pol (Great Gate), built in 1600. This in turn leads to the Tripolia Pol, a triple arched gate built in 1725. The road ahead is lined with shops and kiosks owned by craftsmen and others. The main block of the palace is approached from the Ganesha Deodhi terrace. You enter a maze of narrow passages, steep staircases, terraces, halls, and apartments. You are soon lost in a world of luxury and indulgence.

The Badi Mahal (Great Palace) is a building in Mughal style built around a lovely courtyard with arcades enclosing a square marble pool. This is the highest point of the palace and has wonderful hanging gardens with towers and terraces. In an adjoining hall, miniature paintings and wall paintings are displayed and there is a nice fountain.

Other places of interest within the palace are the Surya Choupad which boasts a huge, ornamental sun – the symbol of the Mewar dynasty – and Mor Chowk (Peacock Courtyard) with its lovely mosaics of peacocks, the favourite Rajasthani bird. The Manek Mahal (Ruby Palace) at the far end of Mor Chowk contains exquisite 19th-century glass and mirror work.

The entry fee for the City Palace museum is Rs250 adult and Rs100 per child. You pay Rs225 for a camera and video recorder. Rs225 per person gets you an audio guide. It takes at least 3 to 4 hours to do some justice to this place. The Palki Khana Restaurant is open from 9 a.m. to 11 p.m.

**Fateprakash Palace** (21 rooms and 41 suites) (http://www.hrhhotels.com/grand_heritage/fateh_prakash_palace/index.aspx), which is now run as a luxury hotel, is part of the complex. It has a crystal gallery that has a range of crystal furniture, crockery and table fountains which have never been used.

There is also a unique jewel studded carpet here. The crystal is spread across the upper-gallery of the glittering Durbar Hall. This hall has some unusually large chandeliers, weapons, and also some unique portraits.

This is probably the single largest private collection of crystal anywhere in the world and frankly it is a monument to excess. It was ordered in 1877 by Maharana Sajjan Singh from the Birmingham-based F&C Osler Company but he died before it arrived and no-one else seemed to take any interest in it until recently. Entry here is Rs550 per adult, Rs350 per child 5 to 12 years, inclusive of an audio guide. Photography, unfortunately, is strictly prohibited.

The other hotel in the complex is the crescent-shaped **Shiv Niwas Palace** (19 rooms and 17 suites) (http://www.hrhhotels.com/grand_heritage/shiv_niwas_palace/index.aspx). It was built in the early 20th century and was originally reserved exclusively for visiting dignitaries and guests of the House of Mewar.

There is an excellent sound and light show here conducted every evening at the magnificent Manek Chowk. The show has been created to spread awareness, interest and pride in the history of Mewar that stretches back 1500 years. The 60-minute show is presented in English and Hindi at the following times: Show in Hindi: 8 p.m. to 9 p.m. (May to August), Show in English: 7 p.m. to 8 p.m. (September to March), 7.30 p.m. to 8.30 p.m. (April)

Entry ticket for the show in English will cost Rs200-500 per adult depending on the seat and Rs100 or 200 for a child between 8 and 12.

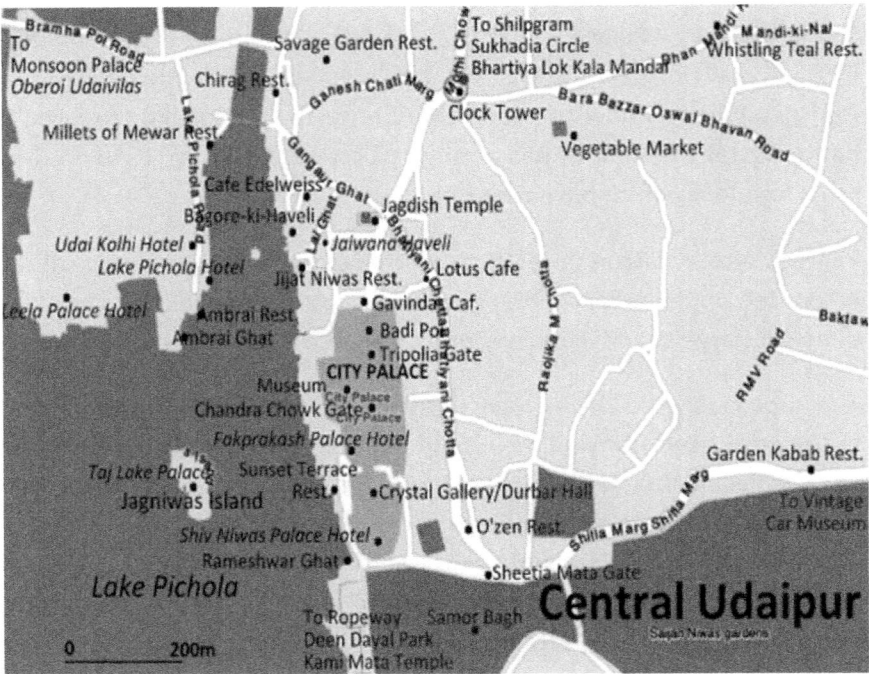

Central Udaipur

**Jagdish Mandir**, located 150 metres north of the city palace, was built in 1652. It is a large, elegant temple with many carvings of Vishnu and a black stone idol of Lord Jagannath. The carvings are typical of Mewar temples. An image of a Garuda (half-bird, half-man), is placed in a separate shrine in front of the temple.

Two huge stone elephants guard the steps leading to the temple entrance. The spire of the main temple is 24m high and it dominates this area of Udaipur. Four smaller shrines dedicated to Lord Ganesha, the Sun God, Goddess Shakti and Lord Shiva surround the main shrine. Several roads radiate in different directions from this point and there are a few good restaurants in the area.

This part of the walled city is a maze of narrow winding lanes fronted by shops and residential buildings. It is easy to get lost but is generally quite safe and you have a great opportunity to see aspects of the local community denied to most tourists. Locals will help you if you ask.

**Sajjangarh** (Monsoon Palace) (http://sajjangarh.com/) is a poorly maintained hilltop palatial residence to the west of the city which was built by a maharani in 1884 in white marble. There are good panoramic views from here. The palace has a grand central court with a staircase and many rooms but, frankly, the building itself is not worth seeing. You can go inside into a couple of rooms but there is little to see.

It is nicely illuminated in the evenings and is a good place to watch the sunset. There are many monkeys hanging around and some have become very adept at stealing from visitors. The palace gained some fame when it was used in the 1983 James Bond film *Octopussy* as the residence of Kamal Khan, an exiled Afghan prince.

The palace can be accessed along a winding road by taxi or private car. Auto rickshaws are only allowed until the gate at the bottom of the hill. Entry to the site is Rs50 and there is a Rs90 charge to take you up the hill from the gate.

Encircling the palace is the **Sajjangarh Wildlife Sanctuary** (https://www.rajasthandirect.com/tourism/wildlife/sajjangarh-wildlife-sanctuary). It covers an area of about five square kilometres and is a reserve for a range of animals and reptiles.

Most visitors consider a boat trip on the glimmering **Lake Pichola** to be a wonderful experience. With the mountains and the city against the backdrop of a beautiful sunset, it is quite magical. Along the way, you see views of historical landmarks dotted along the shore such as the City Palace and the picturesque ghats -- steps leading down into the water that locals use for bathing.

As you travel north you pass various hotels and mansions, the most prominent being the **Bagore ki Haveli** (http://www.udaipurtourism.com/monuments-havelies/bagore-haveli.html) with its triple-arched Tripolia Gate. This is now a museum and is well worth visiting partly because of its magnificent architecture. There is a well-known cultural show here each evening from 7-8 p.m. You need to line up for tickets and seating is on a first-come basis so I advise you to arrive by 6 15 p.m. in the busy season.

The boat then goes south and you will see Mohan Mandir, a delightful perching place for waterbirds that was built by Rana Jagat Singh II in honour of Lord Krishna.

You will also see Arsi Vilas, an 18th-century structure built by Rana Ari Singh II; the 17th century Jag Mandir Island Palace; and Jag Niwas, now the Lake Palace Hotel. You'll also catch a view of the distant Sajjangarh Palace perched on the hills.

One trip allows you to alight at Jag Mandir to do some sightseeing and take a later boat back to the jetty where you started your cruise. Boats depart about every 20 minutes from Rameshwar Ghat in the City Palace gardens (you'll need to pay Rs30 to get inside the City Palace if you're not staying there).

The Regular Boat with a one hour ride across Lake Pichola costs Rs400 per adult, Rs200 per child (5 years to 12 years) while the Sunset Boat Ride costs Rs700 per adult and Rs400 per child.

If you want a cheaper option, the boat stand south of Lal Ghat offers 30 minute boat trips for around Rs250 at any time of the day, although Jag Mandir isn't included.

Udaipur has many vantage points for photography but certainly one of the best is **Ambrai Ghat**, especially at sunset. It's located directly opposite the City Palace and in front of the Lake Palace Hotel, so you have a wonderful view of both as their lights are turned on. To get there, head to the Hanuman Ghat area and keep walking along the road that runs parallel to Lake Pichola as far as you can, past the Amet Haveli Hotel and Ambrai restaurant.

The **Udaipur Ropeway** is another popular attraction. The red cable cars take five minutes to climb up the hill from Deen Dayal Park to the Karni Mata temple. There's a viewing platform there and it's another popular spot for seeing the sunset over the city.

Tickets cost Rs100 for Indian adults and Rs300 for foreign adults. Tickets for children under 110 centimetres tall cost Rs50 and Rs150. The line and waiting time to buy tickets can be lengthy at times.

Near the base of the ropeway is **Dudh Talai**, a pretty lake and the Manikya Lal Verma Garden. Musical fountain shows have also made this sunset point popular with locals and visitors. The old stepwell has been made into a feature in the public garden. Further south, the lakeside drive is beautiful and peaceful.

**Bharatiya Lok Kala Mandaal** (Saheli Marg, Madhuban) is a cultural institution that studies folk art, culture, songs and the festivals of Rajasthan. There is a puppet theatre here where shows are held at regular intervals, and a hall displaying theatre objects.

A neighbouring hall has a collection of tribal folk musical instruments and ornaments. Near the puppet theatre, there are henna handprints, decorated cow dung floors, and terra-cotta small shrines that come from the village of Molela near Nathdwara.

Although it is a few kilometres north of town, **Shilpgram** (meaning "craftsmen's village") (http://www.shilpgram.in/Shilpgram-Udaipur.htm), a rural arts and crafts complex, will be of interest to some. It showcases rural life and traditions from Rajasthan, Gujarat, Maharashtra, and Goa. The complex has typical huts from each of the states. Artisans also sell their wares.

On weekends there are folk dances, horse rides, and camel rides. The complex really comes alive during the 10 day Shilpgram Arts & Crafts

Fair in late December but otherwise it doesn't seem to be on the tourist circuit and it can be quite quiet and unexciting mid-week.

The **Vintage Car Museum** (http://www.udaipurtourism.com/museums/vintage-museum.html) at the Garden Hotel, near Saijjan Niwas Garden is something completely different. This houses the car collection of His Highness, the Maharaja of Udaipur, and other vehicles that have been added recently.

The collection is housed in the original semi-circular Palace Garage, a glorious setting for such a remarkable collection of golden oldies. One of the original Burmah Shell petrol pumps is also still here. The Entry Fee is Rs250 per Adult and Rs150 per Child 5 to 12 years which seems high. There is also a deal which includes lunch or dinner and the museum for Rs400. It opens 9 a.m. to 5 p.m.

There are two lovely gardens in the city. **Gulab Bagh**, also known as Saijan Niwas Garden, is the largest garden in Rajasthan, covering over 40 hectares. Maharana Saijan Singh built this beautiful garden in the 1850s and it has become famous for its numerous varieties of roses. Apart from the roses, there are orchids and lawns, together with a toy train for children, a small zoo, a library and a museum.

**Sahelion Ki Bari** (Garden of Maids) in the northern part of the city was built in the 18th century by Maharana Sangram. It is famous for its lush green lawns, lovely lily pond, elephant statues around another pond and the rainforest area. It is well worth visiting if you are in this area. Entry is Rs5.

Sukhadia Circle is a popular landmark particularly at night when it is illuminated by many lights. It has a nice three-tiered fountain in the centre.

Just a couple of kilometres from the city centre, **Ahar** is famous for being the cremation ground of the rulers of Mewar and it is a renowned archaeological site. There are cenotaphs of the Royal rulers and an archaeological museum which holds a collection of Palaeolithic and

Neolithic material and a good collection of sculpture, both labelled in English.

The **Udaipur Solar Observatory** (https://www.prl.res.in/~uso/), situated on an island in the middle of Lake Fatehsagar, is one of the six Global Oscillations Network Group sites in the world and it now has the country's largest telescope to observe the sun. Unfortunately, there is no public access to the structure.

**Eating and Drinking**

Udaipur is well-known for its vegetarian *Daal-Baati-Churma, Gatte-Ki-Sabzi, Kachori* and *Mirchi Bada*. Meals are usually comprised of lentils, vegetables and a wide variety of spices. Ocra, dried mango and *Sangri* (beans) go together with most of the meals.

*Thali* restaurants are good for all-you-can-eat Rajasthani dishes. They are heavy on roti, savoury goodies and vegetables. Udaipur is also known for its spicy snacks, known as *mirchi bada*.

You will find swanky restaurants through to open-air eateries right in town along the lakeshore. Similar places are along Lake Palace Road and the nearby streets of Jagdish Temple Road and Lal Ghat. For market dining at stalls and standard sit down restaurants, the bazaars in the eastern part of Ganjaur Ghat are good. Here are a few specific eating suggestions.

It's about 25 minutes from the centre of town and despite its design like a traditional village and the dancing troupe and camel rides, **Aapni Dhani** (http://apnidhani.com/) somehow misses out with entertainment and ambience but it probably won't disappoint you on the food front. The standard meal includes *daal baati, bajra khichda, bajra roti*, two varieties of vegetables, *gatte ka saag*, sprouts, *papad*, salad, amazing garlic chutney, white butter, and loads of ghee!

**Ambrai** (http://www.amethaveliudaipur.com/restaurant.html) is an open-air restaurant located on the banks of Lake Pichola. It provides a great view of both the City Palace and Lake Palace. The food they serve up doesn't quite match the amazing ambiance, and the service is poor. The waiter will try to talk you into the most expensive things on the menu but I would resist. The standard dishes are quite good enough and even these will cost Rs1500-Rs3000 for two without drinks.

Much better value in this part of the city is **Millets of Mewar** (https://www.milletsofmewar.org/). This is claimed to be Udaipur's first dedicated health food restaurant. They serve traditional and re-imagined Indian fare, as well as soups and salads, Thai curries, chapatti pizzas, and a wide variety of vegan, raw, and gluten-free options. The top floor has distant water views while the floor below has floor seating and a traveller's vibe. It opens for breakfast, lunch, and dinner.

**Devi Garh** (Delwara, NH8, near Eklingji) (http://www.raasdevigarh.com/) is a multi-cuisine restaurant in a beautiful 18th-century hotel and resort about 25 km north-east of the city. The venue has intimate outdoor spaces, and a wide array of flowers and candles flickering inside in mirrored walls. The cuisine is street food prepared by expert chefs and there are live jal tarang and flute recitals in the background.

Trendy **Upre** (Hotel Lake Pichola, outside Chand Pole) (http://www.lakepicholahotel.com/dinning.html) is a terrace restaurant with fine views and a decidedly aquatic twist. The menu is East meets West, where classic European cuisine gets a creative Indian makeover.

Located inside The Jaisingh Garh Hotel, **Kabab Mistri** (http://www.jaisinghgarh.com/kabab-mistri.html) is a great roof top restaurant serving up excellent Indian food. Many Udaipur restaurants pretty much offer the same menu but here you can try their kebabs, *palak ghosht* and crisp garlic naan and find all are good.

Situated in the compound of The City Palace, **Palki Khana** offers a cafe-style menu. Try their cafe mocha, creamy vegetarian risotto, and the Caesar's salad. The **Sunset Terrace** of the Palace has great water views and opens 7 a.m. to 8.30 p.m.

Once you find **Savage Garden** (https://www.facebook.com/savagegardenudaipur/?rf=1235670710555 75) tucked away in the lanes of Chand Pol you'll be delighted by this indoor/outdoor, all blue restaurant which has Mediterranean and Indian food. They serve amazing spinach and mushroom ravioli and some excellent soups and chicken dishes.

**Sheesh Mahal** (https://www.theleela.com/en_us/hotels-in-udaipur/the-leela-palace-hotel-udaipur/dining/sheesh-mahal), the alfresco fine-dining restaurant at the Leela Palace Udaipur is full of delightful little touches: pouches of spices to freshen the air, scented candles and flowers. A highlight here is the spicy *lal maas* (a local mutton creation). The chefs elevate fine dining to a whole new level with their mix of authentic styles and contemporary nuances.

**Cafe Edelweiss** (https://www.facebook.com/pages/Cafe-Edelweiss/228679873940942) is a small homely cafe located near Gangaur Ghat. It is a great place for a Western breakfast and is always flooded with tourists. They have omelettes, coffee, toast, desserts and their famous chilli brownies. It closes at 8 p.m.

**Brewmen** (https://www.facebook.com/brewmen.in/) is located near Sahelion ki Badi. It has modern decor, courteous staff, sandwiches made with crusty bread, and a wide range of teas and coffee.

Much is written about **Lotus Cafe** (Tel: 291 64208) (https://www.facebook.com/pages/Lotus-Cafe-Udaipur/214085951947616) but I summarise it as a reasonable place to eat 'safe' Indian food in a comfortable environment with other foreigners. You can sit upstairs on the floor around a communal table if you need to meet and talk with other travellers. Ask for 'spicy' rather than 'normal' if you like a bit of bite or you will find the food bland.

Central Udaipur is best explored on foot but unmetered taxis, private taxis, radio taxis, auto rickshaws, and regular city bus services are available for longer trips around town.


## Tours

### Walking tours

There are several companies and private individuals offering one-day walking tours. Most take you into the heart of the old town. One such company is Magic Tours (http://udaipurmagic.com/tour/walking-tour/). **Old City Walk** shows you many heritage buildings between Gangour Ghat and the clock tower, and you also visit Pichola Lake with its ghats and many nearby temples.

It's then off to the shoe market and the vegetable market square where you will see spice sellers, colourful local grocery shops, tea shops, and shops selling fruits, vegetables, and local beauty products

**Food tours** (http://udaipurfoodtour.com/) are the best way of exploring this royal city and its delicious cuisine. Each food tour is a combination of the most popular food and hidden sights of the city. Part of the food tour involves walking in old traditional markets while you drive to some places which are too far away. You sample a mixture of some great street food as well as food from air-conditioned places where you can sit in relative peace and quiet to enjoy the flavours.

### Bicycle Tours

**Udaipur      Old      City      Cycling      Tour** (http://www.indiaunbound.com.au/city/udaipur/).The tour starts with a gentle ride in the back streets of the old city. From here you head to the Clock Tower, a sprawling bazaar that was built in the mid-1800s then through a vegetable & spices market. After a quick drinks break it's down to the bank of Lake Pichola through narrow lanes then behind the

City Palace Complex and into the heart of city, finally ending at Tripolia Gate of City Palace to conclude with tea/coffee and snacks.

**Udaipur Outskirts Cycling Tours.** There are two options for cycling tours outside of Udaipur: 18 or 30 kilometre cycling tours. You will start from the hotel early in the morning, bike past various public buildings and many people on their way to work and school before leaving the city proper and entering into the rural outskirts of Udaipur.

Here the scenery changes to a mixed rural landscape of farms and villages, with cattle, birds and farm-related activity. You'll either carry a packed lunch from the city and have it on the way at a picturesque spot or have lunch at a local restaurant back in Udaipur at the completion of the tour.

## Cooking classes

There are at least a dozen places where you can take cooking lessons. Most offer 3-4 hour classes where you cook then eat a lunch or dinner. Some like Sadhna's Cooking Classes (Tel: 9929394551) have been operating for many years while others such as Enjoy cooking Classes (Tel: 9829107577) only commenced in 2015. I have no experience of any of them.

One that gets good reviews is Shashi's Cooking Classes (18 Gangaur Ghat Rd; Tel: 9929303511). Or you could go out-of-town for the **Devra Cooking Class** (http://www.indiaunbound.com.au/city/udaipur/). Devra is a 'homestay' property, a 15-minute drive from Udaipur's city centre. The owners, Major Durga Das and Jyoti Jasol, are charming and knowledgeable hosts and delightful company. You can spend the morning or afternoon here taking in a cooking class, followed by lunch/dinner.

## Out of Town

There are several places around Udaipur which are popular with visitors. Day tours are available and two have reasonable accommodation if you want to stay longer. The most popular is **Mount Abu**, a hill station situated on a rocky plateau about 160 km west of Udaipur.

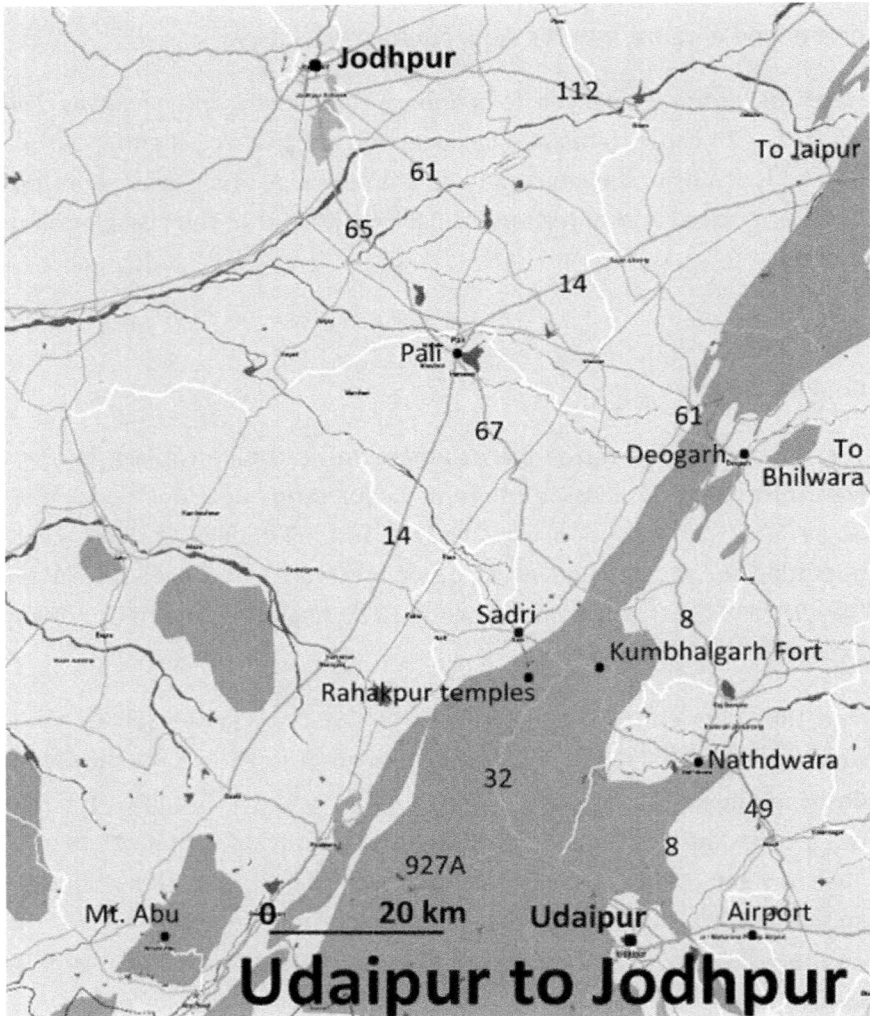

There are rivers, lakes, waterfalls and evergreen forests so locals refer to it as 'an oasis in the desert'. Mount Abu town sits towards the south-west end of the plateau surrounded by the Mount Abu Wildlife Sanctuary.

Nakki Lake is the centre for most activities and boating is popular. You can rent a paddle boat and oarsman. Toad Rock and Sunset point are two places of interest near town. The Wildlife Sanctuary is said to have more than 250 species of birds, and leopard, chinkara, sloth bear, wild boar and langurs can also be found here. There are nature trails through the park and guides can be arranged through the Tourist Reception Centre. It opens sunrise to sunset.

The mountain is famous for its temples. Three in particular are worth seeing; the Adhar Devi Temple carved out of solid rock; the Shri Raghunathji Temple; and a shrine and temple to Dattatreya (Shiva) built in a cave on top of a mountain peak.

Most impressive of all are the Jain temples including the famous Dilwara Temples, a complex of temples carved in white marble that was built between the 11th and 13th centuries. These are some of India's finest temples with spectacular carved interiors. Unfortunately, no photography is allowed inside (though photographs are sold outside). As at other Jain temples, leather articles (belts, shoes etc.) have to be left at the entrance.

The Vimai Vasahi Temple was built in 1031. All the pillars and ceiling and wall panels are beautifully carved. The figures are adorned with figures in various dance movements. Inside the sanctum is a brass-gold idol.

The Luna Vasahi Temple was built in 1230. There is a giant lotus hanging from its dome made from marble that looks like paper. The other three temples are from the 14th, 15th, and 18th centuries. Visitors can enter the temples from noon to 6 p.m.

Hotel prices soar and the place is packed during Diwali (October or November). It also gets pretty busy from mid-May to mid-June, before the monsoon.

You will notice members of the Brahma Kumaris World Spiritual University, a worldwide organisation whose headquarters are here in Mount Abu, in their white clothes. The organisation also runs the Peace Park, located 8 km north-east of town on the road to Guru Shikhar, and the small World Renewal Spiritual Museum in the town centre.

The town of **Eklingji** about 22 kilometres north of Udaipur on Highway 8 is located amidst a beautiful valley. The Eklingji Temple Complex with its 108 temples is one of the most famous temples in Rajasthan. Initially, the temple was built in 734 A.D. but since that time, it has been repaired and modified by various Kings, The main temple is crafted out of white marble. As you wander around the temple complex you'll find a number of carvings from the Kama Sutra.

The double-storied temple has a pyramidal roof, which shelters the huge pillared hall, and a carved tower. There are silver, bronze and stone images of Nandi and a huge black marble four-faced image of Lord Shiva. Many people seem to be attracted by the phallic form of Lord Shiva which is garlanded with a silver snake. Unfortunately, no cameras are allowed in the complex.

There are other ancient temples near Eklingji, such as another Shiva Temple that was built between 1473 and 1509. Deserted **Nagda**, which lies 2 km to the north, is the site of the ancient capital of Mewar, which dates back to A.D. 626. Here you find the ruins of the Saas Bahu, a 10th-century twin temple and the remains of Adbhutji Temple.

**Nathdwara** is a small town about 48 km to the north-east of Udaipur. It is famous for its Shrinathji Temple, a 17th-century temple that is dedicated to Lord Shrinathji. The structure of this temple is simple but the black marble image of Shrinathji with a large diamond between his lips is worth seeing. The temple closes for around four hours in the afternoon so arrive in the morning. During the times of Holi, Diwali, and Janmashtmi, people throng in large numbers and the place gets overcrowded.

About 4 kilometres from the town, **Chetak Smarak** is a memorial built to Rana Pratap's famed horse Chetak who died after helping the Rana escape from the Battle of Haldighati. The memorial is said to have been built at the spot that Chetak died.

Further afield, about 110 km north-east is the town of **Chittorgarh**, named after its most imposing structure, the Chittorgarh Fort which stands atop a 180 metre high hill. The fort houses several magnificent monuments, some unfortunately not in great condition. A one-kilometre road weaves its way to the summit, taking visitors through seven gates before arriving at Rampol (Gate of Ram).

The town has other attractions as well. The Rani Padmin's Palace is built on the banks of a lotus pool and has a pavilion that provides privacy for the women of the royal family. The Vijay Stambh (the Tower of Victory) was built after the defeat of the Muslim rulers of Malwa and Gujarat. The nine-storey tower can be climbed to the terrace where there is a spectacular view of the entire town. Then there is the seven-storied Tower of Fame which was built by a wealthy Jain merchant in the 12th century.

South of Udaipur there are a couple of places of interest. **Rishabdeo** is situated 65 km from Udaipur on the Udaipur- Ahmedabad Road. The main attraction here is the temple of Rishabhadeoji, an important pilgrimage site for followers of the Jain religion, which traces its origin to the 15th century.

When entering this temple, you will see the elephants that are carved out of black stone, the image of Goddess Chakreshvari, the image of goddess Padmavati and the idol of Lord Rishabh Dev also carved out of a single piece of black stone. There are 23 other idols.

Further south is **Dungapur** which was founded in 1358 A.D. by Rawal Veer Singh, the eldest son of the ruler of Mewar. Situated in the foothills of the Aravalli Hills it is a naturally beautiful city. The seven-storey Juna Mahal, a former royal residence, sits on the edge of town.

The first palace on the site was constructed in the late thirteenth century and various extensions and fortifications were added through the nineteenth century by successive rulers.

Unfortunately, its structural integrity is threatened due to insufficient maintenance, and the interior has been vandaalized and the artwork defaced. There is still enough to see to make a visit worthwhile but let us all hope that protection and restoration can be carried out soon.

The other place of note is nestled in idyllic splendour, with the blue waters of Gaibsagar Lake on one side and a cove of private reserve forest on the other. This is **Udai Bilas Palace** now a heritage hotel which is the embodiment of the old world charm of princely India.

## Between Udaipur and Jodhpur

Another popular spot is the village of **Ranakpur** near Sadri town between Udaipur and Jodhpur. It is 91 km from Udaipur, in a valley on the western side of the Aravalli Range and is noted for its temples. We approach here along a narrow, winding road where monkeys regard us haughtily at every turn as if we are invading their territory.

In parts, there is a patchwork of tiny terraces protected by stone walls topped by thorn bushes. We see bullock-powered water wheels and long-tailed sheep being shepherded by young boys who should really be at school.

The **Chaumukha Mandir temple** (a Jain temple) is famous for its exquisite white marble. It is open to tourists in the afternoon only. It is a very big temple and has sculptures of the same quality but of a different type than the Dilwara ones in Mount Abu. It has over 1400 exquisitely carved white marble columns, which are all different.

The temple is dedicated to Lord Adinath. Different doorways allow you to enter the chambers which ultimately take you to the main hall where you see the image of Adinath. The temple ceilings have impressive scrollwork and geometric patterns while five spires and around 20 cupolas rise from the roof.

To enter the temple, you must be appropriately dressed. Women need to cover their legs well below the knee. Leather products (including belts) are not allowed. If you are carrying a camera it will cost you Rs100 for each camera including a mobile (cell) phone with a camera. The guard at the entrance will find it with a metal detector and tell you, "one ticket, one camera."

The **Temple of Parsavanath** is another attraction that is worth visiting. Built in the mid 15th century, the temple is renowned for its engraved windows embellished with Jain figures. Close by there are two other temples dedicated to Neminath (22nd saint) and Surya Narayan (Sun God).

The Surya Narayan Temple dates back to the 13th century but it was rebuilt in the 15th century. It has innumerable circular wall projections and a relief of Lord Surya driven in his chariot by seven horses. The sun god is an ancient and revered deity in India known as Surya.

**Kumbhalgarh Fort** (http://hillfortsrajasthan.nic.in/kumbhal-fort/index.html) is a World Heritage Site about 32 km to the north-east of Ranakpur. It was built in the 15th century by Rana Kumbha the ruler of Mewar state and enlarged through to the 19th century. The fort is built on a hilltop 1100 metres above sea level and has perimeter walls that extend 36 kilometres. Some of the walls are 4.5 metres thick.

There are seven fortified gateways, and over 360 temples within the fort, 300 are ancient Jain and the rest Hindu. The fort remained impregnable to direct assault, and fell only once, due to a shortage of drinking water for the defenders.

It's a steep walk up to the highest point but the views are worth it. You can climb precipitous stairs and lose yourself in corridors, courtyards and pavilions. It is all very interesting. A highlight is the light and sound show held each evening. The whole fort looks so majestic when it is fully lit after the show is over.

The **Kumbhalgarh Wildlife Sanctuary** with its diverse topography is nearby. There are rivers and ranges and it is home to antelopes, leopards, panthers and sloth bears. Once the hunting grounds of royals, this area was declared a wildlife sanctuary in 1971. Treking is allowed but you need a forest guard or a guide with you. Horse safaris organised by local tour operators are very popular. There is also a popular jeep safari and you can stay in Forest Rest Houses with basic facilities.

If you are travelling direct to Pushkar on the NH8 rather than via Jodhpur, a stop at **Deogarh** is worthwhile. This is a popular tourist destination about 130 km from Udaipur with an old fort on a hill and the wonderful **Deogarh Mahal**, a 17th-century palace with glittering mirror-work and murals which is now a heritage hotel.

The 50 rooms are scattered around various wings of a lovely honey-coloured building. Traditional Mewari cuisine, along with Continental and Oriental dishes, is served in the restaurants. The family has also converted one of its forts, Seengh Sagar, into an intimate four bedroom haven in the middle of a lake.

For the nature lover, an alternative is **Deogarh Khayyam** where there are sixteen luxurious, heritage tents, situated in the midst of eucalyptus trees in a beautiful lakeside setting. Morning walks, bird watching and village tours are available, and sitting outside under the starry night sky with a blazing fire is simply divine.

The drive from Udaipur to Jodhpur highlights again the contradictions of rapidly developing India. In parts, there are new six-lane motorways which are largely empty but for the occasional cow or camel, the ever-present motorcycles travelling in the opposite direction to any other traffic, and perhaps a strolling herd of goats. In other parts, there are crowded two-lane roads where traffic slows to a crawl because of markets which encroach onto the pavement.

# 5 JODHPUR – THE BLUE CITY

This region has a long history before the city was founded. For several hundred years the area was part of the Gurjara-Pratihara Empire, whose capital was Kanauji. This slowly collapsed from the 10th century and at the beginning of the 13th century, the most prominent and powerful state in Rajasthan was Mewar.

In 1303 the army of the sultan of Delhi, conquering the Rajput states, including Mewar, however, in 1400, Rao Chanda seized control of Marwar and founded his own Rajput dynasty there. The next few hundred years saw a battle between the forces of the sultan, the Moghuls and various Rajput states.

The city of Jodhpur was founded in 1459 by Rao Jodha, a Rajput chief. Jodha succeeded in conquering the surrounding territory and thus Jodhpur became his capital. The city grew despite the battles raging around but it really prospered under the peace and stability that were a hallmark of the British Raj era.

In 1947, when India became independent, the state became part of the Union of India. At the time of partition, the ruler of Jodhpur, Hanwant Singh, did not want to join India, but finally, it was included in the Indian Republic. Later after the passing of the State Reorganization Act in 1956 it was made part of the state of Rajasthan.

**Jodhpur** is now the second largest city in Rajasthan and has become a popular tourist destination, because of its many imposing buildings and the stark landscape of the Thar Desert. It is sometimes referred to as the "Blue City" due to the vivid blue-painted houses around the huge Mehrangarh Fort. The old walled city circles the fort, however, the city has expanded greatly outside the wall over the past several decades.

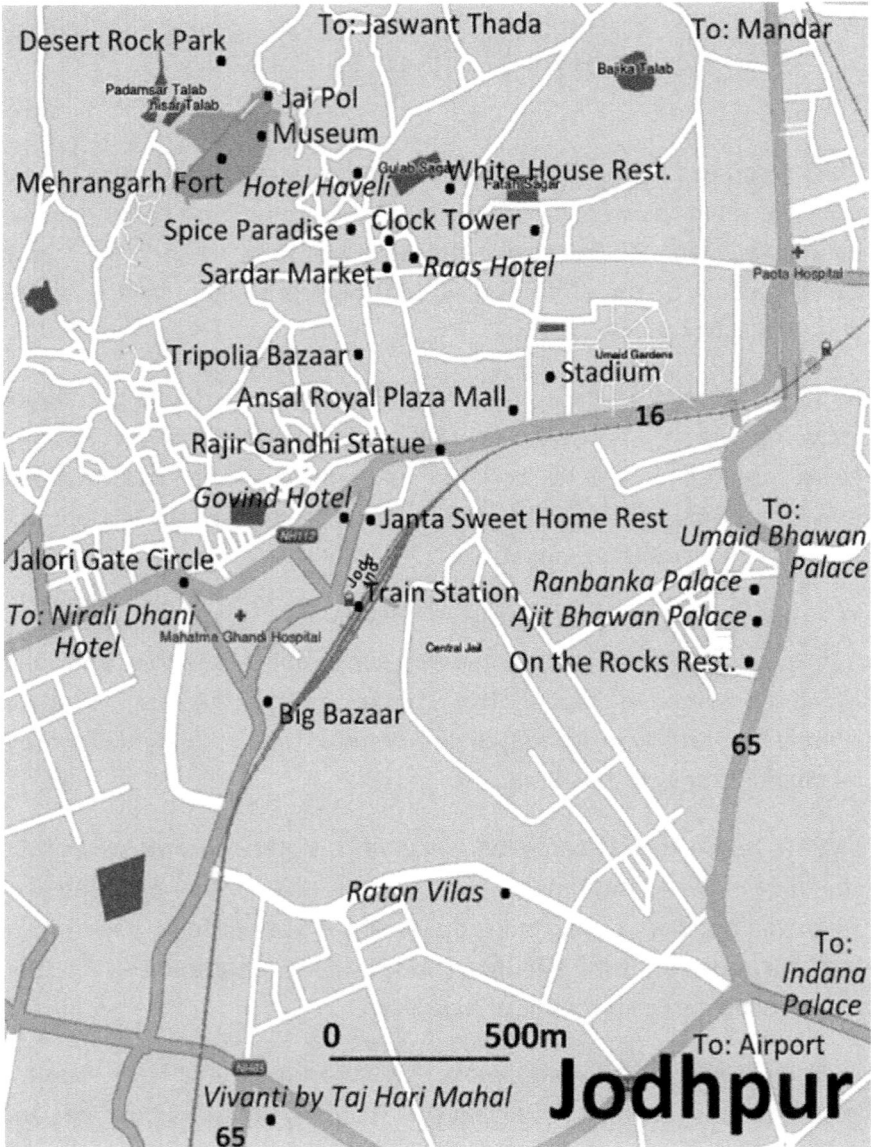

Jodhpur is an imposing sight from the road, a walled medieval city huddled beneath a massive fort. Kipling dubbed this a work of giants and angels and you can see why.

The area has a diverse economy but the handicrafts industry and tourism are the most important. Wheat and the famous Mathania red chillies are grown while gypsum and salt are mined. The city lies about 250 kilometres from the Pakistani border and this location makes it an important base for Indian military forces.

Jodhpur has good air, rail and road links with the other major cities in Rajasthan as well as Delhi and Mumbai. The airport is about 5 km south of the centre while the railway station and bus station are both conveniently close to the Old City. Parts of the walled city can be easily covered on foot but a rented bicycle can be handy.

Inside the 9.5 km-long city walls there is a tangle of winding, crowded, medieval streets, which often lead to unexpected places. It is very easy to get lost. The whole area is scented by incense, roses, spices, cow dung, and sewers and there are shops and bazaars selling everything imaginable. The Sardar Market is the heart of this shopping area and it can be quite frenetic. Areas of the old city further west are just as atmospheric but with far less hustling.

The city as a whole is cleaner than it used to be since shops were banned from giving out plastic bags. This is a comparatively safe city, however, it is advisable to be careful where you go late in the night.

**Mehrangarh Fort** (http://www.mehrangarh.org/) dominates the city and is the largest fort in all Rajasthan. It was started in 1458 and the city has grown around it. It has been an extremely successful structure and withstood many attacks. It occupies the entire top of a 150 m high hill with commanding views all around, with some three kilometres of massive ramparts built around the edges.

The fort houses the Maharaja's palace, several temples and, tucked away in the back, an extensive garden still farmed to this day. The fort has plenty of large spaces around various buildings, and ramps and access ways up to the crenels where you can see the cannons facing the blue city. It's a good idea to buy an elevator ticket (Rs50) and another for entrance to the museum.

The main entrance is the north-east gate called Jai Pol (Victory Gate). This was built by a maharaja in 1808 after the defeat of invading forces from Jaipur. If you plan to walk up from here you have a steep climb and pass through several other gates before reaching Suraj Pol which gives access to the museum. On the way, you will pass local musicians playing folk music, a small craft market, a good restaurant and a couple of cafes serving snacks and drinks.

*Mehrangarh Fort*

The museum is housed in the former palace and is a superb example of Rajput architecture. The carving, in particular, is just beautiful.

Highlights include the Pearl Palace, Mirror Palace, Flower Hall and the Peeping Palace where ladies could look through its exquisite latticed stone screens to observe the ceremonies and festivities in the courtyard below.

The Moti Mahal (Pearl Palace) is decorated with colourful stained glass windows. This is where the Maharaja held his audiences and official meetings. Note the five alcoves on the far wall allowing his queens to listen in without being seen. The royal rooms, the audience hall and the throne hall are superb examples of Rajasthani art using mirrors and coloured pieces of glass.

The display of howdahs (elephant seats) and palanquins (a seat carried by four or more men) is outstanding. As well as these there are examples of swords, cosmetic boxes, pots, silver carpet weights, painted doors, idols, and miniature paintings.

The Sheesh Mahal (Mirror Palace) has large, regular pieces, rather than an intricate mosaic of tiny fragments and there is superimposition over the mirror-work of brightly painted religious figures made in plaster.

The Phool Mahal (Flower Hall) was the Maharaja's pleasure chamber and is the most extravagant part of the palace. This room is beautifully decorated and it has a ceiling rich in gold. There are rare wall paintings, royal portraits and the famous raga mala paintings. Some have a distinct European influence because these decorations were carried out during Maharaj Pratap Singh's reign, who was very much an Anglophile.

Zenana Deodi is the inner sanctum of the palace once guarded by eunuchs. This was home to the Maharaja's wives. The delicate sandstone screens and carvings are exquisite. The Chamunda Mataji Temple is missed by many visitors but it remains a local favourite to this day.

The museum armoury displays swords, spears, knives, pistols and rifles and shows how dangerous life could be outside the palace. There is the Mehrangarh museum shop where you can buy handicrafts, footwear, dresses, etc. Drinking water coolers are installed at several places inside the palace and there is the Cafe Mehran if you need to nibble.

An audio tour is included in the entry fee of Rs600 for foreign tourists (December 2017). A deposit of Rs2000, passport, credit card or driver's license is required. Usage of a video camera is Rs200, and a still camera is Rs100. Indians pay Rs100 for entry to the museum. The fort is open daily from 9 a.m. to 5 p.m.

If you have the time, also venture deeper into the fort (outside the palaces) which will give you a more complete idea of its size. You can also visit the **Chokelao Gardens** (Rs30), which are located outside the inner wall by following the signs for the Flying Fox.

The **Flying Fox** consists of six ziplines ranging from 100 to 300m long. The first zipline is partly over the fort and the rest are on the hill at the back of the fort. There are age and height restrictions; you must be at least 10 and taller than 4'7" to do this attraction. Before you can go on the actual zipline, there is a small demonstration line a few feet above the ground that you will be instructed on. If you are not confident you can bail out at this point. The cost is Rs1900 and Rs1599 for students (January 2017).

**Jaswant**                                                 **Thada**
(http://www.rajasthantourism.gov.in/destinations/jodhpur/jaswanttha da.aspx), one kilometre downhill from Mehrangarh Fort, is a royal cenotaph with a picturesque location next to a little lake. It is an intricately carved white marble memorial built by Maharaja Sardar Singh in 1899 in memory of his father. Some sections of the thin marble walls are translucent, a feature extolled by resident guides as something of a miracle.

The cenotaph has two more tombs within it. Nearby are the royal crematorium and three other cenotaphs. There are nicely maintained lawns and overall it is a clean, shady, beautiful place. Entry for foreigners is Rs50.

**Umaid Bhawan Palace** (https://taj.tajhotels.com/en-in/umaid-bhawan-palace-jodhpur/) is clearly visible on a hilltop to the south of the city. It was only completed in 1944 and is the last great palace built in India. The Maharaja of Jodhpur still lives here, but half the building has been converted into a 5-star hotel. This bagged the 'The Best Hotel in the World' honour at TripAdvisor's Travelers' Choice Awards in 2016.

Only paying guests are allowed inside the hotel and you probably can't visit the Maharaja so you are stuck with an outside view or a visit to the five rooms of the museum (Foreigners Rs50, Indians Rs15, open 9 a.m. to 5 p.m. daily). There is also a heritage vehicle/model train collection. The museum has exhibits of stuffed leopards, a strange collection of clocks in windmill and light house shapes, elegant murals and miniature paintings. The classic cars of the Maharajas are on display in the garden.

This imposing building is one of the world's largest private residences. It is also known as Chittar Palace because of the local chittar sandstone used in its construction. Amazingly, the manually chiselled sandstone blocks have been put together without mortar. There is a good view of part of the city from the parking lot on days without smog.

**Rao Jodha Desert Rock Park** (http://www.raojodhapark.com/) is a park celebrating native Thar Desert plants. It lies at the foot of Mehrangarh Fort and extends across 70 hectares of rocky land surrounding the fort. You can enter the Park from several points.

Go early in the morning to avoid the heat because there is plenty of open walking. You can follow the coloured markers and find your own way around but I feel a guide is a must to fully appreciate the richness of the offerings and of the work that went into creating this gem. It provides an excellent introduction to the ecology of deserts in Rajasthan.

They have four interesting walks, each between 60 and 100 minutes. There are information brochures and a small Visitor's Centre with descriptive posters of how this desert park was created. There is an outdoor cafe, restrooms and a small shop. The park opens from 8 a.m. to 5.30 p.m. from October to March and 7 a.m. to 6 30 p.m. April to September. Entry for adults is Rs100 and students are free. You can hire a naturalist for a tour for Rs200 (December 2017). Walking shoes, a hat, sunblock, and water are a must.

**Spice Paradise** (Girdi Kote in Amar Chok by Sardar Market) (http://www.spiceparadise.in/) is a shop that offers cooking lessons and sells Indian spices. The cooking classes for tourists cover some of the basics of Indian cooking like how to make chai, lassis, chutneys, daal, chapatis, naan, raita, biryani rice and a paneer curry.

It is a hands-on experience so you'll be fully participating in all the steps in preparing the meal. Best of all you eat what you've cooked during the class. Everyone receives a cookbook of all the recipes they have learned.

**Umaid Heritage Art School** (153 Sumer Market, Dhaan Mandi, Near Clock Tower) is a popular art gallery and school. The school tries to impart knowledge to locals and visitors with the help of experts. Unusually, the school tries to preserve traditional artwork by combining it with contemporary art forms. Several famous artists, such as Vijay Raj and Gaurav Solanki are associated with this school. Vijay Raj, who specialises in sketches and Rajasthani miniature paintings, gives free lessons here. You can pick a painting you like and you'll get paints, brushes, and guidance on how to reproduce or modify it.

**Toorji Ka Jhalra** or the stepwell is in the Old city. It was built in the 1740's by Maharaja Abhay Singh's queen consort and has recently been restored. Sets of seven steps connect platforms on three sides as you descend lower. There are no fences, no visitor's fees and the locals use it and keep it clean. The water at the bottom looks clean and there are fish swimming about.

**Jodhpur Government Museum,** located in Umaid Garden, houses a rich collection of relics including armoury, textiles, local art and crafts, miniature paintings, portraits of rulers, manuscripts and images of the

Jain Tirthankaras.

**Jaswant Thada** is a milky white memorial built as a tribute to the leader Jaswant Singh who ruled Jodhpur, and made attempts to bring down the level of crime, subdue dacoits, built railways and broadly worked on raising the economy of Marwar.

**Mahamandir Temple** situated on Mandore road, is supported by 84 pillars and ornamented with detailed designs and figures depicting various postures of Yoga.

## Shopping

The city's main shopping area is Nai Sadak, lined mostly with clothing shops. It leads into **Sardar Market**, a full-on bustling Indian market with the usual riot of sights, sounds and smells. The main entrance to Sardar Market is through Girdikot Gate (crowded gate).

The clock tower in the centre is a useful orientation point. It was built by Maharaja Sardar Singh from whom the market takes its name. Locals hawk bangles, imitation jewellery, fruit and vegetables, spices, pottery, baskets, clothes, and so on. It is best to head into the different shops by yourself, as rickshaw drivers and other locals will try to direct you into certain shops where they can earn a commission for sales.

You can casually look around and see what happens in a typical busy and noisy Indian market. It seems like chaos, with close to 7,000 match-box sized shops full of loud bargaining customers lining both sides of the narrow lanes but it seems to work for the locals. It is certainly an eye-opener for many visitors.

Bazaars offer a wide range of products such as textiles, embroidered leather goods, lacquerware, antiques, carpets, puppets and figurines. A visit is not necessarily a quick affair. Be prepared to spend a good hour or more in a shop chatting with the very friendly owners over a cup of marsala chai.

Popular souvenirs include Bandhej sarees and dress material, *Mojris* or *Jootis* (shoes with a pointed front), handmade wooden pieces (made to look like old antiques), spices and tea, and textiles such as rugs, scarves, duvet covers, and so on.

## Eating and drinking

Restaurants, as you find them elsewhere, are somewhat hard to find in Jodhpur, except in tourist areas such as in front of the Fort or in the major hotels. Otherwise, especially for lunch it's stand-up street food such as samosas.

Don't forget to try the Rajasthani delicacies which include Makhaniya Lassi a yoghurt drink spiced with cardamom and butter, *Mawa Kachori, Panchkuta* (dry curry), and *Gatte ka saag* (curry). Other favourites include *Kabuli* (a rice speciality), *Kaju Draksh ki Sabji* (curry made of cashew and raisins), *Malai Kulfi* (milk ice cream) and *Doodh Jalebi* (sweet dipped in milk).

You should be able to get a good meal at one of the following:

**Darikhana** (http://www.raasjodhpur.com/our-dining-options.html) at the lovely Raas Hotel offers magnificent views of the Mehrangarh Fort, which glows pink in the day and is gloriously illuminated at night. This is a modern and contemporary space with a solid background of tradition serving fragrant dishes which sizzle with the aromas of hand-ground spices. It is not cheap.

**Risala** (Umaid Bhawan Palace, Palace Road, Cantt area) (http://www.tajhotels.com/luxury/grand-palaces-and-iconic-hotels/umaid-bhawan-palace-jodhpur/fine-dining/risala-restaurant.html) serves a blend of imaginative and sumptuous Continental and Indian cuisines. Outside the windows, there are spectacular views of the gardens, the blue city and the Mehrangarh Fort, while the interior of the restaurant is adorned with royal and martial portraits. The menu is claimed to consist of many recipes authenticated by time and honoured by the royal kitchens of the Maharaja.

**Latitude** (Vivanta Hotel, Residency Road) (http://www.vivantabytaj.com/hari-mahal-jodhpur/dining/latitude-restaurant.html) is a popular choice, as it fuses rich flavours and aromas with the sound of cooking and artistic displays. The traditional design and stylish décor make Latitude a lively scene on occasions.

Food stations with chefs cooking live right in front of the guests accompany the breakfast, lunch and dinner buffets at times but there was nothing of this on our last visit. Nevertheless, the food was good and we dined just outside the main restaurant with a lovely view of the pool.

**Mehran Terrace** at Mehrangarh Fort offers a romantic dining experience. It is a place to enjoy a candle-lit dinner under the stars with live music and dance performances. Since it is one of the most popular restaurants in the city, prior reservations are recommended.

**Gypsy Restaurant** (689, 9th C Road, Sardarpura) (http://www.gypsyfoods.com/) is one of the most popular restaurants in Jodhpur, with good quality of food, hospitable staff, and a warm ambience. It has offered vegetarian Indian delicacies, since 1991. Don't miss the special traditional thali here which serves 34 dishes.

**White House Café** (Gulab Sagar, Near Mahila Bag School) (98 2931 6221) is a perfect mix of tradition and modernity. Visit this place for its lively atmosphere, exotic mocktails, fine dining and much more.

**Jharokha** (Hotel Haveli, Makrana Mohalla) (http://www.hotelhaveli.net/facilities.php) is a place to dine out under the open sky. This restaurant offers an elegant seating arrangement, stunning views of the Blue City and many Rajasthani and North Indian culinary delights. For those who love international cuisine, there is Italian for main course and delicious pancakes for desserts.

**Padhro Sa** at the Nirali Dhani Hotel (Chopasani Road) (http://www.niralidhani.com/jodhpur-restaurant.php) has a traditional menu with a great variety of local dishes as well as Continental, Italian and Chinese. The food is full of robust flavours and textures.

**Janta Sweet Home** (Station Road, Ratanada) (https://www.facebook.com/pages/Janta-Sweet-Home/245759382141734) prepares some of the best quality sweets and namkeens in Jodhpur. From *Papads* to sweets and dried fruit, they have everything. *Mawa ki Kachori, Malai Ghewar* and *Mirchi Badas* are three recommended delicacies of this shop.

## City Tours

The half-day **Jodhpur Cycle Rickshaw Tour** operated by City Discovery (https://www.city-discovery.com/jaipur/tour.php?id=14248) leads you into the crowded alleys of Jaipur to see some of the city's most famous sites. Along the way, you'll get a history lesson and hear stories, old legends, and lost myths that shape life in Jaipur.

The **Old City Tour** operated by Jodhpur Cycling Tours (http://jodhpurcyclingtours.com/the-old-city-tour/) is for more active visitors who want an exciting and eco-friendly tour around the streets of Jodhpur. You go out for a two-hour cycling adventure around the alleys and the fort wall and get to know the different communities and the history. Here you will be introduced to the culture and life of today by a local site guide.

## Yoga

Like many Indian cities, Jodhpur has several places where you can participate in Yoga classes. Here are some suggestions:

Priyanka's Yoga Studio (https://www.facebook.com/priyankasyoga/), Sabji Mandi Link Road, Ratanada.

Adhyatma Vigyan Satsang Kendra (www.the-comforter.org), Near Hotel Lariya Resort, Chopasni Road.

Yoga Guru Karan Singh (http://www.yogagurukaransingh.com/about_utamber.html), Utamber Club, Rai Ka Bagh.

## Festivals

There are several festivals in Jodhpur that are worth seeing if you happen to be in the city at the right time. The **Jodhpur Desert Kite Festival** is a 30-day event held in January each year at the Polo Grounds. Helicopters release kites of different shapes and patterns while children release balloons. Many kite enthusiasts from different parts of the country visit Jodhpur to take part in the many competitions during the festival

The **Rajasthan International Folk Festival** is a 5-day festival held in October. Two hundred or more musicians and artists unite to celebrate Rajasthan's folk music and history and you can also see some ethnic dances being performed by the artists here. Every year, to honour the epic heroes of Rajasthan, the two-day **Marwar Festival** is held in September/October. Folk dancers put on a show exhibiting the regal lifestyle and the battle stories of the Kings who ruled Rajasthan. Other forms of entertainment like tattoo and polo also draw many tourists.

Although it is more than 100 km from the city, the **Cattle Fair of Nagaur**, held during January-February, is a major attraction and it has become the second largest festival in India. The 8-day festival is organised for animal trading and something like 70,000 decorated cows, bullocks, camels and horses are traded. During the fair, you can also see tug-of-war, camel and bullock races, cock fights and puppet shows.


## Around Jodhpur

Few tourists seem to do it, but I believe a visit to **Mandore**, seven kilometres outside the city, is well worthwhile. This was the ancient capital of Marwar before Jodhpur was built. It is open to the public free of charge. The lower part consists of small temples and memorials, garden areas, and high rock terraces. The gardens house a government museum, a 'Hall of Heroes', dedicated to various deities and Rajput folk heroes with statues carved out of rock and painted in bright colours.

*Mandore*

Also in the garden is "The Shrine of the Three Hundred Million Gods", filled with brightly coloured images of the various Hindu Gods. The upper part of the complex holds the ruins of the impressive old fort. A large now-ruined temple is a highlight. The whole area would be nicer if there wasn't the usual rubbish you find in many places. It is closed from 7 p.m. to 7 a.m. There are good views from here.

On the way from Jodhpur you pass **Bal Samand Lake**. This is a popular picnic spot, built in 1159AD by Balak Rao Parihar. It was designed as a water reservoir to provide water to Mandore and is now surrounded by parkland. The Bal Samand Lake Palace was built later as a summer palace on its shore.

Today, after the successful completion of an ambitious restoration and modernization program, Bal Samand is a world class Heritage Hotel with modern amenities and an Health Spa of renown. The gracious interiors are matched only by the spectacular views of the pristine lake and the splendid gardens.

Some readers will be interested in visiting the new **Machiya Safari Park**. It is about 1 km away from the Kaylana Lake, and around 9 km to the west of Jodhpur. The major wildlife consists of wild cats like lions and cheetahs, blue bulls, monkeys, monitor lizards, desert foxes, rabbits, and mongoose. This park also has an excellent bird-watching point as well as a fort within its premises. It is still being developed and can be very hot due to lack of trees so a morning visit is advised.

Another worthwhile experience is to visit the **Guda Bishnoi village**. This is located about 22 km from Jodhpur and is the home of the Bishnoi tribal community who take plant and animal life very seriously so they are pure vegetarians. Guda Lake, a few kilometres from the Bishnoi village, is a resting spot for numerous migratory birds.

Probably the best way to visit here is on a **Bishnoi Village Jeep Safari** (http://www.bishnoivillagesafari.org/bishnoi_village_safari/villagefasafa ri.html). This provides a jeep drive through the countryside and gives an opportunity to meet people in their homes and have a meal with them.

The vegetarian community you meet protect the local fauna so you see herds of black buck around the Vishnu's settlements freely and fearlessly running about. The cost is Rs1000 per person.

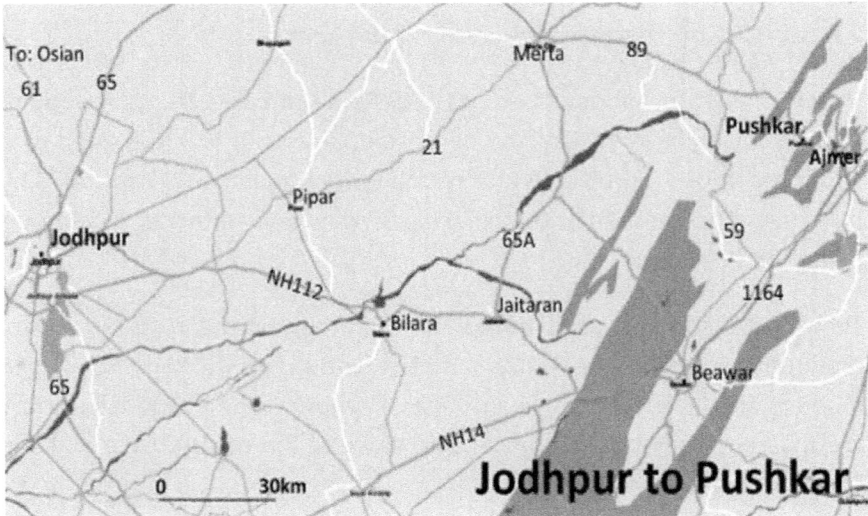

Jodhpur to Pushkar

**Osian** is an ancient town located 69 km north of Jodhpur. The city was a major religious centre of the kingdom of Marwar and today it is famous as home to the cluster of ruined temples dating from the 8th to 11th centuries. The Sun Temple, Sachiya Mata Temple and the Jain Temple dedicated to Lord Mahavir stand out for their grace and architecture. Intricate carvings are a common feature of all the temples.

The Jain Temple was built in AD 775 and is thronged by devotees all year. It is stunning structure that is made of red sandstone and is renowned for its exquisite carvings. The Sachiya Mata temple was originally built in the 8th century, however, the temple complex that you see today 'only' dates back to the 12th century. It has a series of magnificently sculpted arches and inside there are beautiful images and sculptures of Hindu deities.

# 6 PUSHKAR – A PILGRIMAGE TOWN

Pushkar is different from anywhere else in Rajasthan and is one of the oldest cities of India. It is very important to devout Hindus as one of the five sacred pilgrimage sites, so is always busy with visitors. Legend associates Brahma with its creation and the town's holy lake is said to have appeared when Brahma dropped a lotus flower.

Because of this, the town has one of the worlds few Brahma temples, 52 bathing ghats, and 400 other temples, so you are never far from chanting, drums, gongs, and devotional songs. Like so much of India the repugnant and pleasant smells are hard to ignore as you walk along.

The small town attracts Hindu devotees and T-shirted, digital camera-toting foreigners. Opinions will differ on its attractiveness depending on your age, outlook, and experience.

The long main street has colourful shops selling anything that a visitor would ever need. It can take 20 minutes or a whole day to traverse. Despite this commercialism, the town remains quite small and easy to navigate. Although many international visitors are not sure what to expect, some quickly feel that there is a mystic atmosphere to the place.

This leads many to have a respect for traditions by dressing appropriately and abiding by local restrictions. These include not drinking alcohol, eating meat or eggs, and not showing public displays of affection. Pushkar is thus not for every foreigner. As you walk the streets you will see it attracts alternative lifestyle visitors, backpackers and hippies rather than straight-laced types.

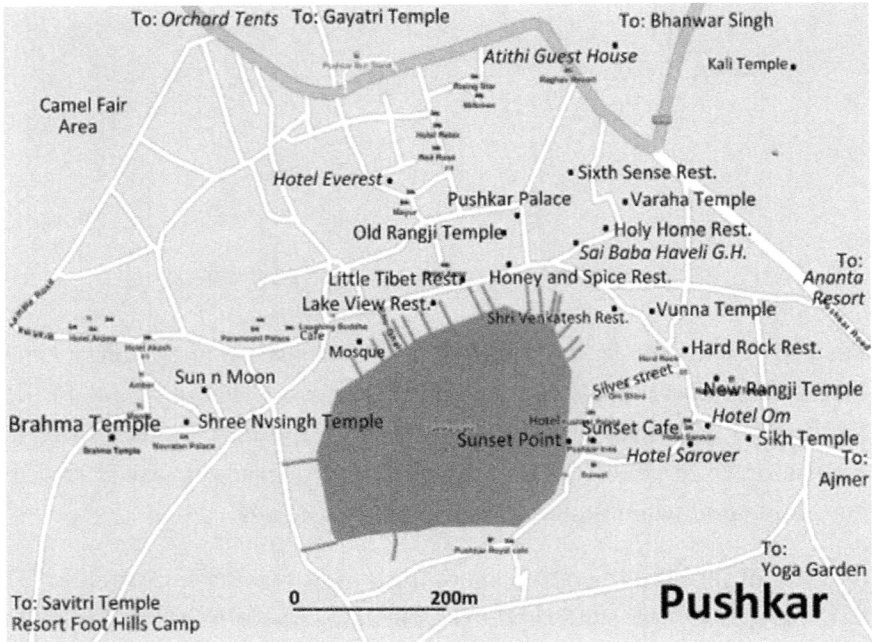

Pushkar

The town is a good place to pick up a few gifts because shopping is less demanding than in larger cities. There are some excellent textiles which are not readily available elsewhere and silver and beaded jewellery. One of the most famous things to purchase and bring home is the *Gulkand*, a sweet and delicious preserve of rose petals prepared and sold everywhere in town.

Pushkar is famous for its spectacular **Camel Fair**, which takes place yearly in the October/November period on the five days before the full moon (Next Dates: 15 November 2018 - 23 Nov 2018). Camels are decorated with great care with silver and bead jewellery. The fair attracts tribal people from all over Rajasthan, pilgrims from all over India, and tourists from all over the world. It is claimed that more than 200,000 crowd into the town at this time.

For international visitors, the camel races are definitely a highlight, although the comical beauty contests featuring elaborately adorned camels are also amusing. There's dancing, folk and fusion music concerts, spiritual and heritage walks, an arts and crafts bazaar, side shows, and a laser show. It is becoming difficult to find accommodation during this period.

At other times most of the sights centre around the lakefront which can be seen on foot. To go further afield you can rent a bike (push/motor) and take in the surrounding beautiful countryside and hidden temples.

Pushkar has many temples. Most are not very old, however, because many original temples were destroyed during the Muslim conquests in the area and what you see today are rebuilt versions. The most famous among them is the **Brahma Temple** (http://www.culturalindia.net/indian-temples/brahma-temple.html) originally built during the 14th century but supposedly established 2000 years ago. This is the only temple that is dedicated to Lord Brahma in India.

Brahma is among the trinity of Hindu Gods, the other two being Lord Shiva and Lord Vishnu. The temple which is set on a high plinth is approached by marble steps leading to an entrance archway and this leads to a pillared outdoor hall and then the inner sanctum. It has a distinct red 210 m high spire.

Look for the silver turtle at the shrine's entrance. The temple holds the images of Brahma seated in a crossed leg position, his second consort Gayatri, and Goddess Savitri. The inside marble floor and walls have been inlaid with hundreds of silver coins by devotees.

The temple is open for worship between 6:30 a.m. and 8:30 p.m. during winter and 6 a.m. to 9 p.m. during summer, except between 1:30 p.m. to 3 p.m. when it is closed. Married men and women are strictly prohibited from entering the sanctum sanctorum or performing any rituals there. They can only offer prayers from the outer hall. Cameras, phones and other devices are not permitted in the temple.

Three *aarties* are held: in the evening about 40 minutes after sunset, about 5 hours past sunset, and about 2 hours before sunrise. Once a year, on the full moon night of the Kartik lunar month (October – November), a religious festival is held and thousands of pilgrims come to bathe in the holy Pushkar Lake. Various rites are also held at the temple during this time.

The market of small shops on both the sides of the main street leading to the Brahma temple is very interesting. There are a number of shops selling different kinds of handicrafts, cloth, wooden and clay toys, medicines, herbs, food items and so on.

Apart from the Brahma temple and other small temples in the Brahma temple campus, there is another large temple of Lord Narsingh located on the street leading to the Brahma temple. This is called the **Shree Narsingh Temple**.

**Kali Temple** is also attractive. This more than 200-year-old temple has been run by the Sarwadia family for generations. An *aarti* is performed several times daily to a god who is seemingly a man-killer and figure of annihilation, but also a mother-goddess.

Brahma's two legendary consorts Savitri and Gayatri also have separate temples erected for them in Pushkar, but on hills at opposite ends of the lake. **Savitri Temple** located on the top of Ratnagiri Hill, behind the Brahma temple, is reached by a one hour's trek on a very steep track with many rocky steps or alternatively by the new Damodar Ropeway. The marble temple built in 1687, houses a statue of goddess Savitri. An early morning visit to the temple provides a good view of the lake. There is a tea/snacks shop at the top.

The **Gayatri Temple** or Pap Mochani Temple is accessible by an easier 30-minute climb from a track behind the Marwar bus stand.

The **Rangji Temple** is dedicated to Rangji, an incarnation of Lord Vishnu. The temple was built in 1823 in a South Indian architectural style, with a few Mughal features. There is a high 'Gopuram' and the temple houses an image of Garuda, Lord Vishnu's mount. It is considered one of the holiest temples in Pushkar.

The **Aptaeshwar Temple** is for the worship of Lord Shiva. This is one of the temples that was destroyed by Aurangzeb and resurrected later. It has sunk over time and is now partially underground. In the centre of the main hallway, is the Shivalinga.

Pushkar Lake is surrounded by 52 bathing ghats (a series of stone steps leading to the lake), where pilgrims come to take a sacred bath. They believe this will cleanse sins and cure skin diseases.

*Pushkar from the lake*

Like many religious places and sacred rivers in India, Pushkar Lake is in urgent need of attention. Tourism and deforestation have adversely affected its water quality, reducing the water levels and destroying the fish population. The lake does not meet the National Water Quality Standards of India.

Development plans aim to improve water quality, increase water storage capacity, prevent encroachment of the lake, and improve the ambience around the lake. This won't address one of the major complaints from visitors, however; aggressive hagglers.

You need to **beware** of men approaching you with a flower to welcome you to Pushkar. It is a scam and you will end up paying a lot of money to get away from them. It is a really distressing and irritating experience for many visitors. Just ignore them and don't take the flower that is almost thrust into your hand.

**Ghats** are built at several points around the lake. These are used for sacred bathing and for other rites. Out of 52 ghats, ten have been declared as 'Monuments of National Importance'.

You should not take a lake bath in the ghats lightly. Shoes must be removed away from the ghats and you should avoid passing comments about Hindu religious beliefs while near ghats. Ghats and the temples are all linked to the divine lake and believers take this very seriously.

If you aren't keen to sit at the ghat itself, there are several restaurants on one side of the lake that give you a lovely view especially at sunset. If you enjoy serenity and calm, a visit to one of these is a must. You can enjoy the scene with a cool gentle breeze and the chimes of the temple bells.

After you have had your fill of temples, there are other things to do. **Yoga Garden** (Vamdev Road, besides Sikh Gurudwara) (http://www.pushkaryogagarden.com) is a yoga centre based on ancient ashram tradition. Here yoga is taught and practiced as a way of life. The house and yoga centre is in a very serene setting surrounded by hills.

During the morning and evening classes, you can hear chanting and music from distant temples. The Introductory course (3 days) and the Intermediate course (6 days) are useful for both beginners and the more experienced. Both teach yoga practices as well as the principles, theories, and philosophies behind them.

The Advance course (21 days) and the Teacher Training course (30 days) are designed for people who would like to adopt yoga as a lifestyle. There are also two 1.5 hour-long yoga sessions each day.

An alternative is the **Pushkar Meditation Temple** (http://meditationinpushkar.in/), a wellness institution where yoga and meditation are practiced, taught and researched as complimentary disciplines. You can enrol for an introductory session, a group of sessions or up to a 21 session course.

**Camel Rides** are popular and this is probably the second best place in India after Jaisalmer, another city of Rajasthan, for its wide array of local camel safari operators. Journeys can be as short as a few hours or as long as a few weeks. The longer trips involve camping out in the desert around the Aravalli Range which has sandy dunes, beautiful hills and lovely sunrises and sunsets.

Tourists can be taken to destinations where you will witnesses small villages and see some of the authentic rural life. Many visitors are saddened to hear the half-naked children they see will never see the inside of a school-house and the girls will likely be married off as young as possible.

I don't find camel riding particularly comfortable and recommend wearing long pants as camel fur is quite scratchy on bare legs. Long sleeve shifts are great for guys; loose fitting lightweight blouses work well for ladies, as sunburn is a hazard. Wear comfortable, slim, closed toe shoes as stirrups can be quite narrow and awkward for rugged boots or thick-soled shoes.

Prices vary with off-season rates starting as low as Rs300 for a few hours, rising to well above Rs2000 and more per day per person during peak season. On short trips, by spending an extra Rs100 you can have your camel outfitted with traditional colourful braided Rajasthani clothes and bells.

## Eating and drinking

Pushkar is any vegetarian and budget traveller's food paradise. Within the town, any form of meat and alcohol is strictly prohibited. Every morning, all along the roads people come with carts and set up *poha* stalls. *Poha* is a kind of flat rice which is cooked with vegetables like potato and peas and served with a garnish of fresh tomatoes, coriander and so on. This simple dish, served in a newspaper for just Rs 5-10, is amazing.

Pushkar is also famous for its '*malpuas*'. This is a sweet dish which looks like yellow round thin bread with holes. It is made from flour, cow milk, sugar, and butter.

The following are a few of many restaurants to try.

**Oasis** (Leela Sevri, 4 km before Pushkar) (Tel: 0145 305 4000) (http://www.anantahotels.com/restaurant-and-bar) is the multi cuisine, 92 seat restaurant in the Ananta Resort. The comfortable and affordable restaurant has Balinese architecture and it faces the beautiful Aravalli Hills. It is on the lobby level overlooking the pool. Prices are high for the area. The adjacent Floats Bar has rich furniture and is a place to watch picturesque sunsets while you enjoy a drink.

The rooftop **Everest Café** (Hotel Everest Kalo ka Mohalla, Badi Basti) (Tel: 0145-510 5103) (http://www.pushkarhoteleverest.com/RoofTopRestaurant.aspx) serves a selection of tasty Indian cuisine, accompanied with panoramic views of the hills and town.

The rooftop **Rainbow Restaurant** (Sadar Bazaar Road, Pushkar Lake) (Tel: 941 426 0770) offers an amazing view. The menu here offers international cuisine.

**Cafe Nature's Blessing** (Panchkund Road) (https://www.facebook.com/cafenaturesblessings/) cooks fresh and crispy vegetables with Indian herbs and spices, and has tofu, mushroom, and vegan-suitable dishes. Open daily 9 a.m.-8 p.m.

**Aroma Royal Restaurant** (Tel: 978 316 2129), in mid-town, serves many types of Indian and continental food. It has become popular with tourists due to the friendly nature of its owner and for the internet facilities and garden setting. Occasionally there are cultural and folk dances.

**Sun-N-Moon** (Bari Basti, near Brahma Temple Road) (Tel: 0145 277 2883) is a wonderful little restaurant for excellent vegan meals. The restaurant with its garden-style seating area has a very warm, homey feel to it. They serve Indian, Chinese, Italian, Tibetan, and local Rajasthani cuisine, all cooked home-style.

**Pawan** (Narsingh Ghat, Opposite Kalu Baba Temple) specialises in various types of falafel wraps. It also serves vegetarian burgers and sandwiches. It is very popular among the back-packing crowd.

**Ganga Restaurant** (Tel: 0145 277 2883), on the main street, is famous for its falafels and pancakes. They have a staggering variety of *falafels*; all are quite heavy so it turns into an entire meal.

The **Little Tibet Garden Restaurant** (Tel: 503 91078) in the centre of town is a hidden gem which you can hardly see from the road. This place has one old tree in a corner and its branches and leaves make the ceiling of this restaurant. They prepare excellent Tibetan food at dirt cheap prices.

**Te.. Lawala** (close to Gau Ghat Badi Basti) (Tel: 0145-510 5455) is a place to enjoy traditional Indian street food inside the Seventh Heaven Hotel. The food served here is tasty, the dishes are economically priced, and the service is quite good. Recommended dishes are *Papdi Chat*, Rajasthani *Thali*, and fruit salad. It operates from 8 a.m. to 8 p.m.

The **Sixth Sense** (Choti Basti) (Tel: 0145-510 5455) is a popular dining place offering beautiful views of the valley, along with tasty vegetarian *thalis*. Other recommendations are pizzas, pastas, spaghetti and puddings. It opens 8 a.m. to 10 p.m.

**Little Italy** (Panch Kund Marg) (http://littleitalypushkar.com/) is a cosy and friendly restaurant serving authentic Italian food. There are bruschettas and pastas to wood fired pizzas and panna cottas. The restaurant uses purely organic ingredients and does not use any artificial preservatives and sweeteners

**Sunset Cafe** (near Pushkar Lake) is a popular cafe and restaurant with spectacular views of the lake and surrounding temples. It offers a selective but interesting menu. You can choose from a hearty *thali* or a *Masala Dosa*, or just try a variety of evening snacks. They also offer fresh juices and other beverages, perfect between those tiring temple visits.

The **Rasta Café** (Atithi Guest House, Choti Basti) is not far away from Pushkar's main market place. It offers beautiful views of the town and sunsets. The ambience is slightly laid-back, perfect for a hot cup of chai or to read books or play games. The Wi-Fi connection at this cafe is quite good. Try their pasta, vegetarian burger or banana Nutella pancakes. It opens 8 a.m. to 9:30 p.m.

**Honey & Spice** (Laxmi Market, off Sadar Bazaar) has yummy banana cakes, tofu steak, sandwiches and a great organic food menu. This is the place where you can enjoy your fruit juices and shakes. It opens 8 a.m. to 9 p.m.

## Ajmer

Pushkar is only 11 km from Ajmer. This city is many times larger than Pushkar but it has less interest for most visitors. Ajmer was founded in the late 7th century and the Chauhan dynasty ruled the city until it was conquered by Muhammad of Ghor, founder of the Delhi Sultanate, in 1193.

Ajmer regained independence under the Mewars in 1365, was conquered by the Marwar in 1532, was ruled by the Hindu Emperor Hemu from 1553, was conquered by the Mughal emperor Akbar in 1559, and control passed to the Marathas In the early 17th century. Later the British used Ajmer as a centre for exercising control over the various kingdoms in the region. It has had quite an interesting history!

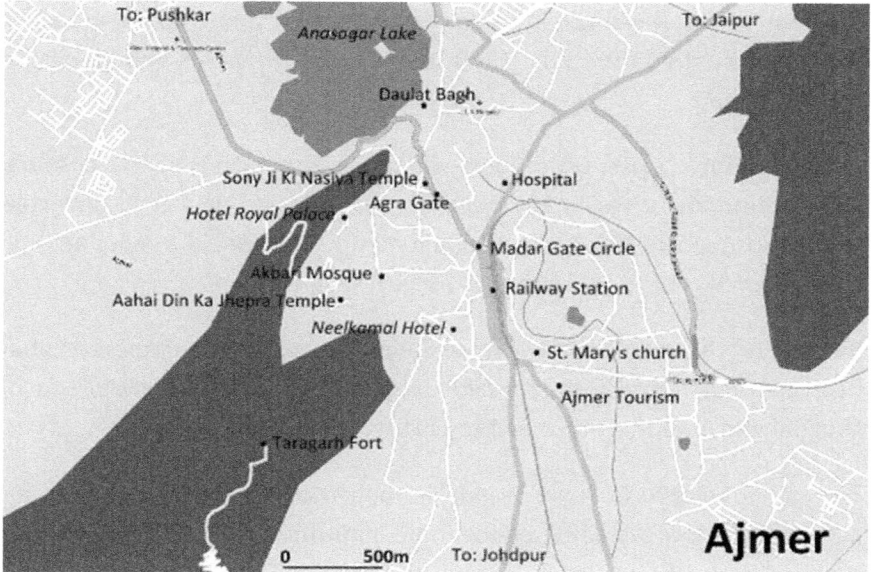

Today it is a Muslim pilgrimage centre for the **shrine of the Sufi Saint Khwaja Moinuddin Chisti**. His tomb remains one of the most important Islamic shrines in the world. He was born in East Persia but spent all his later life in Ajmer. He was revered for his austere life and for distributing gifts from the Delhi Sultanate.

Several white marble buildings arranged around two courtyards are situated at the foot of the Taragarh Hill. You pass through the massive entrance gate and see the 16th-century red sandstone Akbari Mosque, built by the Mughal emperor Shah Jahan and the 15th-century Buland Darwaza.

The main complex contains the Sandaali Masjid, various tombs and the silver Jannati Darwaza. Overlooking these is Shah Jahan's Jami Masjid. The tomb chamber is made of marble and has silver doors. The saint lies under a silver canopy covered with velvet and silk fabrics. The narrow lanes of the bazaars around here retain an almost medieval character, with rose-petal stalls and shops selling prayer mats and beads.

**Taragarh Fort** on the summit of Taragarh Hill was the seat of the Chauhan rulers. It is reputed to be one of the oldest hill forts in India but was partially dismantled by the British. The battlements run along the top of the hill.

Another temple exists on the lower slope of Taragarh Hill. This is **Adhai Din Ka Jhonpda**, a Vaishnava Hindu temple built in 1153 and converted into a mosque in 1193. Much has fallen into ruins, but the relics are still good examples of Hindu architecture and sculpture.

In the city, the **residence of Prince Salim** the son of the Emperor Akbar has been converted into the city's museum. It houses a collection of Mughal and Rajput armour and sculpture.

The famous Mayo College, originally built by the British as a school for princes and now a leading educational institution, is sometimes known as the "Eton of the East". This is one remnant from the past which distinguishes Ajmer from the rest of Rajasthan. The city was sold by the ruling Marathas to the East India Company in 1818 and thus Ajmer was a little Muslim enclave of directly ruled British territory for the next 130 years or so. It became part of Rajasthan in 1956.

Attractive **Anasagar Lake** to the north of Taragarh Hill was built by Maharaja Anaji in the 10th century. On the south-east side of the lake is the Daulat Bagh, a garden with five pavilions, known as the Baradari.

Just to the south of here is **Soniji Ki Nasiyan**, an architecturally rich Jain Temple. It was built in the late nineteenth century. The main chamber has several interesting gold-plated wooden figures.

# 7 JAIPUR – THE WONDERFUL PINK CITY

Jaipur is the capital and largest city (over four million) in Rajasthan. It was founded in 1727 and named after Maharaja Sawai Jai Sing II, the ruler of Amber. It is unusual for an Indian city to have a known beginning date; most began at some unknown time uncounted centuries ago and then grew in a casual, formless way.

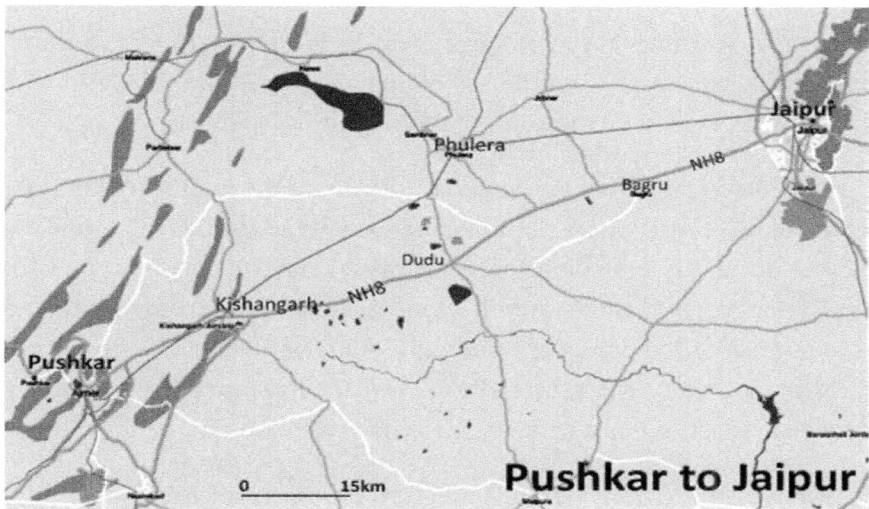

Pushkar to Jaipur

Jaipur is known as the **Pink City** because of its distinctly coloured buildings. It is believed that buildings were painted this colour to imitate the red sandstone architecture of Mughal cities. The present earthy red colour originates 140 years ago when buildings were repainted for a visit by the British Prince of Wales.

Jaipur nestles into the Aravalli Ranges and is surrounded by hills on three sides, each crowned with a formidable fort. The city itself is studded with grand palaces, majestic mansions and gracefully landscaped gardens and parks. It is probably the first fully planned city in India and was laid out with great precision.

The city is thus relatively easy to navigate because of the regularity of its streets, and the division of the city into six sectors by broad avenues 34 m wide. The airport is about 15 km south of the centre and the railway station is a kilometre or so to the east of the main business centre. The city is developing a metro rail system and limited services started in 2015.

Jaipur has a number of important cultural sites and is a major hub for arts and crafts. The Palace Quarter within the Old City houses the fascinating Hawa Mahal, the City Palace complex, Jantar Mantar observatory, formal gardens, and a small lake. Nahargarh Fort, a World Heritage Site, was the residence of the King Sawai Jai Singh II. It is situated on a hill in the north-west corner of the Old City.

Each January, Jaipur hosts what is claimed to be the largest free **literary festival** on earth where a remarkable, witty, sensitive and brilliant collection of authors come together for five days of readings, debates and discussions at the beautiful Diggi Palace. The vastness, youth and exuberance of the crowd is a notable distinctive thing about the Jaipur festival. Bollywood stars, celebrity lawyers, politicians, artists, musicians and economists are just some of the 80,000 who attend.

The biggest attraction in these parts, however, is in neighbouring **Amber** rather than in Jaipur. Amber or Amer was a flourishing settlement dating from the 10th century. Around 1037, Amer was conquered by the Kachhawaha clan of Rajputs and it was their capital until Jaipur was made the official capital on the plains below in 1727.

The town was originally named Ambikeshwara, the name of Lord Shiva, and was later abridged to Amber or Amer. The cobbled streets and the ruins of old havelies (small palaces) give the place an old world feel.

Amber is 11 kilometres north of central Jaipur and the massive **Amber Fort-palace** (http://www.amberfort.org/) complex is built in a combined Hindu-Muslim style. It dates from 1592 and was the royal palace of the Kachhawahas for 130 years. The serene Maota Lake at the base of the hill adds to the beauty of the fort.

The palace was built largely on the profits of co-operation with the Mughals. The earliest rulers of Amber to have contact with the Mughals decided there was nothing to gain by opposition to them and so they joined them. While other rulers fought many historic but useless campaigns against the Mughals, the rulers of Amber and Jaipur gained immense wealth as the spoils of war.

*Entering Amber Fort by elephant*

There are two ways to reach the fort from Amber town. If you chose to go by elephant you will enter through the main gate, Surajpol (Sun Gate), which leads to Jaleb Chowk. This road climbs steeply and switches back on itself so that an invader would be vulnerable to a defending force. If you go by vehicle you will enter through the Moon Gate on the opposite side of Jaleb Chowk. This is the main courtyard from where you can walk up the stairway that leads to the palace.

Before you enter the palace there is a steep narrow staircase leading up to the impressive Kali Temple also called Shila Devi Temple, famous for its mysterious history, its huge silver lions and its silver doors with raised relief.

Lion Gate leads to the second courtyard of the fort which houses the Diwan-I-Aam or the 'Hall of Public Audience'. This beautiful hall has two rows of ornamented pillars and is open on three sides. This is where the king used to listen to the needs and complaints of the people. There are nice views over the city from here.

Residential apartments of the Maharaja are located behind the exquisite Ganesh Pol (Ganesh Gate) with its beautiful carved statue of Lord Ganesha. On top of the gate is a chamber with marble grills from where the ladies of the royal family used to watch the proceedings at Diwan I Aam.

The Jai Mandir, the Hall of Victory, is famous for its inlaid panel and dazzling mirror ceiling. It is said that the reason behind this was because in ancient days the queen was not allowed to sleep in the open air but she loved to see the stars shining. So the king ordered his architects to make something which could solve this problem.

They were highly successful as two burning candles can be converted into thousand of stars. Much of it had deteriorated with time and there is on-going restoration being undertaken.

The Diwan-e-Khaas or the 'Hall of Private Audience' in the third courtyard has delicate mosaic work in glass which resembles the stained glass windows of European cathedrals. In this hall, the king used to meet special guests from other states, ministers, and his friends. The third courtyard also has a nice Mughal-style garden. It is laid out with narrow channels lined with marble around a star shape pool with a fountain at the centre.

The Sukh Niwaas (Summer Palace), which is opposite the Diwan-e-Khaas, has doors made of sandaal wood and ivory. There is a channel running through the hall, which carried cool water that worked as an air cooler, with the aid of a breeze. It is said that the kings used to spend time in this hall with their queens and sometimes with their mistresses. From here you can also view the fort rampart and its reflection in Moata Lake.

The Zanani Deorhi or the Palace of the Women is in the fourth courtyard. The rooms are connected through a common corridor but are ingeniously designed to ensure privacy to each room.

Because the fort sprawls over the hill, this is a place where an audio guide or a real guide is useful. The fort also contains a cafe, money changer and book shop. Most foreign tourists ride elephants to the top although there is considerable debate about the treatment of these lovely animals. In order to get an elephant, you need to arrive there before 11 a.m.

The elephant ride costs Rs900 plus tip (fixed government price) for one or two people. A guide through the fort will cost about Rs200 Entry to the fort is Rs25/10 for Indian adult/child and Rs200/100 for foreigner adult/child. A camera is free and audio guides are Rs150.

The Amber Fort **Sound and Light Show** is held in the Lower Amber Fort each evening at 7 p.m. You will experience some of the history, culture and life of Amber through this spectacular show but don't forget the mosquito repellent. Entry to the English language show is Rs200.

While in Amber there are three other places worth visiting.

**Jaigarh Fortress** is a one kilometre walk uphill from Amber Fort. It was never conquered in battle and was considered the strongest of the three forts in the area. It is one of the few military structures of medieval India preserved almost intact. Jaigarh Fort and Amber Fort are supposedly connected by subterranean passages and can be considered as one complex even though they are treated differently by visitors.

It is best known as the site of the world's largest cannon on wheels at the time of its manufacture. The Jaivana weighs 50 tonnes and the barrel has a diameter of 280mm, but it was only test-fired once.

Another attraction is the **Anokhi Museum of Hand Printing** (Anokhi Haveli, near the Badrinath Temple) (http://www.anokhi.com/museum/home.html), a well-kept museum dedicated to the traditional art of hand block printed textiles. The museum is in a heritage haveli (private mansion) well sign-posted from the fort. There is a small cafe, clean toilets, small shop, friendly staff, and a printer and block carver demonstrating his crafts.

Located near the Anokhi Museum, **Panna Meena ka Kund** is an eight storey staircase pool or stepwell. Built in the 16th century, this place earlier served as a community gathering area, where people would come to swim, relax or chat with a neighbour. The architectural arrangement of stairs in a criss-cross manner, the recessed doorways and the octagonal gazebos make this place an attractive tourist spot.

Before leaving Amber you should consider **Elefantastic** (90 Chandra Mahal Colony, Delhi Road) (http://elefantastic.in/) which provides an opportunity to take an elephant ride or safari or spend some personal time with elephants.

As part of this later experience you can wash the elephants, feed and water them, have a painting class and learn about elephant-decorations, ride them to the lake for a swim and a scrub, watch the elephants fall asleep at night, and wake up with them in the early morning.

In my mind, the most interesting ride is a 1.5 hour ride which takes you to the villages surrounding Amber. It is a chance to see village life and get a feel of how things work further away from the busy streets of the cities.

Safaris are also offered. These can be through the jungle areas surrounding Amber which gives a chance to see animals in the wild. You are likely to see peacocks, deer, and snakes, and you might even spot a leopard. A meal and drinks are included. An alternative is through the villages surrounding Amber, during the sunset hours. The safari starts before sunset and ends after dark.

After seeing Amber, it is a good idea to visit some of Jaipur's own attractions but on the way back stop at **Jal Mahal**, a palace located in the middle of the Man Sagar Lake. It is an architecturally beautiful building.

The palace, built in red sandstone, is actually a five storied building with four floors under water when the lake is full. The palace can only be viewed from the banks of the lake but I was told by a guide that it was under renovation and will eventually become a hotel. This may not happen because of an ownership dispute and the cost involved.

Back in the city, the first place to visit is the **City Palace** (https://royaljaipur.in/), a large complex in the centre of the Old City. The outer wall is original, while the actual palace has been enlarged and extensively changed over the centuries but despite this it is a striking blend of Rajasthani and Mughal architecture. Unlike many other Rajput palaces, the fortifications are separate to the palaces.

The palace today is only partly Sawai Jai Sing's work as the maharajahs who succeeded him all built extra private apartments to accommodate their wives and concubines while never demolishing the work of their predecessors. The result is that the palace area is a maze of doorways, passages and ramps.

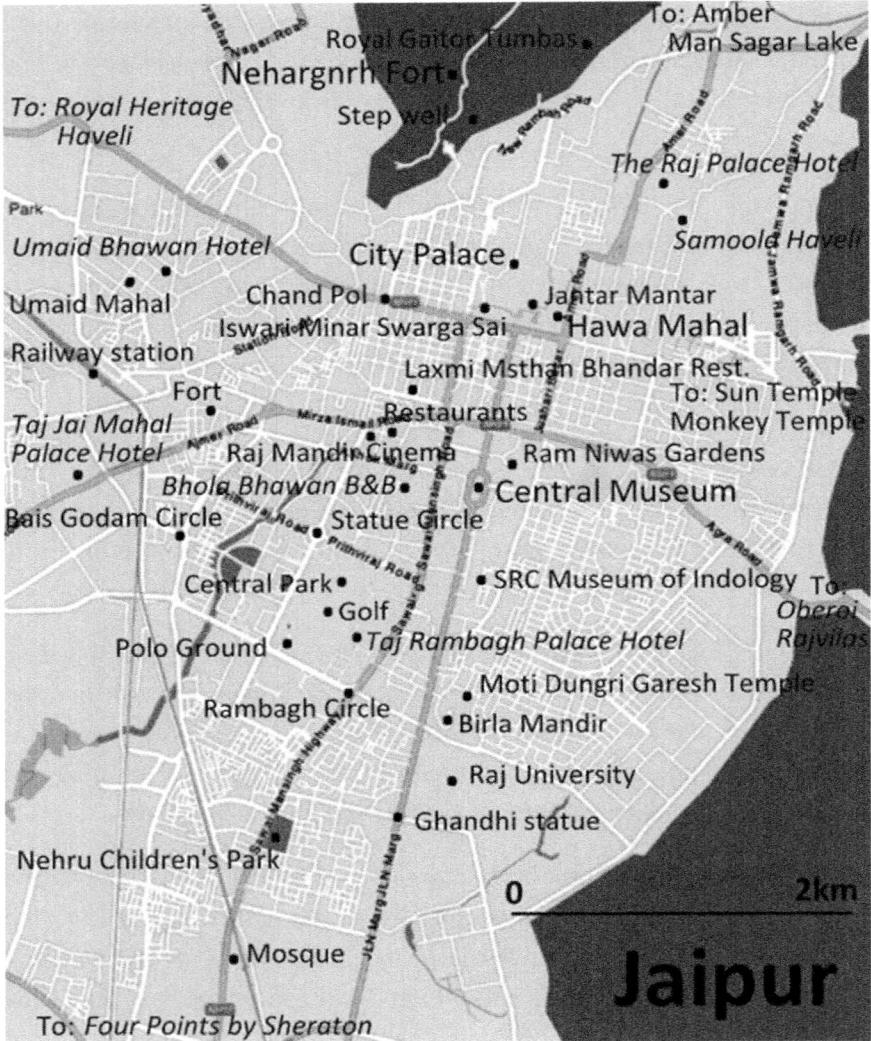

You enter through Virendra Pol, and see the double storey marble Mubarak Mahal (Welcome Palace). The multi-arched and colonnaded building now forms part of the Maharaja Sawai Mansingh II Museum containing a collection of royal costumes and valuable artefacts. Of most interest perhaps are the costumes of one of Jai Singh's sons who was over seven feet tall and weighed 250 kg. The building is divided into a regular grid and is beautifully decorated.

North of here the grand Rajendra Pol has brass doors, walls covered with precious stones and is flanked by carved elephants. Between the Armoury and the Diwan-I-Aam art gallery is an open courtyard. At its centre is a pink-and-white, marble-paved gallery containing two enormous silver vessels which are claimed to be the world's heaviest. Each has a capacity of 4,000 litres and they were filled with water from the holy Ganges River for the personal use of the maharaja during visits outside of India.

The art gallery has a collection of illustrated manuscripts, beautiful Sanskrit books, early manuscripts on palm leaves, and miniature copies of holy Hindu scriptures, which could be easily hidden in times of danger. The hall still has its beautifully preserved painted ceiling, some fine carpets on the walls, ornate pillars with brightly painted Jaipur designs and an enormous crystal chandelier.

The Armoury, which has one of the best collections of weapons in the country, is in the Maharani's Palace. Many of the pieces have a history attached to them, such as a sword inscribed for Shah Jahan, and a sword encrusted with rubies and emeralds that was presented by Queen Victoria to Maharaja Ram Singh. The 19th-century mirrored and gold-inlaid ceiling, decorated with a gorgeous floral pattern and women in various moods, is impressive.

The crowded Carriage Museum houses a collection of carriages and palanquins, with some showing covered versions for palace women.

Four glorious gates representing the seasons are in Pitam Niwas Chowk towards the palace's inner courtyard. You enter the courtyard through the Peacock Gate which depicts autumn and see the Lotus Gate which signifies summer, the Green Gate signifying spring, and the Rose Gate signifying winter.

Beyond this chowk is the private palace, the Chandra Mahal, which is still the residence of the descendants of the royal family and where you can take a 45-minute guided tour (Rs2500) of select areas. When the family is at home the family standard of five bands of colour is flown from the battlements.

Although outside the walls, the early 18th-century Govind Devji Temple is part of the City Palace complex. It was situated so that the maharaja could see the deity from his palace. The temple is in nice gardens and is a popular place of worship.

Admission to the City Palace is Rs500 for foreigners (which includes a camera fee and entry to Jaigarh Fort above Amber Fort) and Rs130 for Indians, plus Rs75 for a still camera. It opens daily from 9.30 a.m. to 5 p.m.

There is also a new feature which some will enjoy. Called Museum at Night costs Rs450 for foreigners. Departures are at 6.30 p.m. daily.

One of the most fascinating sites in the city is **Jantar Mantar** (http://www.jantarmantar.org/), an observatory adjacent to the City Palace. It was begun by Jai Singh in 1728 and contains a collection of bizarre-looking structures which are now on India's list of World Heritage Sites.

Jai Singh liked astronomy and he built five observatories but this is the largest and best preserved. If you are interested in astronomy, paying for a guide is worthwhile. Entry is Rs200 for foreigners and Rs50 for Indians.

You can't miss the massive Brihat Samrat Yantra (King of the Instruments) sundial. The shadow cast by the 27 m-high arm moves up to four metres in an hour, and helps in the calculation of local and meridian time. Those who believe in astrology gather here during the full moon in June or July.

The Laghu Samrat Yantra is a smaller sundial of red sandstone and white marble with two quadrants. Nearby is the Dhruva Darshak Yantra, used to find the location of the Pole Star and the 12 zodiac signs. Other structures can help determine the positions of constellations, calculate the date of the Hindu calendar, and aid in the calculation of the altitude of celestial bodies.

You will see a cluster of 12 yellow instruments, the Rashi Yantras, representing each of the 12 zodiac signs. There are instruments resembling two huge slotted bowls, a pair of metal wheels, and miniature coliseums made of 12 upright slabs and 12 horizontal slabs. The complex has a cafe and there is a Sound and Light Show about 6 p.m. in winter (later in summer) with a Rs200 entry.

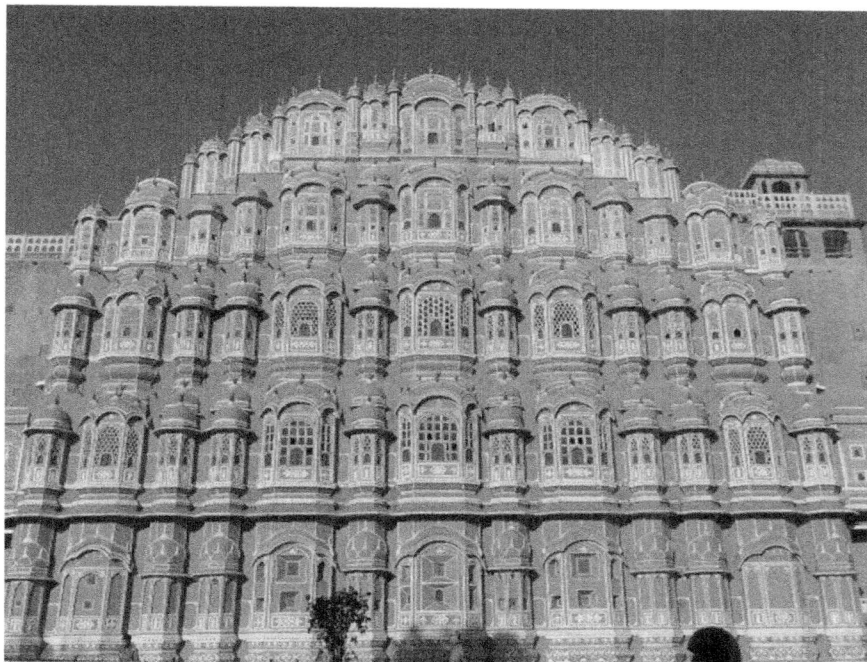

*Hawa Mahal*

The **Hawa Mahal** (http://www.hawa-mahal.com/) built in 1799 is Jaipur's most distinctive landmark. It is an extraordinary, five storey, fairy-tale, pink sandstone folly which enabled ladies of the royal household to watch the life and processions of the city without being seen. It consists of 953 balconies decorated with stone lattice work screens but is only around one room deep, with narrow, delicately scalloped walkways.

Most people come here to get a view of the facade but you can also climb to the top by paying a small entry fee at an entry up a side street to the right. It's still a great place for people-watching from behind the small shutters. The top offers stunning views over Jantar Mantar and the City Palace one way and over Siredeori Bazaar the other. There is also a small archaeological museum here.

The **Iswari Minar Swarga Sal tower** near Tripolia Gate is a handy landmark among the chaos of the Old City. The minaret was erected by Jai Singh's son, Iswari, who later killed himself rather than face the advancing Maratha army. You can take the spiral walkway to the top of the minaret for excellent views over the old city. The entrance is a bit hard to find so you may have to ask someone. There is an admission charge of Rs200.

The **Raj Mandir Cinema** (C-16, Bhagwandas Rd) (http://therajmandir.com/) is in a different area to all the above attractions but it is worth seeing. The highlight is the stunning art-deco-India-style interior. It was once known as the best movie theatre in India and is still probably the best in Rajasthan.

If you want to view an Indian movie (and you should) this is the place. There is general chaos in the ticket line, and inside the audience laughs, cheers, claps, and consistently talks through the entire film. The movies themselves are always interesting as they often combine action, drama, mystery, suspense, and dances. Box seats at Rs120 are best. There are shows at 6:30 p.m. and 9:30 p.m.

The **Central Museum** in Albert Hall in the Ram Nivas Garden (Ram Nivas Bagh, south of the Old City) (http://alberthalljaipur.gov.in/) was established to house and care for documents, antiques, and articles of importance to the city.

The building was built in the mid-1800s to greet the Prince of Wales on his visit to India. It is modelled after the Victoria and Albert Museum in

London. The sandstone and marble structure was designed by an English architect and it was originally meant to function as a town hall.

The museum has an assortment of rare articles on display including textiles, carpets, paintings, metal and wood crafts, pottery, arms and weapons, flora and fauna, toys, and dolls. One section of the museum, also known as Darbar Hall, is supposed to have the largest floor covering in the world.

This museum opens every day from 9:30 a.m. to 4:30 p.m. Entry is Rs300 for foreigners and Rs40 for Indians. Photography isn't permitted. The Central Museum sits within the Ram Niwas Gardens, and the 13-hectare garden also includes a small zoo and bird park, a theatre and a few small cafes and picnic spots.

Constructed by Seth Jai Ram Paliwal, the **Moti Dungri Ganesh Temple** is located on a small hill on Jawaharlal Nehru Marg to the south of the Central Museum. This temple was initially built to house the idol 'Ganesha' then later the Moti Dungri palace complex, an imitation of a famous Scottish castle, was built around the temple. The Moti Dungri Ganesh Temple is carved out of stone and is known for its amazing lattice work on marble.

The grand **Birla Mandir Temple** (http://www.culturalindia.net/indian-temples/birla-temple-jaipur.html) is located at the base of Moti Dungari Hill just a little to the south. The enormous temple, which was built in 1988 by the Birla Group of Industries, looks stunning at night.

The Temple is dedicated to Lord Vishnu and his consort Lakshmi. Stained glass windows depict scenes from Hindu scriptures. Hindu deities are depicted inside the temple, and on the outside walls great historical and religious figures are shown, including Socrates, Zarathustra, Christ, Buddha, and Confucius.

There are three large domes said to represent the three major religions in India and this is aimed to show the secular nature of the temple. It is surrounded by large lush green gardens. The Birla Temple also has a museum which showcases the ancestral valuables of the Birla family. The museum is open every day from 8 a.m. to noon and then from 4 p.m. to 8 p.m. There is no entry fee to visit the museum.

The **Rambagh Palace** (Bhawani Singh Road) (https://www.tajhotels.com/en-in/our-hotels/hotels-in-jaipur/) is not far from here to the west. It is the former residence of the Maharaja of Jaipur and is now a luxury Taj Palace Hotel. The first building on the site was a garden house built in 1835. In 1887, during the reign of Maharaja Sawai Madho Singh, it was converted into a modest royal hunting lodge.

In the early 20th century, it was expanded into a palace. After India became independent the palace became the Government House and in 1957 it was converted into a luxury hotel. The hotel is proud of the fact that in 2009 it was rated as the best hotel in the world by *Conde Nast Traveller* magazine.

There are two temples on the eastern edge of the city where both locals and tourists go to feed the surprisingly tame monkeys, use the temples, and enjoy the views. To reach **Galwh Bagh** (the Monkey Temple) you climb to the top of the hill and then go down into the valley, all the while in the company of countless monkeys, goats, and other animals.

Unfortunately, the place is not well kept so you are likely to encounter dirt and rubbish, as well as pseudo holy men coercing people for money. Most visitors are only interested in the 5000 or so monkeys that inhabit this place but the assorted shrines themselves are attractively atmospheric.

To reach **Surya Mandir** (the Sun Temple) you turn right at the top of the hill. There is an excellent view from here, especially at sunset. If you want monkey food it is available for purchase at the bottom of the hill. Entry to the temples is free, but local religious people will ask for donations and there is a Rs50 charge for using a camera.

There are still a few other interesting sites to visit

**Royal Gaitor Tumbas** is the cremation ground of the Royal Maharajas of Rajasthan. It is in a dramatic rocky setting at the foothills of Nahargarh Fort to the north of the central city. There are good views over the city and of the snaking city wall.

These cenotaphs are a combination of Islamic and Hindu temple architecture, among which the cenotaph of Maharaja Sawai Jai Singh II is considered the most impressive as it is made of white marble with intricate carvings on it.

Twenty ornately carved pillars depict scenes and figures from Hindu mythology. It is interesting to note that the carvings on each cenotaph are a reflection of the taste of respective Maharajas. Unfortunately, the whole site seemed a little run-down. There is litter and building debris in the car park. Entry is Rs15 for adults and the area opens from 10 a.m. to 5 30 p.m. daily.

Above Gaitor and reachable via a steep path lies the Ganesh Mandir, the second of the city's two major Ganesh temples. This huge building has a large swastika painted on its side.

**Nahargarh Fort** is the smallest of the three forts in the Jaipur area, notable primarily for excellent views over Man Sagar Lake and the vast sprawl of Jaipur. The fort was initially built by Sawai Jai Singh in 1734 and was subsequently developed further. The fort also houses the deteriorating Madhavendra Bhawan Palace. Entry is Rs50 for Indians and Rs200 for foreigners. It opens 10 a.m. to 5.30 p.m. daily.

**Chokhi Dhani Village** (http://www.chokhidhani.com/resort/food-joints.html) is a nicely landscaped area spread over four hectares, at the Chokhi Dhani Resort. Different folk artists perform at different places and a village fair is hosted every evening displaying the rich and wonderful cultural heritage of Rajasthan. The cost to enter is Rs700 but this includes a meal which can be a buffet or individually plated.

Your experience will depend on the number of visitors. At times it becomes overcrowded and the staff simply can't cope. Entry can be confusing and slow because various food options are not clear to visitors and there is difficulty finding a seat to eat once you are inside. Weekends are particularly bad but in the low-season mid-week the whole thing can be excellent.

The **SRC Museum of Indology** (24, Gangwal Park) is a private museum located at Jawaharlal Nehru Marg. The collection consists of thousands of items divided into 18 sections. There is a huge collection of paintings done on different media including cloth, skin, glass, paper, wood and ivory using water colour, lacquer and oil paint. There is also a large collection of manuscripts with around 15,000 on display. The designer-woven textile collection has over 6000 items.

The **Jawahar Kala Kendra** arts centre (Jawaharlal Marg opposite Rajasthan Commerce College) is a place, where something is always happening - drama festivals, music performances, art exhibitions, craft fairs, workshops, discussions and seminars, or film screenings. Jawahar Kala Kendra is open throughout the week from 10 a.m. to 5 p.m. There is no entry fee.

The **Khole Ke Hanuman ji Temple** (Laxman Dungri on the Delhi bypass) is dedicated to the Lord Hanuman. It is considered to be one of the most ancient and famous temples in Jaipur. The compound is huge and it attracts a large number of devotees. The zigzag path leading to the temple is quite long and there is considerable walking involved if you want to see everything.

Some visitors will rate a visit to **Rusirani Village** highly while others will think it offers little of interest. The village is about 2.5 hours north-east of Jaipur and you need to visit on a tour. It is a good place to experience the traditions and beauty of Rajasthan in a very laid-back way.

A walk in the village takes you back to the past, where people were helpful and simple in their living. It also gives you a chance to meet the locals and eat in a local house, and see the local market, a few temples and lush green fields.

## Shopping

Even if you have no interest in buying anything, you need to visit the bazaar in Jaipur's city centre. An evening visit will overpower you with colours, sights, sounds and smells. There are different specialist zones for each item. Be wary of gem scams and people who seem eager to hang out with you.

You will see Jaipur's famous 'Rajais' (a type of light quilt stuffed with cotton) everywhere but these are not ideal to take home because of their bulk. You can shop in the main market area or elsewhere but remember to bargain everywhere for nothing in the city is 'fixed price'.

Jaipur is a renowned handicraft centre and there are both tourist souvenirs and quality arts and crafts available. The city is known for producing exquisite gold jewellery enamelled or inlaid with precious stones, blue pottery, wood carvings, block printing, tie-dye textiles, leather articles, hand-made paper and more.

Miniature paintings made from vegetable dyes, and sometimes gold and silver, are popular with visitors. So too are paper-mache birds which are exquisitely designed. Watch out also for wide-eyed puppets with curling moustaches or nose rings as they are traditional Rajasthan designs.

One of the highlights of most of Rajasthan is the chance to interact with the friendly people, and shopping provides a good opportunity for this. You will find that many middle-class young people are curious of foreigners and are keen to find out what you think of their city.

Jaipur has a reputation as a good place to buy gems and jewellery. I believe this may be correct if you are an expert but as an unprofessional visitor you are likely to get conned. Shop keepers will regale you with beguiling tales about how you can buy gems in Jaipur and sell them back home for a massive profit.

This generally does not work, of course. What is more likely is you will end up with a handful of worthless cut-glass "gems" wondering where all the mysterious entries on your credit-card bill came from. So be very aware.

## Other activities

Jaipur has many places where you can spend time with elephants – Elefantastic (http://www.elefantastic.in/elefantastic-farm/), Elefriend, Eleday, Elephant Joy and so on. I do not know which is currently considered the best to visit as I have serious problems with the treatment of the elephants in such places.

There are various tours on offer around Jaipur. The **Free Walking Tour** (http://www.freedaytour.com/) is the perfect introduction to Jaipur, and a great way to orientate yourself in the city at a price to suit everybody's budget. It operates every day from 8:15 a.m. to 10:45 a.m. with an English speaking guide.

The tour is free but donations would be appreciated. You need to book this tour in advance as the operators do not take more than 10 people on each tour.

**Jaipur Cultural Walk** (http://www.jaipurculturalwalk.in/) operates twice a day from 10 a.m. to 2 p.m. and 4 p.m. to 8 p.m. I prefer the morning tour which starts with a hot breakfast then continues with a tour through the spice bazaar and flower market, followed by the vegetable and fruit markets. You next explore the narrow streets where artisans and handicraft makers ply their trade before a short tea break.

Then it's time for a rickshaw ride around the old city back to the vegetable market, where you will make the choice of fresh vegetables for dinner. Finally, it's on to the home of a local Indian family for an 'interactive' cooking session and culinary experience after which you sit down and enjoy a meal together.

If cycling is more your style try the **Pink Inside Cycle Tour** (http://www.cyclinjaipur.com/). This operates from 6:45 a.m. to 10 a.m. everyday but booking is required. You make your way along the narrow alleys and actually get to take a peek into homes, kitchens and artisans' workshops. You will get to know about the lives of the locals, and enjoy a traditional Rajasthani meal with an Indian family in the heart of the old city.

The same company operates the full-day **Jaipur by Insiders Tour** (http://www.cyclinjaipur.com/#!day-tours/sxvke). This starts with the Pink Inside Cycle Tour then follows with a cooking class from market to table, a yoga class, and a spa break to enjoy a traditional Ayurveda massage.

**Hot Air Balloon** rides are offered by SkyWaltz (http://www.skywaltz.com/destinations.html) from September through until March in both the morning and evening. It is too hot for the rest of the year

Many of the major hotels in Jaipur have luxury **spas** which are available to those who are not guests at the hotel. Some of the well-known ones are Jiva Grande Spa at the Taj Rambagh Palace, the Spa and Fitness Centre at The Oberoi Rajvilas, and Jaipur Marriott Hotel's O2 Spa. There are plenty of options as well outside the hotels. Try Kerala Ayurveda Kendra (Tel: 141-5106743), Vipassana Center (Tel: 9536590801) or Aura Thai Spa (Tel: 141-6001 000).

## Getting around

**Walking** is always my preferred travel mode but in large cities it is not always practical. In the Tripolia Bazaar, it is a treat to walk, although side streets are a bit less welcoming and you will quickly see the poverty faced by many. For short distances inside Jaipur, try the reasonably-priced cycle rickshaws which are slower but usually cheaper than autos.

**Autos** are also a cheap way to go around the city, however, foreigners are often charged much more than the local rate. You can hire an auto rickshaw driver for a day and this cuts down on the hassle.

The **taxis** in Jaipur are very convenient and comfortable. These are much safer than auto rickshaws in traffic, and the drivers are generally polite. If there is not one outside your hotel, ask the hotel to call for one, as it can be difficult to hail one on the street. Taxis generally have yellow license plates with black letters and some are painted in yellow and black.

A limited **metro rail** service started in March 2015 and construction is on-going. Phase 2 is scheduled to open in March 2018.

## Eating and drinking

India is a large country so it is no surprise to learn that each area has its own food specialties. In Jaipur, I recommend you try a range of local dishes from daal, *baati* and *churma* to the spicy *laal maas* which is an absolute delight for non-vegetarians.

There are also sweets like *ghewar* which is a speciality of this royal city, and piping hot *pyaaz kachoris* which are popular with locals with a cup of tea. *Thalis*, or meals on a platter, have always been an integral part of the dining experience in Rajasthan and I strongly urge you to try this while in Jaipur.

The combination of *daal, baati* and *churma* becomes a complete meal in itself. The daal, or lentil curry, is served with baked *baati*. *Churma* is a sweet dish made with flour, sugar and ghee. The local way to eat this is to break the *baati*, mix in some *daal* and *churma*, and pour ghee over the whole lot.

*Ghewar* is popular during festivals like Teej and Gangaur and it is available in several varieties. It is a deep fried sweet with a sweet crust.

*Laal maas* was originally a Royal dish but it is now found everywhere in Jaipur. Made with spicy dry red chillies, other spices and red meat, it is the most recommended and popular non-vegetarian dish in Jaipur.

You can explore the cuisine of Jaipur by taking a Rajasthani food tour. You can choose half-day or full-day food tours which cover some 'must see' attractions as well as excellent food from multiple places located all over the city. You will find some advertised on the web.

Some of the most popular restaurants in Jaipur, where you can have some Rajasthani food, are among the following. I have not tried all of them but I have never been disappointed whenever I have eaten in the city.

There are several **Laxmi Misthan Bhandar** (LMB) restaurants in the city but the easiest one to find is, located in Johri Bazaar. Try the typical Rajasthani sweets like *ghewar* and *mawa kachori*. You can also have a filling and authentic Rajasthani *thali* that includes Rajasthani **kadhi**, 5 different vegetables, *papad mangori* soup, *ker sangri* and 3 types of bread. The price ranges between Rs80 and Rs350

**Surya Mahal Restaurant** (Tel: 236 2811) (http://www.suryamahal.com/) on MI Road serves authentic Rajasthani cuisine and you could also try other popular dishes from the north and south. A meal will cost approximately Rs700 for two, excluding alcohol.

Adjacent **Natraj** (Tel: 237 5804) serves simple and inexpensive north Indian and Rajasthani *thalis* with different breads, *gatta*, *sangri* and yoghurt salads.

Nearby **Handi** (Tel: 237 2275) (http://handirestaurant.com/), also on MI Road, is a must-visit place for meat-eaters. It serves tender mutton cooked in traditional pots (*handis*) smoked with burning charcoal, along with wafer-thin *roomali rotis*.

For something really upmarket it is hard to go past **Suvarna Mahal Restaurant** (Tel: 238 5700) (https://taj.tajhotels.com/en-in/taj-rambagh-palace-jaipur/restaurants/suvarna-mahal-restaurant/) in the famous Rambagh Palace. With a menu that offers authentic Rajasthani cuisine and more, this place has excellent service and splendid decor.

It serves one of the best *thali* spreads of its type and I can personally recommend it. The appetisers include vegetable kebabs and barbequed lamb, and among the main courses is *lal Maas*, and *gatte* among others. For dessert, there are the rich *malpuas* (deep-fried pancakes) and *rasmalais* (cottage cheese balls in sweet cream).

Another top restaurant is **Gulab Mahal** (Tel: 222 3636) at the Jai Mahal Palace You can feast on an extensive Rajasthani menu, surrounded by a royal, lavish ambiance. The chef presents a repertoire of delicacies once prepared in the royal kitchens. A meal for two here can cost you around Rs2500.

At **1135 AD** (Tel: 98290 37170) in Amber Fort, you'll be served your lunch on pure silverware and matching cutlery, and you'll eat it under a recast roof with gold inlay and leaf work. You could start the meal with stuffed roasted *paneer* (cottage cheese) and follow it with a *thali* of ten items served with flavoured rice and naan bread. If the food isn't captivating enough, there is live folk music and dancing in the courtyard.

**Around Jaipur**

**Ramgarh** is approximately 35 km from Jaipur city and it attracts hundreds and thousands of tourists every year. The artificial Ramgarh Lake, spread across 4 km, is the most popular tourist attraction in Ramgarh. The lake offers boating between the months of October and June and it is also an interesting place for bird watchers. The thick forest within **Jamwa Sanctuary** is home to many wildlife species and wildlife safaris are available.

The Polo Ground at Ramgarh is regarded as one of the best polo grounds in India. It is located between Ramgarh Lake and the Aravalli

Hills. Jamwa Mata temple is another attraction.

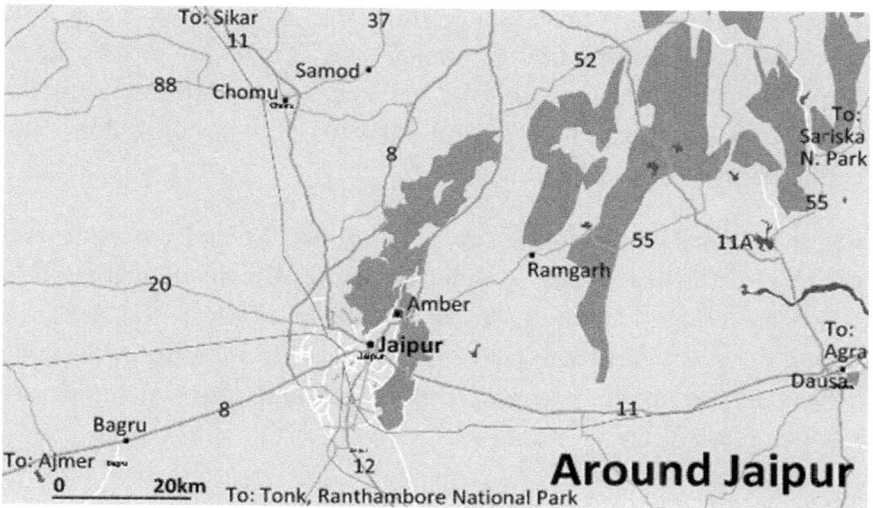

Sleepy **Samode** village is tucked around a low-lying outcrop of the Aravalli Hills about 45 km north of Jaipur. The village walkways are inhabited by various craft communities engaged in block printing, lacquer work, weaving of carpets, traditional and modern silver jewellery, stone and paper painting, gem stone cutting, pottery, traditional *jooti*-making (shoe making) and metal works.

A **camel ride** in Samode can be an adventure. The camels take you on a leisurely ride along the Aravalli foothills, weaving their way through a treasure trove of artisan workshops. You can soak in the landscape dotted with ancient *havelis*, *bawadis* (stepwells), cenotaphs and temples.

Musicians with their vibrant attire and unusual instruments provide great evening entertainment. The instruments include one-stringed fiddles, country violins, bagpipes made out of goatskin, a dried gourd, castanets, and Jew's harps. The villagers sing with plaintive abandon under the starry desert sky.

The 400 years old **Sheesh Mahal** (Palace of Mirrors) with its unique architecture and famous garden is a must-see. Samode Palace, about 10 km from the village, is a charming and romantic edifice which has been converted into a heritage hotel. Other stay alternatives are a local home, where you share the patterns of daily life and are introduced to Samode's crafts and craftspeople, or experience a farm stay on the outskirts of Samode, where the rural lifestyle includes agriculture and cattle rearing.

**Bagru** is a small village on the Jaipur-Ajmer road 35 km from Jaipur. It is popular for block or wooden printing commonly known as 'Bagru Prints'. These are created by an exclusive technique in which the design is carved on a wooden block which is then used to reproduce the same design on the fabric. Excellent bed covers and other materials are manufactured by these villagers.

**Tonk**, 96 km south from Jaipur, is renowned for its old *havelis* and mosques. This elegant town was once ruled by the 'Pathans' of Afghanistan. The ancient town takes pride in its beautiful architectural wonders, established during the Mughal era.

Sunehri Kothi, declared a historical monument, is also known as the Mansion of Gold and is the main attraction. Its interiors are decorated with mirrors, gilt, stucco and stained glass. The Arabian and Persian Research Institute houses rare and beautiful collections of Arabic and Persian books, some adorned in gold and precious stones. The Jama Masjid, in the Delhi Mogul style of architecture, is one of the biggest mosques in India.

**Ranthambore National Park** is situated 160 km south-east of Jaipur city in idyllic scenery in the Sawai Madhopur district of Rajasthan. It is one of the largest and most famous National Parks in India. Once known as the hunting base for the Maharajas of Jaipur, the park today is a major tourist destination and is well known for its tiger sightings. It is probably the best place in India for spotting wild tigers.

There are Wildlife Safaris, and Jeep Safaris which take about three and half hour to tour the entire park. Other than the majestic tigers, visitors may see leopards, deer, hyenas, crocodiles, and many more animals. The best time to visit is between December and April when the weather is pleasant. The park remains opens from 6 a.m. to 6 p.m.

## Jaipur to Agra

**Sariska National Park** (http://www.sariskanationalpark.com/) in the Alwar district is not on the direct road but is one of the most visited national parks. Located around 107 km north-east of Jaipur, this national park covers a vast expanse of 800 square km. The sanctuary is home to a variety of wildlife species such as leopards, Sambar deer, hyenas, crocodiles, and many avian species and marsh animals.

If you are looking for a relaxed excursion to an idyllic location, the Sariska National Park has plenty to offer. It is relatively easy to get to and has a wide range of flora, fauna as well as dazzling scenery. The park surrounds a couple of historical spots that many tourists visit such as the ancient 'Kankawadi Fort', the 'Nilkanth Temple', and the Sariska Palace.

Because of these monuments located within the park boundaries, the park authorities keep the park open throughout the year. Most visitors arrive in winter but the summer months are better for animal viewing. They can become extremely hot, however, and it can be very uncomfortable waiting to see animals in the blazing heat.

**Dausa** is 55 km to the east of Jaipur on National Highway 11. It is named after a hill near the city which has a fort, built by Badgujar kings, who were the original rulers of this area. The Krishna Temple on the main highway just to the east of Dausa is of interest. The highlight of the district, however, is in the small village of Abhaneri.

To reach here you go along highway 11 to Bamanpra then turn left onto the SH25. Around 6 km along this road turn right at a crossroads then it's about 4 km to **Abhaneri Village**. Unfortunately, there is no clear signage but the village and the monuments are well worthwhile checking out. Abhaneri is famous for its early medieval monuments, in particular, the **Chand Baori** (Stepwell) and the Harshat Mata Temple, but you also should spend a little time looking at life in the village. It is quite fascinating.

The Chand Baori is located next to the Temple and it is one of the oldest and most attractive landmarks in Rajasthan yet it is rarely visited by international visitors. It was built by King Chanda of the Nikumbha Dynasty between 800 and 900 AD.

This incredible square structure is 13 stories deep, and lined along the walls on three sides are many double flights of steps. 3,500 narrow steps arranged in perfect symmetry descend to the bottom of the well. Chand Baori extends approximately 30 m into the ground making it one of the deepest and largest stepwells in India. One side of the well has a pavilion and resting room for the royals.

Jaipur to Agra

In addition to conserving water, Chand Baori also served as a sort of community centre for the locals. The townsfolk used to sit around the step well and cool off during the summer days. It is claimed that at the bottom of the well the air is about 5-6 degrees cooler than at the top during the summer heat.

**Harshat Mata temple**, which dates back to a similar time, is protected by the Indian archaeological department. Though the temple is in ruins, you can still see the beautiful craftsmanship in its construction. Harshat Mata is regarded as the goddess of happiness but there is little evidence of this in this very poor village. Visiting the temple is worthwhile, thanks to its amazing architecture which takes us back to the glory of medieval India.

The ruined images in the temple indicate that the temple was actually dedicated to Lord Vishnu. It was destroyed during the Islamic time and several broken columns are a testament to the destruction. The site is still an active religious site for locals so visitors must remove their shoes when visiting. No charge is levied at present at the stepwell or temple.

There is another interesting spot a little further along the highway. **Mehandipur Balaji Mandir** is about 40 km from Dausa. The temple is located 3 km south of the Jaipur - Agra highway from Brahmbad.

This extremely popular pilgrim site is said to have miraculous powers to exorcise a person possessed with an evil spirit or a victim of black magic. Thousands of people who are apparently under the spell of evil or possessed by ghosts flock to this temple to offer different kinds of prayers to seek relief.

It requires nerves of steel to watch some of the exorcism rituals that are practiced here. To a non-believer it makes absolutely no sense at all. At the rear of the temple there is a large hall where people sit on the ground and get beaten. Elsewhere women swirl their hair and hit their heads against the rock. In a secluded area, men, women and even children are chained to big rocks for long periods without food and water and are regularly beaten.

It is worthwhile to make a small detour to **Bharatpur** a city a few kilometres north of the highway. Located within the Bharatpur Palace is Kamra Khas, a museum that contains a vast number of antiques, including stone sculptures, local art and craft wares and ancient scriptures. The palace itself was built in stages by various Maharajas and is a fine fusion of Mughal and Rajput architecture. The Ganga Mandir, in the centre of the city is one of the most beautiful temples in Rajasthan.

Just north of here is Lohagarh Fort which withstood many attacks by the British. It is not flamboyant, but is clearly rugged and strong. The fort is surrounded by a moat which originally was filled with water to keep enemies out. Interesting monuments inside the fort are Kothi Khas, Mahal Khas, Moti Mahal and Kishori Mahal.

The **Keoladeo National Park** just south of the city and adjacent to the road is a major wintering area for aquatic birds. It is recognised as one of Asia's finest birding areas with over 380 resident and migratory species. You can walk or cycle through the park but the best way to see the birds is to rent a rickshaw with a puller who has been trained by the park management. Boats are also available for rent.

The most interesting site of all is nearby **Fatchpur Sikri**. This is covered in the next chapter.

# 8 AGRA – NOT ALL ABOUT THE TAJ MAHAL

Agra is a city on the banks of the Yamuna River in the state of Uttar Pradesh, 200 kilometres south of the national capital New Delhi. The early history is obscure but it may have been a Hindu stronghold for many centuries. Reference to it was made by a Persian poet in the 12th century when it was noted that Mahmud of Ghazni had so ruined the city when he invaded that it never recovered.

Sikandar Lodi made Agra his capital in 1501 and he built a fort and laid out a city. This was destroyed by an earthquake within a year but he rebuilt part of it immediately after. Virtually nothing remains from that period. He died in Agra but is buried in Delhi.

The golden age of the city began with the Mughals under the leadership of **Babur**. It was known then as Akbarabād and remained the capital of the Mughal Empire under the next three Emperors. Barbur was only 13 when he inherited from his father a small principality called Ferghana in what is now eastern Uzbekistan.

Over the next few years, he lost this area to others but turned his attention south and established a realm that eventually became the nucleus of present-day Afghanistan. From here he invaded south-eastwards into India.

Babur came from the cool fertile uplands of Turkestan so the dry, dusty plains of Hindustan and the town of Akbarabād would have been very unattractive to him. To help overcome this deficiency Babur laid out the Arām Bāgh or Garden of Relaxation on the banks of the Yamuna River.

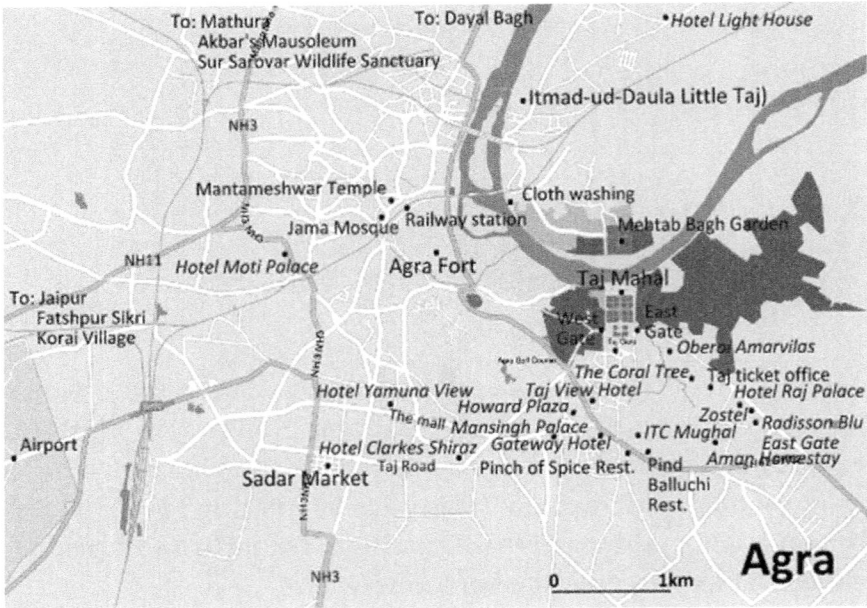

To: Mathura
Akbar's Mausoleum
Sur Sarovar Wildlife Sanctuary

To: Dayal Bagh

*Hotel Light House*

NH3

*Itmad-ud-Daula Little Taj)*

Mantameshwar Temple

Cloth washing

Jama Mosque  Railway station

Mehtab Bagh Garden

NH11  Hotel Moti Palace

Agra Fort

Taj Mahal

To: Jaipur
Fatshpur Sikri
Korai Village

West
Gate

East
Gate

Oberoi Amarvilas

The Coral Tree. Taj ticket office
Hotel Yamuna View   Taj View Hotel        Hotel Raj Palace
                Howard Plaza.
                The mall Mansingh Palace    Zostel. Radisson Blu
Airport                                   .ITC Mughal      East Gate
                Hotel Clarkes Shiraz  Gateway Hotel      Aman Homestay
                        Taj Road                 Pind
Sadar Market                 Pinch of Spice Rest.  Balluchi
                                              Rest.

NH3

0          1km

**Agra**

Unfortunately in 1530, after only four years of rule, Babur died and his eldest son, **Humayun**, was named as successor. He was, however, opposed by many enemies and was forced out of India for many years after being defeated in the Battle of Kanauj. He eventually triumphed over his many rivals and returned to Delhi as emperor once more but he died in a strange accident by tripping over his robe and fracturing his skull.

Humayun left his shaky kingdom to his son **Akbar** who was only thirteen. It turned out that Akbar was a brilliant administrator, general, ruler and judge of men. He built the great Red Fort in Agra, besides making the city a centre for learning, arts, commerce and religion. He also built a new city on the outskirts of Akbarabād called Fatehpur Sikri.

By the time of Akbar's death, his empire stretched across the whole north of the sub-continent. The domain was extremely well-run; revenues and resources were immense. As well, he had given the office of Mughal emperor a status far above that accorded to previous dynasties of Muslim rulers.

His son **Jahāngīr** succeeded his father as Emperor in 1605. His reign was characterized by political stability, a strong economy and impressive cultural achievements. He had an interest in gardens and laid out many inside the Red Fort. Jahangir was fascinated with art and architecture and was a naturalist as well.

**Shāh Jahān**, Jahāngīr's son, was a pious Muslim and was known for his keen interest in architecture but he destroyed many Hindu temples during his reign. He built much of what you see today in Agra Fort but is probably best known as the builder of the Tāj Mahal in memory of his wife Mumtāz Mahal. Shāh Jahān later shifted the capital to Delhi, but his son **Aurangzeb** moved the capital back to Akbarabād, imprisoning his father in the Fort there.

Aurangzeb ruled for almost fifty years and shifted the capital to Aurangabad but the Mughal Empire was in decline. Akbarabād came under the influence of the Marathas and was renamed Agra, before falling into the hands of the British Raj in 1803.

Agra is known world-wide for the **Tāj Mahal** (http://www.tajmahal.gov.in/), one of the most famous buildings in the world. It has been voted as one of the New Seven Wonders of the World along with the Great Wall of China, the Colosseum in Roma, Petra, Chechen Itza, Machu Picchu, and Christ the Redeemer in Rio. It is one of the three World Heritage Sites in Agra.

Completed in 1653, the Tāj Mahal is finished in marble and is perhaps India's (and the world's) most beautiful building. This perfectly symmetrical monument took 22 years and 20,000 workers to build and is set amidst landscaped gardens. While the white domed marble mausoleum is the most familiar component of the Tāj Mahal, it is actually an integrated complex of structures. There is a mosque, museum, fake mosque, water supply buildings and worker's accommodation.

The compound is bounded on three sides by red sandstone walls while the river side is left open. Polluting traffic is now not allowed near the complex and tourists must either walk from parking lots or catch an electric bus. There are three entrances to the compound and these days there is quite good security to pass through.

*Inside the Tāj Mahal compound*

Built by the Persian architect, Ustād ʿĪsā, the Tāj Mahal is on the south bank of the Yamuna River near the centre of town. It cannot be seen from much of the city but is visible from Agra Fort from where Emperor Shāh Jahān gazed at it for the last eight years of his life.

The entry to the main complex is through the impressive three-storey Great Gate with its 22 small domes representing the number of years it took to build the marvellous building. You see three styles of decoration on the gate in black slate – flowers, calligraphy in the form of verses from the Koran, and a geometric pattern. These are repeated on the Tāj itself.

The gate leads to a monumental avenue with a paved footpath leading to the mausoleum divided by a spectacular water channel and bronze fountains between a double row of cypress trees. The whole plan is a superb combination of harmoniously balanced buildings and jewel-like finishes so it can be enjoyed from afar as well as in the examination of details.

The Tāj Mahal was built on a marble platform that stands above a sandstone one. The dominant structural material throughout the complex is local red sandstone which is abundant in the area. Marble, however, had to be brought on elephant-drawn carts from 300 km away in Rajasthan. Semi-precious stones were brought from sources further afield: jasper from the Punjab, jade from China, and chalcedony from Sri Lanka.

It is the white crystalline marble facing of the main mausoleum that makes the Tāj so stunning and as the colour white symbolizes mourning throughout the Islamic world, white marble is particularly suited to use in the construction of tombs.

The large, elegant dome of the Tāj Mahal has a diameter of 18 m, and a height of 24 m. and the top is decorated with a lotus design. The tomb of Mumtāz Mahal is under this dome. Shāh Jahān's tomb was placed next to hers by his son Aurangzeb. The interior walls are about 25 metres high and are topped by a "false" interior dome.

There is only one access to the plinth and tomb. Shoes must be removed at this point or plastic overshoes put on. Socks are allowed if you prefer. The interiors are decorated with fine inlay work, incorporating semi-precious stones. There are 47 different materials in the inlay work including coral from the Red Sea, melinite from Russia, cornelian from Baghdad, lapis from Afghanistan and so on. It must have been even better before a warlike people called the Jats looted the place in the 18th century.

What you see are not the actual tombs. These are under the central chamber directly below the visible tombs and they cannot be visited.

This arrangement was common when the building was constructed. The replica tombs are elaborately inlaid with semi-precious stones and enclosed by white marble screens so delicately fretted as to suggest the finest lace.

This is one of the wonderful things about the building. It somehow manages to successfully blend subtlety with grandeur. There is no doubt that the design of the building is stunning but this is matched with the intricate execution of details.

The complex is set in a large 300-metre square Mughal garden. Raised pathways divide each quarter of the garden into 16 sunken flowerbeds. A reflecting pool runs between the tomb and the Great Gate with a raised marble water tank halfway between them. This is great place for a photograph.

The main building changes colour and texture during the day depending on atmospheric conditions. Some visitors are initially disappointed when they visit in foggy conditions but this has its own magic. Many like to visit early morning when the building has a soft dreaminess but I consider it equally attractive in the dazzling whiteness of midday or the cold splendour of moonlight.

The grounds are open from 6 a.m. to 7 p.m. weekdays, except for Friday when the complex is open for prayers at the mosque between noon and 2 p.m. The complex is open for night viewing on five nights at full moon time, excluding Fridays and the month of Ramadan.

There has been more written about the Tāj Mahal than practically any other building on earth and everyone has seen photographs of the amazing structure. Most visitors have experienced this hype and I was wondering if I would be somewhat let down after expecting so much. In fact, there is something mesmerizing about the tomb and its surrounds and no one goes away disappointed.

For security reasons only five items—water in transparent bottles, small video cameras, still cameras, mobile phones and small ladies' purses—

are allowed inside. Admission is Rs1000 for most foreign visitors, Rs530 for those citizens of SAARC and BIMSTEC countries and Rs40 for Indians. Children below the age of 15 are free.

A longstanding myth claims that Shāh Jahān planned his own mausoleum to be built in black marble across the Yamuna River from the Tāj Mahal. Blackened marble ruins in the so-called Moonlight Garden, were used to support this legend, however, according to a book by Ebba Koch, excavations carried out in the 1990s found that they were discoloured white stones that had turned black. Others claim they are the remains of walls and pavilions in one of Babur's old gardens.

About 500 meters from the east gate, on Fatehabad Road, you'll find a **forest reserve** that provides a unique opportunity to view the monument in different hues. There are four main photo points, six metre high watch towers in different locations, and a 9 kilometre walking trail.

This is a great way to escape the crowds of Agra with wonderful views of the Tāj Mahal. It costs 100 rupees (for tourists) to walk around this clean and peaceful garden. There is a playground inside and a shop where you can buy drinks. We also saw lots of peacocks.

**Agra Fort** (or Red Fort) (http://agrafort.gov.in/) probably existed for centuries before the present structure was commissioned by the great Mughal Emperor Akbar in 1565. It is another of Agra's World Heritage Sites. The red sandstone fort was converted into a palace during Shāh Jahān's time and many of the original buildings were replaced by more sumptuous marble ones. Today about 30% is open to the public while 70% is used by the Indian army. Entry is Rs550 for foreigners, Rs40 for Indians.

It looks forbidding from the outside but inside the crescent shaped fort is very interesting. It is ringed by red sandstone ramparts and a wide and deep moat and there are four gates.

The monumental Delhi Gate built in 1568 is considered the grandest. It is embellished with inlay work in white marble but is not used by the public; visitors enter via the Amar Singh Gate.

The gateway leading to the great courtyard of the Diwan-i-Aam is reached by a steep ramp. This double gate, with interior platforms on both sides and double arches, has the typical features of Shāh Jahān's monuments. The Diwan-i-Aam, constructed in 1628 and built in red sandstone on a raised platform, has a total of 48 large pillars over which the engrailed arches support the flat stone roof. The Hall is open on three sides with multi-foiled arches.

The citadel contains several beautiful palaces such as the Khas Mahal, a building comprising open terraces and a hall, flanked by a pavilion on either side. The palace is laid out in three receding levels reflecting the fine aesthetic sense of Shah Jahan. It was meant for the royal ladies.

Another feature is the Shish Mahal, (Palace of Mirrors) so named because of the fine, profuse embellishment of mirrors on the arches, walls and the ceilings. This served as the luxurious bath of the Khas Mahal. The Emperor used these chambers to hold secret meetings and today you can only look in from an entrance.

The great sandstone Jahangir Mahal is considered by some to be the finest building in the fort. This has intricate carvings of birds, lotus and other designs in the Hindu style. Every part of the walls and ceiling of the library and the porch of this building is adorned with brilliant colours and gold leaf. It was probably built by Jahāngīr for his Rajput wife, Jodha Bai.

Then there is the spacious octagonal tower of Muhammam Burj constructed by Shāh Jahān for his beloved queen Mumtaz Mahal. This is where the emperor was imprisoned by his son for eight years until he died.

The elegant Diwan-i-Khas, built in 1637, consists of two large halls, an outer columned hall and inner closed hall, both connected by three multi-fold archways. The court met every day here to decide appeal cases and for considering the policy matters of the Empire. Besides, important persons and ambassadors of foreign countries also met the Emperor here.

This is where the bejewelled Peacock Throne once stood. The double columns of this building are said to be the most graceful of all in Shāh Jahān's buildings.

Two very beautiful mosques, the Pearl Mosque, constructed in 1646-53 in red sandstone while the entire interior is finished in white marble, and the later Nagina Masjid for ladies, are other highlights. It is interesting to see the tomb of the British governor is here within the compound.

A Sound and Light show is held every evening at a cost of Rs200 for foreigners, Rs70 for Indians.

The **Jāma Masjid** is opposite the Agra Fort and near the Agra Fort Railway Station. It is popularly known as the Friday Mosque. It is one of the larger mosques in India but is a very simple structure of red sandstone with a little white marble. The mosque was built by Mughal emperor, Shāh Jahān in 1648 and dedicated to his favourite daughter. It is beautifully decorated and is crowned by three large sandstone domes distinguished by their zigzag bands of marble.

The **Mankameshwar Temple** near the Jāma Masjid is one of four ancient temples located on the four corners of Agra City. Many of the surrounding markets date back to the Mughal Era. You'll find a tangle of narrow lanes housing a variety of wares including spices, clothes, saris, jewellery, and shoes.

If you get hungry there are also snack stalls. It's also a place to find traditional arts and crafts, such as marble work. This area, known as Kinari Bazaar, can be very confusing for first time visitors but getting lost can be quite fun and you will find your way out.

Across the river there is more to see. The **Mehtah Bagh Garden** was the last of eleven Mughal-built gardens along the Yamuna River opposite the Tāj and the Agra Fort. The garden complex, square in shape, is perfectly aligned with the Tāj Mahal. It was created as "a moonlit pleasure garden" with white plaster walkways, airy pavilions, pools and fountains.

Frequent floods and villagers extracting building materials nearly ruined the garden but restoration began in the 1990s and the garden's original ambiance was restored using plants that the Mughals used in their gardens. It has now become a very good location to view the Tāj Mahal particularly during summer when the sun is higher in the sky.

Take the time to stop off by the railway bridge over the river as you return. You will be rewarded by the sight of many men and women washing and drying hundreds of pieces of fabric which will be sold in the city's shops and markets. It is a fascinating and very colourful sight.

Nearby is the **Itmad-ud-daula** (baby Tāj) (http://agra.nic.in/historyof_ITMAD-UD-DAULA.html). The Empress Nūr Jahān built this tomb for her father, Mirzā Ghiyās Beg, the Chief Minister during the reign of the Emperor Jahāngīr. The mausoleum is set in a nice garden, criss-crossed by water courses and walkways. Entry is Rs110 for foreigners and Rs10 for Indians.

Although it is not built on a grand scale, it is a charming, intimate place with a gentle serenity. Its garden layout and use of white marble, inlay designs and latticework were mimicked later by the Tāj Mahal. Take note of the latticed screens of intricately carved white marble which allow light to reach the interior.

The yellow marble tombs of Nūr Jahān's father and mother have been set side-by-side, a formation replicated in the Tāj Mahal.

To the north of here is **Chini ka Rauza**, the tomb of Afzal Khan, a Persian poet who was the Prime Minister in the court of Shāh Jahān. This tomb, built in 1635, is a landmark of Indo-Persian architecture and is the first building in India to be adorned with glazed tile work. There is free entry.

Just a little further north is the **Rambagh Gardens**, one of the oldest gardens to be built by the first Mughal Emperor, Babur. It was built in a Persian style with ample pathways and canals, representative of the Islamic idea of paradise. Unfortunately, the condition of the Rambagh gardens today has changed for the worse due to heavy renovation and restoration in the past and lack of maintenance today. However, the place is of great interest to history buffs. There is an entry fee of Rs100 for foreigners.

Outside the immediate city there is much to see. **Akbar's Mausoleum** (http://asi.nic.in/asi_monu_tktd_up_akbartomb.asp) is the last resting place of Akbar the Great. It is on the Delhi-Agra Highway at Sikandra, 13 kilometres from Agra Fort. The vast, beautifully carved, red-ochre sandstone tomb is set in a lush garden.

As was the custom at the time, Akbar himself planned his own tomb and selected a suitable site for it. Akbar's son completed construction of this pyramidaal tomb in 1613. The 99 names of Allah have been inscribed on the tomb.

The main entrance is from the south. From the huge main gate, a broad paved causeway leads through the garden to the mausoleum which consists of three red sandstone stories topped with a final one in white marble. The actual tomb of the Emperor is in an underground chamber reached by a sloping corridor. Foreign entry is Rs210.

Nearby is **Guru ka Tal**, an historical Sikh pilgrimage place dedicated to the memory of the ninth Guru Sri Guru Tegh Bahudar Jr. The structure was originally built in 1610 to collect and conserve rainwater and the Gurdwara was built in the 1970s. There are elaborate stone carvings and eight ancient towers. It is clean, calm & divine. You will find yourself in a very peaceful atmosphere away from the busy outside world.

**Dayal Bagh** (http://agra.nic.in/whatto_see.html) is a pilgrimage site just north of Agra, which is popular for the memorial of Shiv Dayal Sahib, the founder of the Radha Swami Satsang Movement which started in 1861. The structure is a blend of mosque, temple and gurdwara architecture. The building of the white marble structure started on 1904 and is still ongoing. Some of the inlay work is quite outstanding but the present construction rather dampens some visitor's enthusiasm.

**Wildlife SOS** (https://www.facebook.com/wildlifesosindia/) is something completely different. This organisation was established in 1995 by a small group of individuals hoping to protect and conserve India's natural heritage, forests and wildlife. India's wildlife is under severe threat and many animals are becoming rare. The organisation also wants to eliminate exploitation of animals.

For more than 400 years, the sloth bear has been a target for human exploitation. A nomadic tribe known as the Kalandars began dancing sloth bears for emperors in the Mughal era. In more recent times, the dancing bear trade became entertainment for villagers and tourists who paid for pictures. Fortunately, in the last ten years, more than 600 bears have been surrendered voluntarily to Wildlife SOS and it is believed that there are no more used for entertainment.

Apart from its work with dancing bears they also work to protect the Asiatic Black Bear and other animals. Visitors can now see the Agra Bear Rescue Facility (http://wildlifesos.org/visit/) which is located inside the **Sur Sarovar Bird Sanctuary**. A new feature is the Education Conservation Walkway. There is also an Elephant Haven for rescued elephants.

The bird sanctuary itself can be visited but as one reviewer said, "The Sur Sarovar Bird sanctuary is an almost unknown sanctuary to all including the birds." This is a bit harsh and the man-made Keetham Lake can be a good place for a relaxed outing.

The **Kalabriti Cultural and Convention Centre** is an arts, culture and conventional centre which aims to celebrate the beauty and uniqueness of Indian culture and heritage. The centre offers visitors a chance to view intricate inlay work on marble and there is a handicrafts showroom where you can purchase items made of marble, metal, wood and thread.

This is also the location of an evening show that depicts the romantic love story of Emperor Shāh Jahān and his beloved wife Mumtaz Maha. Over 80 talented artists perform a story *Mohabbat The Taj*. The show is really great, packed with dance and musical performance. It's like seeing a live Bollywood movie. Headsets are provided to understand the dialog in several languages. Unfortunately, no photography is allowed.

The **Taj Mahotsav** is an annual 10-day festival held in February. With the majestic Taj Mahal as a backdrop, it is a great cultural event to attend. Every year, the Taj Mahotsav has a different theme and is a celebration of the rich arts, crafts and culture of India. Artisans from all over the country come together and display their works. Apart from this, there are also folk and classical music and dance performances by talented artists.

**Tours**

The **Mughal Heritage Walk** is a community-based tourism initiative of the Center for Urban and Regional Excellence and the Uttar Pradesh government. It aims to help villagers make an income from tourism and thus improve their living conditions. The one-kilometre walk is along the riverside opposite the Tāj Mahal and it goes through Kachhpura village. You'll see several lesser-known monuments of the Mughal Era, make contact with the village communities, and enjoy a fabulous view of the Tāj Mahal as well.

Daily tours are conducted by **U.P. State Tourism Development Corporation** (http://www.tajmahal.gov.in/tours.html) for local sightseeing in Agra. There is a full-day tour that includes the Tāj Mahal, Agra Fort and Fatehpur Sikri departing at 10:30 a.m. and they also operate a half-day tour to Fatehpur Sikri. The full day tour costs Rs3000 for foreigners, Rs650 for Indians.

For something different, you could try the **Agra Cultural Tour** (http://www.urbanadventures.com/Agra-Culture-Tour) operated by Urban Adventures. You will discover the city's hidden alleyways and lively spice markets, hop on a cycle rickshaw and admire colourful Hindu temples and traditional mosques then indulge in a variety of savoury Indian snacks and sweet treats. You visit the magnificent Agra Fort, Ambedkar Park, and the Radha Krishna Mandir Temple.

**Eating and drinking**

There are a variety of restaurants and bars to choose from in Agra. For the better restaurants try the Sadar Bazaar and Cantonment areas. If you are looking for inexpensive eating places try the streets in Taj Ganj, around the Tāj Mahal. The five-star hotels have good restaurants, which serve authentic Mughal cuisine. If the local fare is not your thing there are Chinese and South Indian restaurants in various areas of the city.

Bars are popular. One of the best known is the Downtown Club. The Tequila Bar at the Mansingh Palace (http://www.mansinghhotels.com/Mansingh-Palace-Agra/dining) in Agra Fatehabad Road is another. Others will prefer the roof top Mughal Bar (http://www.hotelclarksshiraz.com/food-and-beverage.html) which is situated in Hotel Clarks Shiraz.

It's no surprise that the Muslim empire left indelible imprints on Agra's cuisine. You see it in the creamy, boldly flavoured curries; lots of ground and whole spices, dried fruits and nuts; and roasted meats.

One of Agra's specialties is *petha*, a soft and delicious sweet made out of white pumpkin. It is available all over Agra. Another favourite is *daal moth* a crunchy, savoury snack item made out of black lentils. It makes for a great accompaniment with tea.

If you want to experience a range of food the Agra Food Walk – **Explore Agra By Mouth tour** (http://travelgenestours.com/packages/agra-food-walk-tour/) is interesting. It is operated by Rituraj who can be contacted on Tel: 97 139 931.

Some of my favourite eating places are the following:

**Esphahan** (Tel: 223 1515) (https://www.oberoihotels.com/hotels-in-agra-amarvilas-resort/restaurants/), probably Agra's finest traditional Indian restaurant is located inside the beautiful Oberoi Amarvilas Hotel. Every evening, they have two sittings, one at 6.30 p.m. and the other one at 9.30 p.m.

The menu might not be as extensive as in other places but the dishes are all exquisite and include excellent North Indian tandoor dishes. Rice with Kerala shrimp curry is a must-try on their menu. The atmosphere is very romantic, as you dine listening to live *santoor* players.

Opposite The Gateway Hotel on Fatehabad Road is a groovy graffiti-filled cafe called **Sheroes Hangout**. This inspiring place is completely staffed by women who are survivors of horrific acid attacks in India. The idea is to raise awareness of this dreadful issue and give the women confidence to show their faces in public after being disfigured. The cafe serves tasty food and beverages and has a library and an exhibition space. The menu has no prices--just pay what you think the food is worth or make a donation to the cause! If you are in Agra - go there.

**Jhankar Restaurant** (Gateway Hotel, Fatehabad Road) (Tel: 223 2400) (https://gateway.tajhotels.com/en-in/fatehabad-road-agra/restaurants/jhankar/) serves traditional Indian food while offering live entertainment with music and dances. The place itself is very charming and elegant. Their specialty is the *aloo dum chutneywale*, potatoes with herbs and dried fruits in a coriander and mint sauce. Another delicious treat is the *magazi murgh korma*, chicken in yogurt, cashews, and poppy seeds, garnished with rose petals and melon seeds.

**Pinch of Spice** (Fatehabad Road) (Tel: 404 5252) (http://www.pinchofspice.in/about.php) is probably the best North Indian restaurant outside a five-star hotel. This is an elegant multi-cuisine non-touristy restaurant and bar with a smart white décor. The cuisine ranges from Indian Mughal to Chinese to a few Italian items. There is another outlet at Wazirpura Road, Sanjay Place, opposite the Sanjay Cinema.

There is a good range of vegetarian and non-vegetarian dishes with the *murg boti masala*, a chicken *tikka* in a very rich and somewhat spicy local gravy a favourite of mine. Dishes are all authentic, and the exclusive fine dining experience extends beyond the food to the service and ambience.

**Shankar Ji** is more down to earth. It is a local *dhaba*, or snack bar, close to a rickshaw stand. It is basic and simple but is welcoming and the menu is written in English.

**Joney's Place** (Tel: 733 9686) is an affordable but tasty Indian restaurant. The restaurant itself is very small and cosy and the dishes are all prepared in front of you. It does a good Indian style breakfast of *puris* and *cholley*. They have been serving deliciously creamy lassies since 1978.

The restaurant serves vegetarian and non-vegetarian curries, pancakes, macaroni, pasta, and sandwiches. The *malai kofta* is also one specialty that comes highly recommended. It opens from 5 a.m. to 10:30 p.m. daily.

The **Pind Balluchi** chain of restaurants (http://www.pindballuchi.com/restaurants.html) is all over India but the Agra outlet (Tel: 653 4777) (Opposite Saga Emporium, Fatehbad Road) is especially attractive as it has a spacious village-style setting. The village look is completed by the waiters who serve you in the colourful Punjabi *kurtas* and *patialas*.

They serve typical North Indian cuisine and I especially recommend their tasty drinks like seasonal mango juice and good appetizers like *Banta* and *Jaljeera*. Apart from being very tasty, the food here is well-cooked and homely without too much oil or fat.

**Mama Franky House** is a very cheap and popular street food joint situated in Sadar Bazaar. From Indian rolls to barbecue there are good options available in vegetarian as well as non-vegetarian. You can eat in the open air or inside but there are no seats. At night they have some foot tapping music. Dinner time is better than lunch because there is much more variety.

**Lakshmi Vilas** (50A Taj Road, Sadar Bazaar) (Tel: 222 5616) is a good place to experience South Indian cuisine at reasonable prices. The interior decoration is very simple and the atmosphere is relaxed. The most popular meal is their thali, which is served for lunch and dinner.

The **Mandarin** (6B The Mall Road, inside now closed Hotel Yamuna View) (Tel: 329 3777) is one of the best Chinese restaurants in Agra and offers a change from Mughal food. The restaurant offers a wide selection of Chinese dishes including stir fries, honey chicken and chilli garlic noodles. The interior is warm and inviting helping ensure that you have a pleasant dining experience.

## Outside Agra

One of the best trips outside Agra is to **Fatehpur Sikri** (http://agra.nic.in/historyof_fatehpur.html), about 35 km from Agra. The city was founded in 1569 by Akbar and served as the capital of the Mughal Empire from 1571 to 1585. The planned walled city which took fifteen years to construct contains a series of royal palaces, harem, courts, a mosque, private quarters and other utility buildings.

The city, however, was a disaster and was abandoned in 1585, shortly after its completion, due partly to reasons of state and partly to a lack of water. The capital was then shifted to Lahore before moving back to Agra in 1598.

Fatehpur Sikri had a romantic beginning. By the time Akbar was in his late twenties he had great power but he lacked an heir. A Muslim saint in the village of Sikri prophesied that the emperor would eventually have three male children. On hearing this Akbar sent one of his wives to live in the saint's house and before long there were beneficial results; she produced a healthy son who would become the emperor Jahāngīr.

It is said that Akbar was so impressed that he resolved to transfer his capital to the site of the Muslim saint's home. Soon a great palace complex was under construction, built in the same red sandstone that Akbar had used in the walls of the Red Fort in Agra.

The city comprised a series of palaces, public buildings and mosques, together with living areas for those associated with the court and the army, , and for an entire population of ordinary people whose history has not been recorded.

Today, much of the imperial complex which spreads over quite a large area is largely intact but there is no life here. It still has an eight-kilometre long wall built during its original construction, on three sides. However, apart from the complex containing the imperial buildings, few other buildings remain. It is now a World Heritage Site and is much loved by tourists.

There is much to see. You have to take a bus from the parking lot. This costs Rs10 each way. The city had the usual Diwan-i-Aam or Hall of Public Audience, where the ruler met the general public every Friday. The multi-bayed rectangular structure fronts a large open space.

The Diwan-i-Khas, or Hall of Private Audience, is a plain square building with four domed shaped pavilions on the roof. The highlight here is its central pillar which supports a circular platform connected to each corner of the building by stone walkways.

Other monuments are the Panch Mahal, whose elevation of four recessed storeys recalls certain Buddhist temples, the pavilion of Anup Talao, the palace of Jodh Bai, the palace of Birbal, and the stables. The complex also contained a vineyard despite the Muslim ban on alcohol. It is believed up to 300 concubines were housed here as well as the three wives of the Emperor.

One of the most impressive structures is the 53 m-high Buland Darwāza (gate) which was not part of the original plan but was built to commemorate a military victory. It is made of red and buff sandstone and is decorated with carvings and marble inlays. An inscription on the central face is a message from Jesus advising his followers not to consider this world as their permanent home.

The gate towers above the courtyard of the Jama Masjid, one of the most spacious mosques in India. This was perhaps one of the first buildings to be built in the complex. Within the courtyard is a white marble tomb of the Sufi saint, Salim Chishti.

*The impressive Buland Darwāza*

To the east, stands the red sandstone tomb of Islam Khan I, grandson of Shaikh Salim Chishti. The tomb is topped by a dome and thirty-six small elevated dome-shaped pavilions, and contains a number of graves.

For something completely different, **Korai Village** (http://www.koraivillageagra.com/) can be visited on the way to Fatehpur Sikri. It's located just off the highway, about 10 kilometres before you reach there. Korai is a tribal village, whose inhabitants once kept dancing sloth bears. They've been struggling to earn an income and survive since the bears were taken away.

If you have concentrated on India's cities, your trip to this village will be an eye opener as you'll experience what rural life in India is like and you will get an opportunity to see how the villagers live. You will get to see their huts, the way they cook, the place where they sleep and the way they procure their water.

It is possible to make a day trip to **Gwalior**, an historic city located 120 kilometres south of Agra. The majestic cliff-top fort is known as the Gibraltar of India and it is both imposing and impressive, with its facade of yellow and blue tiles and pictures of elephants. It has been praised for the architectural design and its resilience.

The Jain rock sculptures, carved out of the mountain are definitely not to be missed and the nearby mother/sister-in-law temples are somewhat reminiscent of Mayan architecture and are wonderfully peaceful.

The Jai Vilas Palace and Scindia Museum in town is also worth visiting. Jai Vilas is an Italianate structure which combines Tuscan and Corinthian architecture. It is outrageously opulent - simply dripping with quirky splendour! There are gilded ceilings, heavy drapes and tapestries, fine Persian carpets, and antique furniture from France and Italy.

On the way, stop off in **Dholpur** a lovely, agricultural village that does not see many tourists. The people are friendly and it gives a different perspective to the major monuments you see elsewhere.

Another place worth a visit is **Mathura**, a city approximately 50 kilometres north of Agra on the way to Delhi. This is a very old region and Mathura was once an important centre on old caravan routes. Mathura is said to be the birthplace of Lord Krishna and it is one of the seven cities considered holy by Hindus.

Mathura was the capital of the Surasena Kingdom, ruled by the uncle of Shri Krishna in the 6th century BC. The city was later ruled by the Maurya Empire then the Sunga dynasty. Later, the Kushan dynasty had Mathura as one of their capitals.

Visitors today are attracted by the many temples and the general 'religiousness' of the place. Thousands of devotees come here each month and some of the temples are worth visiting even if you are a non-believer.

The Krishna Janambhoomi Temple complex (http://mathuravisit.com/mathura/krishna-janambhoomi.html) is located near the Bhuteshwar railway station. Hindus consider it to be one of the most sacred places as they believe that the temple stands on the same place where Lord Krishna was born. The complex has a Keshavdev temple and a museum, where excavated articles relating to the story of Shri Krishna' birth are displayed.

The temple shares a common wall with the Eidgah mosque so there is heavy security here. The mosque houses the tomb of the Mughal governor. The present temple was built in the 20th century and can be visited between 7 a.m. and 8 p.m.

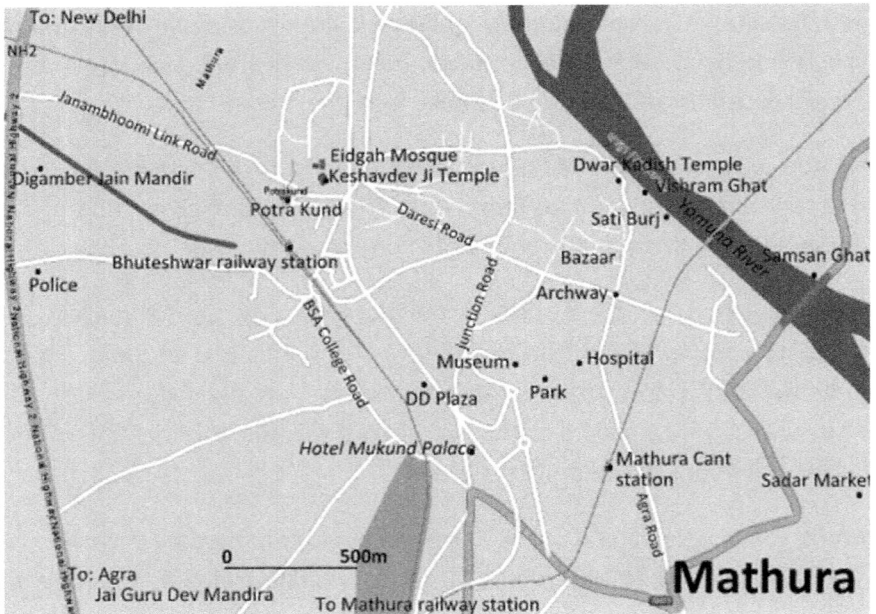

The Dwarkadish Temple, built in 1814, is a popular temple near the banks of the Yamuna River. It is well-known for its amazing swing festival at the start of the monsoons. This temple is managed by followers of Vallabhacarya. The temple is fairly interesting architecturally.

The Gita Mandir is situated about five kilometres from Mathura Junction towards Vrindaban. The magnificent temple was built by Birla, one of the leading industrial powers of India. The excellent architecture of the temple attracts tourists from all over India. The whole of Gita, the sacred book of the Hindus, is inscribed on the temple and beautiful carvings and paintings enhance the structure. There is a beautiful image of Lord Krishna in the sanctum.

The Jai Gurudev Temple has some resemblance to the Tāj Mahal in that it is built with white marble. I was told that you are prohibited from donating if you are a non-vegetarian.

Mathura Jain Chorasi is a worship place of Jains. There is a large statue of Lord Jambu Swami made from granite.

Apart from the temples, there are three further places worth visiting. The Government Museum (http://mathuravisit.com/mathura/government-museum.html) at Dampier Park has the biggest collection in Asia of Mathura and Gandhar sculpture. Rare items from the Gupta and Kushan period (400BC-1200AD) are on display.

Vishran Ghat is a bath and worship place, on the banks of the river. It is the main ghat of Mathura city and is central to 25 other ghats. Lord Krishna is said to have rested at this place.

Potra Kund is a water enclosed area close to the Keshavdev Ji Temple, and it is said that the mother of Lord Krishna washed his clothes in the Kund. It is constructed of huge red sandstone blocks and famous temples enclose the area. The stepped structure attracts tourists to visit the holy site. The water of the pond is considered very holy and it is possible to bathe in it.

Mathura has a twin town close-by at **Vrindavan**. This is the site of an ancient forest where, according to an ancient text, Lord Krishna spent his childhood days. The town is about 10 km away from Mathura. There are hundreds of temples here and some have appeal to foreign visitors.

One problem for visitors is that Vrindavan is absolutely infested with monkeys, who are adept at stealing cameras, glasses, food and anything you're not keeping a close eye on. They are a real nuisance. You can often get the item back by paying a fee to a young boy who will retrieve it for you by giving the monkey some food.

There are too many temples to detail and actually many are not worth your time if you are not Hindu. Some of the following, however, will have appeal.

The Madan Mohan Temple is the oldest temple in Vrindavan. The temple is closely associated with the saint Chaitanya Mahaprabhu. The two phallus shaped structures on top of the hill can be reached via a steep flight of steps. There is a newer temple at the foot of the hill.

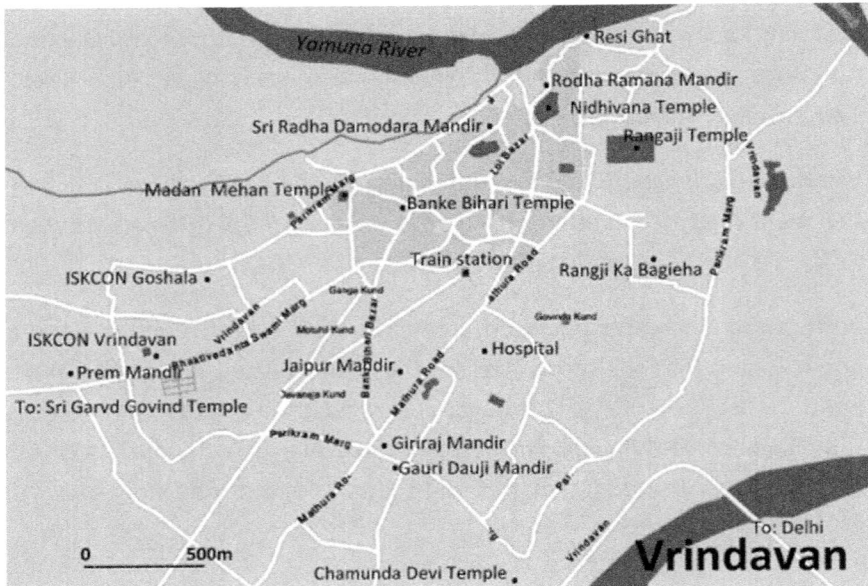

Vrindavan

The Garud Govind Temple was built in 1590 and is one of the most ancient temples here. Some sources claim that some form of temple has existed here for 5000 years. It is a bit out of town past the Prem Mandir.

The ISKCON Temple is well maintained and clean, and it has a good restaurant called Govinda with reasonably-priced food, and a relaxed atmosphere. There is also an awesome bakery. The evening aarti, held at 7:00 p.m. in summer and 6:30 p.m. in winter, is a beautiful spiritual drama of singing, dancing & chanting.

The Vrindavan Chandrodaya Mandir (http://www.vcm.org.in/a-unique-temple) will be the world's tallest temple (213 metres high) when completed. It will be one of the most expensive temples in world. It is being built by the International Society for Krishna Consciousness (ISKCON). Construction started in August 2014 and ISKCON is hoping to conclude the temple construction within the next five years.

The Banke Bihari Temple, built in 1862 is one of the most popular shrines in Vrindavan. It is home to a Krishna idol known as Thakur-ji. The idol's eyes are said to be so powerful that it is kept hidden from view most of the time. The temple is closed from noon to 4:30 p.m. but at other times it is always overcrowded.

The Prem Mandir is a beautiful and clean, religious complex situated on a 20 hectare site on the outskirts of Vrindavan, however, in some regards it is almost an amusement park. It is one of the newest temples dedicated to Divine Love. The main structure built in marble has figures of Shri Krishna and his followers depicting important events covering the main temple.

Morning *parikrama* and evening *parikrama* are worth seeing as is the musical fountain show at 7.30 p.m. A canteen welcomes you with vegetarian food and you can also buy books and other things in the shop. There are few restrictions on where you can go and unlike some other temples, you can take as many pictures as you like. It is superbly lit during evenings.

The Govind Dev Temple which is built in the form of a Greek cross was once a magnificent seven storeyed structure. The temple combines western, Hindu and Muslim architectural elements and was built at astronomical cost. It was destroyed by Mughal ruler Aurangzeb and now only two storeys remain.

Rangaji Mandir is the largest temple in Vrindavan. It was built in 1851 in a South Indian style, with eight *gopurams*, one of them is six storied and totally covered with beautiful carvings. Inside is a 15 m-high wooden chariot, taken out yearly for festivals, and in the inner courtyard is the 15 m-high gold-plated pillar known as Dhwaja Stambha.

Kesi Ghat is the principal bathing place in the town. This ghat is named after Lord Krishna's killing of the demon Kesi. You can enjoy a cheap, nice boat ride at this spot.

# 9 A BRIEF HISTORY

North-west India, where the Golden Triangle is located, has a very long history. The Bronze Age began around 3300 BC with the early Indus Valley Civilisation. This spread and flourished for 1400 years and was the first major civilization in South Asia. It developed into a sophisticated and technologically advanced urban culture in the Mature Harappan period, from 2600 to 1900 BC.

At its peak, the Indus Civilization may have had a population of over five million. The Indus cities are noted for their urban planning, baked brick houses, elaborate drainage systems, water supply systems, and clusters of large non-residential buildings.

Particularly note worthy was the ancient Indus systems of sewerage and drainage which was far more advanced than any others and even more efficient than those in many areas of India today.

## The establishment of Hinduism and Buddhism

The Indus Valley Civilisation collapsed around 1800 BC and was later followed by the Iron Age Vedic Civilisation, which extended over much of northern India and beyond. This was partly founded by The Aryans who came from central Asia in waves of invasions. This was the start of the caste system with the Aryans becoming the priests, rulers and warriors, and the subdued people becoming the slaves, labourers and artisans.

The Vedic period, lasting from about 1750 to 500 BC, saw the foundations of Hinduism and other religions and many of the concepts of Indian philosophy can trace their root to the Vedas. Over time the Aryans developed a settled and ordered society and this allowed trade and commerce to flourish.

People began to live in towns again and writing was re-invented as a highly civilized society emerged. It was during this time that the Magadha kingdom was established in north-east India, and Mahāvīra and Gautama Buddha established Jainism and Buddhism.

Most of the region was conquered by the Maurya Empire during the 4th and 3rd centuries BC and this developed into the largest ever in the Indian subcontinent. The empire was established by Chandragupta Maurya and he went on to reconquer the north-western parts of the subcontinent that had been previously conquered by Alexander the Great. The empire flourished under the reign of Chandragupta's grandson, Ashoka.

This was an era of social harmony, religious transformation, and expansion of knowledge. Maurya embraced Jainism and introduced social and religious reform across his society, while Ashoka's embrace of Buddhism saw social and political peace and non-violence across all of India.

The Mauryan king was assassinated in 185BC during a military parade by the Brahmin general Sunga, who then took over the throne and established the Sunga dynasty. This patronized Indian culture at a time when some of the most important developments in Hindu thought were taking place.

The Śātavāhana Empire covered much of India from 230 BC onward. Sātavāhanas started out as part of the Mauryan dynasty but declared independence with its decline. They had battles with the Sunga Empire but later, they played a crucial role in protecting a huge part of India against foreign invaders

The fall of the Mauryas left the Khyber Pass from Afghanistan unguarded, and a wave of foreign invasion followed. The Greek Syrian King Demetrius capitalized on the break-up, and he conquered southern Afghanistan and parts of north-western India around 180 BC, forming the Indo-Greek Kingdom.

There were on-going battles between the Sungas, the Indo-Greeks and others, however, the Indo-Greeks and the Sungas seem to have reconciled and exchanged diplomatic missions around 110 BC. Roman trade with India started around 1 AD

The Kushan Empire expanded out of what is now Afghanistan into the north-west of the subcontinent about the middle of the 1st century AD. They played an important role in the establishment of Buddhism in India and its spread to Central Asia and China but by the 3rd century AD their empire had collapsed.

Various parts of India were ruled by numerous kingdoms for the next 1,500 years, among which the Gupta Empire stands out. This period, with its Hindu religious and intellectual resurgence, is known as the Golden Age of India. During this period, aspects of Indian civilization, administration, culture, and religion spread to much of Asia.

The Gupta period (4th-6th centuries AD), was a period of prosperity and peace, however, Hun invasions from the north-west contributed to the collapse of the Gupta Empire and afterwards north India reverted to small republics and small monarchical states ruled by Gupta chiefs.

A new dynasty known as the Pratihara Empire emerged in the 6th century. One branch established the state of Marwar, based at Mandore near modern Jodhpur, and this grew to dominate Rajasthan. Later parts of Malwa were conquered.

The 7th - 11th centuries saw considerable cultural development with Hindu numerals introduced and Indian mathematics influencing the whole Arab world.

Until the end of the 12th century, the Rajasthan region was concentrated in the hands of the Hindu ruling classes, of which the Rajputs are the best example. They were descended either from the Huns who settled in North and West India during the 6th century AD or from other Central Asian tribes who accompanied the Huns. The Rajputs boasted a proud warrior heritage and considerably raised the concepts of loyalty, honour in battle and bravery.

In the Delhi region, Anangpal, a Tomer ruler possibly created the first known regular defence-structures and a town called Lalkot in what is now South Delhi. Later a city called Qila Rai Pithora was created by Prithviraj Chauhan after his ancestors captured Lalkot. The ruins of the fort ramparts are still partly visible in the area around Qutb Minar.

**The Muslim invasion**

Mahmud of Ghazni, a local Muslim ruler in Afghanistan, saw India as a wealthy place with fertile lands. He launched regular raids during the harvest season and financed his struggles in Central Asia from them. The north Indian temples and palaces, with their enormous wealth in cash, golden images and jewellery, made them natural targets.

Mahmud routinely captured gold and other wealth but he also had a religious motive. He attacked and ransacked the wealthy Hindu centres of Mathura in 1017, Thanesar in 1011, Somnath in 1024 and Kanauj.

The Rajput clans fought many battles against each other in the 11th and 12th centuries until a new threat emerged. In the late 12th century Muhammad Ghuri entered India by the Gomal Pass and by 1191 he had overrun quite a considerable area. The Rajputs decided it was time to act. On the plains north of Delhi, they gathered together and won a first battle, but were only able to hold off the Muslim threat for a year.

In 1192 a second battle was fought in the same place and the Chauhan kingdom fell to the invaders. Muhammad pressed on and took Ajmer in Rajasthan. In 1206 he was assassinated, but his policy to retain his Indian acquisitions was followed by his successors. The early rulers of what came to be called the Delhi Sultanate were Turks, mainly from

Central Asia, who had settled in Afghanistan.

On Muhammad's death, control passed to Qutb–ud–din–Aibak who established a policy of conciliation and patronage in Delhi. He converted the Old Hindu stronghold of Qila Rai Pithora into his Muslim capital and commenced a number of magnificent building projects, such as the Quwwat-ul-Islam mosque and the Qutb Minar, a victory tower.

Later leaders built magnificent buildings such as the Red Forts at Agra and Delhi, Humayun's Tomb in Delhi, the Itmad-ud-Daula and Taj Mahal tombs at Agra, Akbar's beautiful new capital at Fatehpur Sikri, and the pavilions and mosques at Ajmer in Rajasthan.

The Delhi Sultanate ruled the major part of northern India in the early 14th century but declined in the late 14th century, and this allowed the emergence of several powerful Hindu states. The final blow came in 1498 when Timurlane, a descendant of Genghis Khan attacked and destroyed Delhi and massacred many of the inhabitants.

## The Mughals

In the 16th century, Muslim Mughals came from Central Asia and gradually established an empire. The beginning of the empire is often considered to be 1526 when the founder, Barbur, defeated Ibrahim Lodi in the first Battle of Panipat.

The resulting Mughal Empire did not eliminate the local societies it came to rule, but rather balanced and pacified them. Considerable change occurred, however, as the Hindu majority were ruled over by the Muslim Mughal emperors. Most leaders, including the famous emperor Akbar, who was the grandson of Babur, showed religious tolerance and were great patronisers of Hindu culture.

However, later emperors such as Aurangzeb tried to establish complete Muslim dominance, and as a result several historic Hindu temples were destroyed during this period and taxes imposed on non-Muslims. The region's economic progress declined rapidly after his death under a series of ineffective rulers.

The resulting unrest allowed groups in northern and western India, such as the Hindi warrior group the Marathas, the long-established Rajputs, and the Sikhs under Ranjit Singh, to gain support and military and governing ambitions during the latter periods of Mughal rule.

In 1737, a Maratha general invaded and plundered Delhi. In 1739, Nader Shah, emperor of Iran, defeated the Mughal army at the huge Battle of Karnal. After this victory, Nader captured and sacked Delhi, carrying away many treasures, including the Peacock Throne.

## The British

The Gurkha Wars of the early 19th century saw the inclusion of parts of northern India into the territory of the East India Company. They then came into conflict with the Sikhs. The Sikhs had become a strong regional power in north-west India during the 18th century by establishing their own empire under Ranjit Singh. They proved to be no match for the British, however, and later proved to be loyal subjects.

The British absorbed many of the Indian princely states into the Company's territories or gained indirect control of those who remained independent. It was not done without conflict, however, and this eventually led to a Mutiny which broke out in 1857. The British regained control but were obviously shaken by the experience, and from then on adopted a more conciliatory attitude towards Indians.

The British also developed infrastructure. The railway system was rapidly expanded during this period, linking regions together economically, and enabling the rapid movement of vital supplies during times of crisis. Canals permitted the irrigation of larger areas of the Ganges plain and the Punjab in the north-west of the country.

The numbers of British in India were small, yet they were able to rule two-thirds of the subcontinent directly and exercise considerable leverage over the so-called princely states that accounted for the remaining one-third of the area.

In 1911 the capital was transferred to Delhi, which meant that the north became the region of India receiving the most attention. To mark this occasion the British Empire builders started building another new city in the Delhi region. New Delhi was built to a grand plan but the British only enjoyed the benefit for a short while. Within 15 years of the new city's completion, the British Indian Empire came to an end.

From 1920, leaders such as **Mahatma Gandhi** began highly popular mass movements to campaign against the British Raj using largely peaceful methods. Some others adopted a militant approach that sought to overthrow British rule by armed struggle but all had the same aim – Indian independence.

### Indian independence

In parallel with the desire for independence, tensions between Hindus and Muslims had also been increasing. By 1940, the Muslims were demanding their own separate state. This was opposed by many Hindus.

In 1942, the Indian parliament demanded that the British leave India. The British responded by imprisoning their leaders, including Gandhi. This caused further tension and in 1944 most were released.

In 1946, the British Viceroy appointed an interim cabinet with Jawaharlal Nehru as prime minister. The Muslims, however, were not satisfied with this and continued to agitate for their own state. It became clear that this was the only way forward.

Independence came after a remarkable struggle using non-violence. The Partition of India into two countries, India and Pakistan, along religious lines, however, let loose violence which is said to have led to the death of 500,000 people.

The transfer of power and boundary delineation resulted in a horrible period as millions attempted to relocate to their chosen country. This was one of the largest mass migrations ever recorded in modern history, with a total of 12 million Hindus, Sikhs and Muslims moving between the newly created nations.

The violence threatened to overwhelm the country but Gandhi ultimately controlled it by threatening to fast to death unless the violence stopped. Some extreme Hindus became angry with Gandhi because of the partition and one of them murdered him on 30 January 1948.

Independence saw the redrawing of state boundaries along linguistic grounds and the establishment of local control over village administration.

A new constitution came into force in January 1950 and India became a secular state. Prime Minister **Nehru** introduced a 'mixed economy' of some state-owned industry and some private enterprise and the emphasis in the first Five Year Plan was on industrialization.

In the 1960s, India fought two wars: against China in 1962 and Pakistan in 1965. Nehru died in 1964 and Indira Gandhi became prime minister in 1966. In 1971, India fought another war with Pakistan.

Since then, progress has been mixed. In the 1970s, the nationalisation of banks was carried out, and many other socialist economic and industrial policies enacted. India took part in the Bangladesh War which took place in Pakistan's eastern half and resulted in the formation of a new country. India had adopted a non-aligned foreign policy but relations with the United States deteriorated, and India signed a 20-year treaty of friendship with the Soviet Union.

Economic and social problems, as well as allegations of corruption, caused increasing political unrest across India. In 1975, Mrs. Gandhi advised the President to declare a state of emergency then she suspended many civil liberties, postponed elections, and imprisoned nearly 1,000 opposition political leaders and activists. In 1977, Morarji became Prime Minister but Indira Gandhi returned to power heading a

Congress Party splinter group.

In 1984, Gandhi directed troops to storm the Golden Temple (the Sikhs' most holy shrine) to flush out Sikh militants demanding self-rule. In October 1984, the Prime Minister's own Sikh bodyguards assassinated her. This resulted in anti-Sikh riots causing the deaths of thousands.

Elections since then have seen wins by the Congress Party and the Hindu-nationalist party Bharatiya Janata Party. Prime Ministers have come and gone while only small changes have been made to the economic liberalisation that India badly needs.

At the last national election in early 2014, the BJP party gained an absolute majority and formed the government, under the Prime Ministership of **Narendra Modi**. It was the first time in 30 years that a single party had won a parliamentary majority on its own. This has led to renewed hope among many Indians for a brighter future. Business cheered the BJP's election victory, relieved by the end of a ten-year Congress government tainted by corruption scandals and incapable of the reforms the economy needed.

But things have not gone so well for the new government. BJP is a Hindu-nationalist party and there are influential members within the party who want India to become a Hindu state. At the election, it persuaded enough voters that the Hindu-nationalist part of its agenda was marginal. Now after several high-profile racial excesses which the government didn't directly condemn many worry that Hindu nationalism is a pillar of Mr Modi's vision after all.

In recent times the government has alienated India's non-Hindu minorities, its liberal intelligentsia, and important section of domestic and foreign opinion. Alarmed intellectuals have protested. Leading historians are aghast at the situation" while dozens of people have returned government awards and prominent Christians have denounced "the growing intolerance in the country".

In May 2017, the government banned the sale of cows -- an animal considered taboo by the country's Hindu majority -- for slaughter, sending the meat industry into a frenzy. While the ban was suspended by India's Supreme Court in July, the policy confusion has had a chilling effect.

Modi's campaign pledge to grow India's economy is being stymied by political opposition, partly from Hindu nationalists in his own party. Some experts warn that the government may be squandering a unique opportunity to secure foreign investment and take advantage of China's slowing economy.

India is still reeling from two shocks within 12 months -- Modi's sudden ban in November 2016 of 86% of the country's cash, and a sweeping overhaul of the tax system aimed at turning the country's 29 states into a single market.

India's Supreme Court dealt the economy another blow in April, banning the sale of alcohol within 500 meters of national highways. The court eased the restrictions in August, but many within the industry said they had already lost millions.

India faces huge hurdles to growth, including widespread corruption, a suffocating bureaucracy, enormous social spending, a stifling business environment, and woeful infrastructure. Mr. Modi's popularity has diminished as observers question his desire or ability to implement economic changes.

# 10 PRACTICAL INFORMATION

## Passports, Visas and Customs

All foreign nationals entering India are required to possess a valid international travel document in the form of a national passport with a valid visa. Until recently, this involved making an application to an Indian Mission or Post abroad and perhaps even visiting that office.

A Visa on Arrival Facility is now available for holders of a passport of many countries. See https://indianvisaonline.gov.in/evisa/tvoa.html for current information.

The process involves applying and paying the visa fee on-line, and receiving an Electronic Travel Authorisation which is valid for entry through designated airports. You print out this ETA and take it with you when you fly to India.

Foreigners are given an arrivals form and a separate customs form by your aircraft crew. These need to be completed before you land to avoid holdups. You will need to stand in line for immigration clearance and the officer will stamp your passport and customs form. You then collect your luggage and chose the Red or Green channel through customs depending on what you are carrying. In either case you will hand your customs form to an officer and you are liable for a search.

**When to Go**

The climate of parts of the Golden Triangle (including Delhi) is monsoon-influenced humid sub-tropical bordering on semi-arid, with high variation between summer and winter temperatures and precipitation. In **Delhi**, summers start in early April and peak in May, with average temperatures near 32 C (90 F), although occasional heat waves can result in highs close to 45 C (114 F) on some days.

The monsoon starts in late June and lasts until mid-September, with about 800 mm (31 inches) of rain. Winter starts in November and peaks in January, with average temperatures around 12–13 C (54–55 F).

The climate in **Agra** is less humid and hotter. During the summers, the daytime temperature hovers around 46-50°C and the humidity can be exhausting. Nights are cooler but may not fall below 30°C. Winters are a bit chilly but are the best time to visit Agra. The minimum temperature sometimes goes as low as 2-4°C but usually hovers in the range of 6-8°C. Average maximum temperatures are from 23-30°C.

**Jaipur** has a hot semi-arid climate and the temperature remains relatively high all through the year. During summer, temperatures can be a scorching 35-48°C. The monsoon is not regular in this part of the country though there is often medium to heavy rainfall from July to September. From December to February the temperature can touch a low of 4°C and this is the most ideal time for sightseeing, and doing other tourist activities.

The weather in **Jodhpur** is dry and hot, typical desert weather. The average annual rainfall is approximately 32 cm. In summer, the maximum temperature is around 42°C and the minimum temperature is around 37°C. In winter, the average maximum temperature is 27°C and the minimum temperature is around 15°C. Jodhpur is bright and sunny throughout the year. The best season to visit the city is between October and March.

**Udaipur** is one of the only places in Rajasthan that has quite a moderate climate throughout the year. In summer, it can be hot whereas in winters the weather is pleasant. The summer season runs from mid-March to June and temperatures can reach 38°C. Monsoons arrive in July heralded by dust and thunderstorms and the city receives around 640 mm of rainfall in this period.

## Population

The current (end 2017) estimated population of India is 1.33 billion which means that over 17% of the world's population is in India. This figure is just marginally below that for China. More than 50% of India's current population is below the age of 25 and over 65% is below the age of 35.

India has the largest illiterate population in the world. The literacy rate of India as shown in the 2011 Population Census is 74.04%, with the male literacy rate at 82.14% and the female rate at 65.46%. The sex ratio for the entire country is 940 females to 1000 males.

As far as the Golden Triangle area is concerned, the population is large. Delhi has an estimated population of 20 million (end of 2017) and Delhi is a part of the NCR (National Capital Region) which has an estimated 27 million. This is estimated to rise to 30 million by 2025.

South of Delhi is the state of Uttar Pradesh which is currently home to 16% of India's total population (around 210 million). Uttar Pradesh plays a key role in the economic development of India as it is the most populous state and the fastest growing. The Agra district has around 4.4 million people.

The rest of the Golden Triangle is in the state of Rajasthan which has an estimated current population of 74.5 million. The Jaipur region houses around 6.7 million while Jodhpur has 3.7 million and Udaipur has 3.1 million. The literacy rate and the sex ratio in both Uttar Pradesh and Rajasthan are noticeably below the national average.

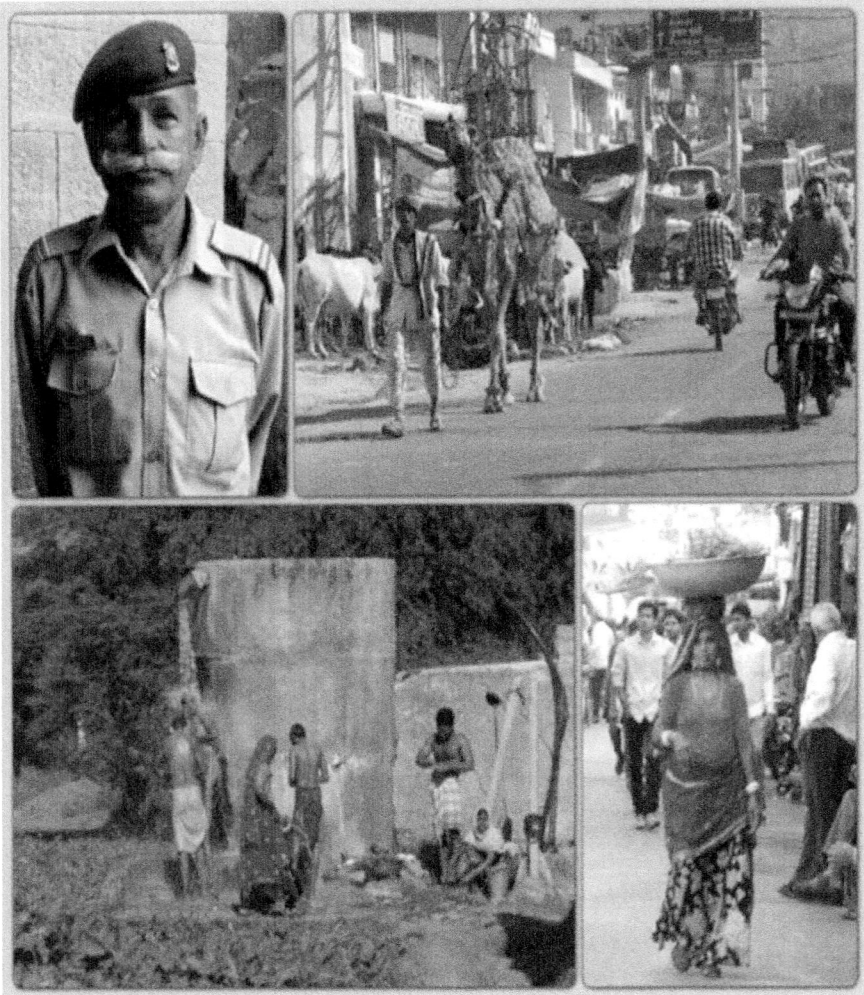

## Geography

India lies in the northern hemisphere between 8°4' and 37°6' north latitude and 68°7' and 97°25' east longitude. It is the seventh largest country in the world, by area. It stretches over 3,200 km from north to south and nearly 3,000 km from east to west. It has a land frontier of 15,200 km and a coastline of 7,500 km.

India is bounded on the south-west by the Arabian Sea, to the south-east by the Bay of Bengal and by the Indian Ocean to the south. The northern frontiers are defined largely by the Himalayan mountain range where there are boundaries with China, Bhutan, and Nepal and its western borders with Pakistan lie in the Punjab Plain and the Thar Desert, the seventh-largest desert in the world.

The famous Ganges is the longest river originating in India and the Ganges-Brahmaputra system covers most of northern, central and eastern India.

The Golden Triangle is located between the Himalayan mountain range to the north; the broad and flat alluvial plain of the Ganges River to the east and the desert to the west. All three regions have an influence on the Golden Triangle but it is not totally contained within any of them.

## Religion

More than 80% of Indians are Hindus but there are other faiths as well. The different religious groups have coexisted peacefully for generations but at times, in parts of the country, disharmony has occurred. This is particularly so with Muslims who are the largest minority group.

It is almost impossible to generalise about **Hinduism** because of its many varied and contradictory beliefs. No short-time visitor will ever understand the many complications of the religion or the place of many gods within it.

As I understand it, gods and humans are subject to the same law of cause and effect (karma) and the universe goes through endless cyclic repetitions which includes your soul reincarnating, and evolving through many births until all karmas have been resolved.

Hindus believe in a one, all-pervasive Supreme Being and that divine beings exist in unseen worlds and that temple worship, rituals, sacraments and personal devotionals create a communion with these Gods. They, however, believe that no religion teaches the only way to salvation above all others, but that all genuine paths are deserving of tolerance and understanding.

Ethical teachings are inspired by two great ancient epics, the Ramayana and the Mahabharata. The latter consists of 100,000 verses and is still influential in Indian life.

Brahma is the god of creation and one of the Trimurti, the others being Vishnu and Shiva. Brahma is four-headed and carries a water pot. His consort is Saraswati, the goddess of knowledge, who rides on a swan. Vishnu is often depicted reclining on a many-headed serpent but can also be seen as Rama carrying a bow or as Krishna, who is blue and plays the flute. His consort is Lakshmi, the goddess of wealth. She is seated on a lotus between two elephants.

Shiva has many representations and has a consort called Devi who also has various forms. The most widely worshipped god is Ganesha, their elephant-headed son. He is said to be the remover of all obstacles so the faithful make a prayer to him before a journey, a performance or a business venture. Ganesha is depicted as dwarfish and potbellied and he carries the rice balls he likes to eat and a broken piece of his tusk.

Many visitors are surprised to find that **Buddhism** is not prominent in India as this is where it all started. It began around 550 BC when Prince Gautama, the son of the king became Buddha, the Enlightened One. Buddha attacked the injustice of the caste system and the ritualised worship of deities so was a serious threat to the supremacy of the Brahmins.

Buddhism appealed to the merchant and lower castes as it provided the means to escape brahmanical oppression and for some time it was extremely influential in India. It spread to other Asian countries as a religion but was ultimately swallowed and regurgitated by Hinduism in India. It is ironic that Buddha, who denied the existence of God, has now become another incarnation of the god Vishnu.

**Islam** is followed by about 10% of the population, making India one of the largest Islamic nations in the world. In the Golden Triangle region Arabs, Turks and Moghuls came as conquerors, sometimes converting Hindus by force, destroying temples and imposing taxes and laws against Hindu customs. They have had a profound impact on culture, food, architecture, social life and attitudes towards women.

A Muslim has five prayer times a day, must fast during the month of Ramadan, should give a portion of their income to the mosque, and make a pilgrimage to Mecca at least once during their lifetime. Muslims do not eat pork and other meat must be ritually slaughtered. They are not supposed to drink alcohol. The Muslim holy day is Friday.

**Jainism** was established at about the same time as Buddhism but it has survived as a separate religion in parts of the Golden Triangle area. Jains are vegetarian, do not wear or use any leather products, and will not work in occupations like construction or farming because small creatures will be killed in digging the soil.

Hinduism assimilated Jain ideas and Jainism includes the Hindu ideas of karma, reincarnation and so on, so there are few concepts that absolutely set Jainism apart from Hinduism. The Golden Triangle area is one of the centres for Jainism and today there are about four million people following this religion.

Visitors will likely visit some of the older Jain temples. Most are beautifully and intricately carved but remember to remove your belt and wallet before entering.

**Sikhism** was founded by Guru Nanak around 1500. It preaches a message of devotion to God at all times, truthful living, equality of mankind and it denounces superstitions and blind rituals.

Sikhs believe there is only one God and he is the same God for all people of all religions. It preaches that people of different races, religions, or sex are all equal in the eyes of God. It teaches the full equality of men and women.

Sikhism does not have priests and any Sikh is free to read the Guru Granth Sahib in the Gurdwara (a Sikh temple) or in their home. All people of all religions are welcome to the Gurdwara. A free community kitchen can be found at every Gurdwara which serves meals to all people of all faiths. One of the more noticeable features of Sikhism is the uncut hair (required to be covered with a turban for men) and the Kirpan (ceremonial sword).

**Christianity** is believed to have been introduced into India by one of the disciples of Jesus. It was further encouraged by Portuguese and British missionaries but only about 2.5% of Indians are Christians. Many of these are located in the southern states of Kerala and Goa but Christian churches exist in Delhi and other areas.

Visitors should be aware that temples, *gurdwaras*, mosques and churches are places of worship. If they also happen to be places of interest to tourists, it is up to you to follow the rules of the religion or individual building.

A good example of this is removing your shoes before entering and to dress conservatively. Some temples allow you to take photographs (often by paying a fee) while others strictly forbid the practice.


## Language

Hindi, written in Devanagari script, is the most prominent language spoken in the country. This is the main language of people in the Golden Triangle area. British colonial legacy has resulted in English being the primary language for government, business, and education. English, along with Hindi, is one of the two languages permitted in the Constitution of India for business in Parliament.

Hindi is not too difficult to learn but short-term visitors to the Golden Triangle region will generally be able to travel without speaking any of the language. As with most countries, however, locals do appreciate foreigners trying a few words. The following may help:

| | |
|---|---|
| Hello - | namaste, namaskar |
| Hi - | suno, suniye |
| Mr. - | shrimaan |
| Mrs. - | shrimati |
| Miss - | kumaari |
| Master - | kumaar |
| Bye - | alvida |
| Thank you - | dhanyavaad |
| Good morning - | shubh prabhat |
| Good evening - | shubh sandhya |
| Good night - | shubh ratri |
| See you later - | phir milen-gey |

| | |
|---|---|
| I - | mein |
| He - | woh / usne |
| She - | who |
| You - | tum, aap |
| It - | yeh |
| What - | kya |
| My, mine - | mera |
| Our, ours - | hamara |
| Me - | mai |
| Us - | hum |
| Your, Yours - | aapka, tumhara |
| We - | hum |

| | |
|---|---|
| How are you? - | Aap kaise hain? |
| I am fine - | Mai achchha hoon |
| You are welcome - | Aapka swagat hai |
| Let us meet again - | Fir milenge |
| My name is | Mera naam ----- hai |

What is your name?-    Aapka kya naam hai?

Can I help you?        kya mein aapki madad kar sakta/ sakti (female)
hoon?

Can you help me?       kya aap meri madad kar saktey hain?

Where is the (bathroom/ pharmacy)? aucaghara/ pharmacy kahaan hai?

Excuse me              kshama keejeeae

How far to go?         Aur kitni door jana hai ?

Where are you coming from? -Aap / tum kahan se aa rahe ho ?

How much is it? -      Yeh kitne ka hai?

I don't understand -   Mujhey samajh mein nahi aataa

Can you say it again? - yaa aap issey dohraa saktey hain?

| | |
|---|---|
| One: | ek |
| Two: | do |
| Three: | teen |
| Four: | chaar |
| Five: | paannch |
| Six: | chheh |
| Seven: | saat |
| Eight: | aath |
| Nine: | nao |
| Ten: | dus |
| Twenty: | bees |
| Thirty: | tees |
| Forty: | chaalees |
| Fifty: | pachaas |
| Sixty: | saath |
| Seventy: | sattar |
| Eighty: | assee |
| Ninety: | nabbe |
| Hundred: | sau |
| Thousand: | hazzar |

## Health and Safety

Medical facilities in India's major cities providing an adequate standard of treatment are available, however, in rural areas facilities can be very limited. In the event of a serious illness or accident, medical evacuation to a destination with appropriate facilities may be necessary. If you or someone you are travelling with needs hospitalization, go to a well-known private one in the nearest big city.

More than anything else in India, the water is likely to make you ill. For this reason, you should not only avoid untreated drinking water but be on your guard against any food product that is washed with water or has had water added to it.

Remember not to clean wounds, cuts, or sores with tap water, instead, douse and cleanse them with antiseptic solution, cover them with an adhesive bandage, and consult a doctor if it doesn't heal quickly.

Most bottled water is safe, but always ensure the lid seal is intact and check that the bottom of the bottle hasn't been tampered with. Use bottled water when cleaning your teeth.

Medicines are widely and easily available in India even those that would require a prescription back home but it is wise to take your own. Pack medications in their original clearly labelled containers. A signed and dated letter from your physician describing your medical conditions and medications, including generic names, is very useful. You'll be able to buy many medications over the counter in India but it can be difficult to find some drugs at times.

Traveller's diarrhoea is by far the most common problem affecting travellers to India with many people suffering from it within weeks of starting their trip. Traveller's diarrhoea is usually caused by a bacterium in the water and therefore it normally responds promptly to treatment with antibiotics.

Much of the Golden Triangle is very hot in summer. Dehydration is the main contributor to heat exhaustion. Symptoms include feeling weak, headache, irritability, nausea or vomiting, sweaty skin, and a fast, weak pulse. Even on a cloudy day sunburn can occur rapidly. Always use a strong sunscreen (at least factor 30), making sure to reapply it after a swim, and always wear a wide-brimmed hat and sunglasses outdoors.

Visitors should be wary of animal bites and scratches as these can lead to serious diseases such as rabies. As a visitor, it is advisable to not touch or feed any animals while in India. Seek medical attention promptly if you are bitten or scratched as rabies, for instance, can be fatal.

Even if you are fit and healthy, don't travel without health insurance – accidents happen and illness can affect anyone. It's wise to declare any existing medical conditions you have as the insurance company will check if your problem is pre-existing and will not cover you if it is undeclared.

Some policies ask that you telephone back (reverse charges) to a centre in your home country where an immediate assessment of your problem will be made.

India enjoys a low incidence of violent crime, and the vast majority of visits to India tend to be trouble-free but petty crime, like pick-pocketing, has become a problem. Avoid wandering around back alleys at night, and don't flash valuables or wads of cash. Avoid provocative debates and arguments where alcohol may be involved and avoid political demonstrations.

Religious ceremonies and gatherings attended by large crowds can result in dangerous and life-threatening incidents, such as stampedes. Always be aware of your surroundings and check out an escape route. Unfortunately, foreign women can be subjected to unwanted attention and more serious harassment and assault on occasions

Theft is a risk on buses and trains so keep luggage securely locked and lock your bags to the metal baggage racks. Thieves tend to target popular tourist train routes, such as Delhi to Agra but take care everywhere. If travelling on local buses, padlocking your bags to the roof rack is also a sensible policy. The safest place for your money and your passport is next to your skin, either in a money belt or a secure pouch under your shirt.

India has an unenviable reputation for scams. Be highly suspicious of claims that you can purchase goods cheaply in India and sell them easily at a profit elsewhere. Precious stones and carpets are favourites for this con. Operators who practise such schemes can be deceptively friendly.

Don't be taken in by a sign saying "government-approved". Often it means exactly the opposite.

Be cautious when sending home goods that you have bought. Shops have been known to swap what you purchased for junk when posting goods to home addresses. If you have any doubts, send the package yourself from the post office.

Be very careful when paying for souvenirs with a credit card. Make the trader carry out any credit-card transaction on the counter in front of you. Alternatively, take out cash from an ATM and avoid the risk.

There will be times when you need to be very firm (and even rude) but never pay for services you have not requested. It is the same when you are approached on the street. Often the only way to get rid of a persistent tout, beggar, or con artist is to ignore him and keep walking.

## Currency and banking

The currency used in India is the rupee (Rs), which is divided into 100 paise. Rupees are available in the following denominations: Notes come in denominations of Rs5, 10, 20, 50, 100, 200, 500, and 2000. The Reserve Bank of India has released four new currency notes – Rs 50, Rs 200, Rs 500 and Rs 2,000 - since devaluing big banknotes in November

2016 in an effort to crack down on black money. Plans to introduce a new Rs 1,000 note are also reportedly afoot. Coins exist to the value of 5, 10, 20, 25, and 50 paise and Rs1, 2, and 5.

In December 2017, the exchange rates for the rupee in India were: Rs64 per US$1, Rs86 per €1, 85Rs per GBP1, Rs48 per AUD1, and Rs50 per CAD1.

There are Authorized Foreign Exchange dealers in most big cities, and banks will also change your currency at a fair rate if you have time for the paperwork. Major currencies such as US dollars, UK pounds and euros are easy to change throughout the Golden Triangle. A few banks also accept Australian, New Zealand and Canadian dollars, and Swiss francs. Private moneychangers accept a wider range of currencies.

A good way of getting your local currency is via an ATM but beware of hidden bank charges, both from the bank providing the ATM and the card-issuing bank. There are ATMs in most towns and these are recommended for cash withdrawals. The average daily limit for withdrawal of money from an ATM appears to be Rs10,000.

Traveller's cheques are cashed at almost all money exchange counters, but avoid hotels and airports as they do not give the best rates. Visa, MasterCard and American Express are usually accepted in tourist hotels and many other shops. Debit cards are also widely accepted.

## Tipping

While India culturally does not have a strong tipping tradition, in most of the tourist towns tips are expected and you will be frowned upon when they are not offered. As you are likely to have considerably more wealth than most people you meet, tipping should be part of your normal pattern in India even if it is not in your home country.

It can be a problem to know when to tip and how much to give. Visitors are not expected to tip taxi drivers as locals very rarely do. Hotel, airport and train station porters should be tipped approximately Rs20/bag. Tip private guides Rs500 and drivers approximately Rs300 per day. In restaurants, if the service was good, tip anything between 5-10% of the bill.

## Budgeting for your Trip

Travel costs in India are some of the lowest in the world. Much of your travel budget here will depend on where you go and your travel style, as well as how much shopping you want to do. There are some costs, however, that you cannot avoid.

Foreigners are usually charged more than Indian citizens for entry into tourist sites (sometimes up to 10 times more), and there may also be additional charges for still and video cameras. You will also be encouraged to hire a guide or rent an audio guide for your visit.

Some of India's top-end hotels are among the world's finest, but be prepared to fork out from US$200-$600 per night at the better properties. The good news is that many 4 and 4.5-star hotels cost under US$100, while three-star properties can be as low as US$30. At the bottom of the market you can get a bed for a few dollars.

Throughout the Golden Triangle area, it will cost roughly US$25 per day if you stay in the cheapest hotels, do limited sightseeing and eat basic meals. Budget US$75 if you wish to stay in midrange hotels, dine at nicer restaurants, do a reasonable amount of sightseeing and largely travel by auto-rickshaw and taxi.

Eating out in India is often great value, with budget restaurant meals for as little as Rs100, and at least triple that for a lower midrange restaurant feed. At the more up-market urban restaurants, main dishes can cost between Rs300 and Rs600 to which you'll need to add the cost of side dishes, such as rice, and (usually) a tax of 10% to 12.5%.

A Western fast-food meal will cost around Rs200-250, a domestic beer Rs100, a soft drink Rs30 and bottled water Rs15.

When travelling between towns, there's a range of classes on trains and several bus types. Domestic air travel has become a lot more price competitive and safer over recent years. Within towns there's inexpensive public transport.

## Public Holidays and Festivals

India, being a culturally diverse society, celebrates a whole range of holidays and festivals. At times it will seem like there are more reasons for celebration than there are for work. In fact, there are only three national holidays in India: Independence Day on 15 August, Mahatma Gandhi's birthday on 2 October and Republic Day on 26 January.

States and regions have local festivals depending on prevalent religious and linguistic demographics and these are what sometimes come unexpectedly. In addition to the official holidays, many religious, ethnic, and other traditional holidays populate the calendar.

Hindus celebrate a number of festivals all through the year. Hindu festivals have one or more religious, mythological or seasonal significance. In addition, there are Islamic holidays, and Christian, Sikh, Buddhist and Jain holidays. Frankly, it is all a bit confusing.

The best known annual festivals are strikingly different from one another. Navaratri is celebrated in September or October to commemorate the victory of Durga over the buffalo-demon Mahishasura. It culminates on the tenth day which marks Rama's victory over Ravan, when Ravana effigies are burnt on huge bonfires.

Soon after comes Divali, the festival of lights where small oil lamps are lit on a moonless night and there is feasting and fireworks in honour of the goddess Lakshmi and in celebration of Rama's return from exile.

Holi is a spring festival held in February or March which is also known as the Festival of Colours or the festival of love. Holi celebrations usually start with a bonfire on the night before Holi where people gather to sing and dance. The next morning is a free-for-all carnival of colours, where participants play, chase and colour each other with dry powder and coloured water. In the evening, people dress up, and visit friends and family.

## Health and wellness Tourism

This is the industry in which people travel to other countries to get medical and dental care, and at the same time, visit the local attractions of that country.

In the past few years, Asia has taken the lead as one of the most preferred destinations for medical value travel. This has been helped by low priced treatment options, cheap international travel, the availability of a variety of treatments, improved infrastructure in terms of healthcare facilities, and attractive locations for spending time after treatment.

India, Thailand and Singapore are the three Asian countries that receive the most medical tourists. All three countries have low cost treatments, quality healthcare infrastructure, and availability of highly-skilled doctors but India adds a very strong pharmaceutical industry to the list.

Major private corporations have made significant investments in setting up modern hospitals and tourism-related services to cater to the new breed of visitor from abroad. Many hospitals and clinics have obtained the approval of overseas regulators.

There are certainly economic advantages in choosing English-speaking India for certain procedures. For example, a heart bypass procedure costs roughly 10% of Western prices at one of India's leading surgery centres. Heart care has become a specialty in India, with centres such as Fortis Wockhardt (Mumbai) and Apollo (New Delhi and Chennai) being very popular. Success and morbidity rates are said to be on par with those found in the US and Europe.

Procedures such as hip and knee replacement, face lift, and gastric bypass are far more affordable in India, including the cost of travel and accommodation, compared to Western countries.

While cost is the big driver of this industry, there are some negatives attached to it. When things go wrong you might find it difficult to claim for damages, simply because insurance laws vary between countries. Even though hospitals and dental care clinics in India have insurance for medical malpractice, the actual settlement that you might be able to ask for might not be the amount that you expect.

The quality of post-operative care that you'll receive will depend on the hospital. Certainly in many places it will not be the same as that supplied by the US and European private hospitals and clinics, and generally you are away from your support network of relatives and friends.

The patient is usually in hospital for just a few days, and then goes on the holiday portion of the trip or returns home. Complications, side-effects and post-operative treatment can then be the responsibility of the health care system in the patients' home nation and this can lead to expensive costs. It is best to plan on a longer stay in India to avoid this.

The solution is to seek out accredited institutions and don't buy into Internet hype or word-of-mouth recommendations. Thorough research may save you thousands of dollars and may even save your life.

India is also home to a number of alternative medicine techniques such as Ayurveda, Sidha, Unani, Yoga, Acupuncture and Homeopathy which are very popular among foreigners. Indian visitors will find an array of courses and treatments that strive to heal mind, body and spirit. Some offer spiritual enlightenment within five-star accommodation, while others offer basic dwellings and harsh discipline.

Meditation and yoga are attracting an ever-increasing number of visitors, prompting the spread of facilities that are convenient for Westerners. Many centres within the Golden Triangle region have facilities.

## Wildlife Viewing

Many Golden Triangle visitors assume that they will have the opportunity to view wildlife including tigers during their visit but unfortunately, most go home disappointed. There are certainly places where wildlife can be seen but these are not on the standard tourist routes and will add days to your other itinerary.

**Ranthambore National Park** attracts large numbers of travellers to witness the elusive Royal Bengal Tiger because this is supposed to have the richest concentrations of animals in the world. Sawai Madhopur is perhaps the best approach as the park is around 11 km from the railway station. If you wish to explore the varied topography of the National Park then an Open Jeep Safari is the best way to see the wilderness.

The park is now open all through the year but the best time to visit is from October through June when the weather is most pleasant. Visitors need to book safaris in advance and this can be done by visiting the web site https://www.ranthamborenationalpark.com/safari-timing.html

Another place to visit is **Sariska National Park** north-east of Jaipur. Although larger than Ranthambore, it is less commercialised and has less tigers but a similar topography. The park is home to numerous carnivores including leopard, wild dog, jungle cat, hyena, jackal, and tiger. These feed on an abundance of prey species such as sambar, chitel, nilgai, chausingha, wild boar and langur. Sariska is also well known for its large population of Rhesus monkeys. Further information can be had from http://www.sariskanationalpark.com/info-about-sariska.htm

## Arriving in Delhi by Air

The Indira Gandhi International Airport, which now is the busiest airport in South Asia, is located to the west of central Delhi. There are two terminals - T3 (international) and T1 (Domestic) - which are eight kilometres apart. A free shuttle bus is available between the two terminals.

T3 was built in 2011, so it is equipped with all the amenities an international traveller needs - a huge variety of duty-free shopping, currency exchanges offering reasonably good rates, Airtel sim cards in case you want to turn your overseas phone into an Indian phone while in India, rooms for sleeping off your jet lag, comfortable seats, and loads of restaurants. Just to confuse things this terminal also has a domestic wing catering to some flights inside India.

There are various modes of transportation from T3 to the city. The Metro train will take you to New Delhi for less than US$1 and you can take a taxi from there to wherever you need to go. Alternatively, prepaid taxis (Black and Yellow coloured) are available at a booth inside the arrival terminal as well as at two booths outside near the taxi bay. These taxis will drop you at the doorstep anywhere in Delhi for a fare under US$10.

Metered Radio taxis are a little more expensive than prepaid taxis and are lined up in front of the terminal building as in any airport in the world. They are run by some private companies, use air-conditioned later model vehicles and are probably worth the few extra dollars. There are air-conditioned buses available to a few destinations including the major railway stations and bus terminals.


## Getting around the Golden Triangle

The best way is to **rent a car and driver** through a tour company. This is also probably the most expensive way. Remember that India is a cheap country so you can avoid many pitfalls for a relatively low price.

Whether you need to pre-book accommodation will depend on the time of year and what level you expect. I recommend booking something in Delhi to give you peace of mind then play the rest by ear.

Travelling by road in India can be dangerous, accidents are commonplace and the number of road traffic deaths is high. Traffic drives on the left so this can be confusing to some visitors. Local driving practices are often undisciplined and aggressive, and vehicles are often poorly maintained.

Many roads are of poor quality and congested, and you will be sharing with pedestrians, carts, cattle and other livestock. Trucks like to keep in the fast lane of divided highways so passing on the left is common.

Travelling by road at night is particularly dangerous due to insufficient or non-existent street lighting and the presence of other vehicles driving with headlights off or on high beam. Vehicles may travel in the wrong direction, often without warning, even on four-lane divided highways. They are usually near the road edge but I have seen several vehicles travelling at high speed in the fast lane completely ignoring on-coming traffic.

*Train travel can be fun but trains are often crowded*

India has an incredible **rail system**. Some say that no visit to India is complete without experiencing the bustle of Indian railway stations and a journey on an Indian express train. On a long distance express in an AC Chair car or an AC1 or AC2 sleeper, all seats and berths are reserved and it's a safe, civilised, cheap and comfortable way to get around India.

Even long distances such as Delhi to Udaipur can be covered more time-effectively and at less cost than flying, using overnight AC Sleeper trains.

On all long-distance trains, you need to make a seat or berth reservation. Trains do get fully booked often weeks or even months in advance, so you should make reservations as far in advance as possible.

You can also evoke the luxury of a bygone era by travelling on one of the luxury trains of India. You can soak in the sights of various parts of India on trains that take you back in time and provide the same impeccable service and luxury to which the Maharajas were accustomed. Some of the popular ones are Palace on Wheels, Royal Rajasthan on Wheels and the Deccan Odyssey.

**Bus travel** has become more popular as roads improve and there are more than 800 bus operators online. You can choose from air-conditioned or non-air-conditioned buses, luxury, and sleeper buses. All air-conditioned buses are fitted with upholstered seats that can be reclined and most offer entertainment in the form of Hindi movies as well.

## Tourist Information

The Ministry of Tourism is the agency for the formulation of national policies and programmes and for the co-ordination of activities of various Central Government Agencies, State Governments/UTs and the Private Sector for the development and promotion of tourism in the country. There is a vast amount of information on their web site http://tourism.gov.in/ but it may not be of direct interest to people looking for general information.

The Incredible India web site https://incredibleindia.org/ is of more use.

# 11 EATING AND DRINKING

Hinduism has a profound effect on what most Indian eat and drink. A love of nature and the importance of living a simple, natural life are the basis of Hinduism. Followers of the religion believe that the body is made up of natural elements: earth, air, fire, water, etc. The proper balance of these elements indicates good health, while an imbalance indicates the opposite.

It was explained to me that "food is considered to be a source of the body's chemistry, which affects one's consciousness and emotions. Thus, the soul depends on the body, which depends on the food. A proper diet is considered vital for spiritual development in Hinduism". The Hindu diet code divides food into three categories, based on the food's effect on the body and the temperament:

Tamasic food is leftover, stale, overripe, spoiled or other impure food, which is believed to produce negative emotions, such as anger, jealousy and greed. This is food to be avoided.

Rajasic is food believed to produce strong emotional qualities, passions and restlessness in the mind. This category includes meat, eggs, fish, spices, onions, garlic, hot peppers, pickles and other pungent or spicy foods.

Sattvic food is the most desirable type of food as it is non-irritating to the stomach and purifying to the mind; it includes fruits, nuts, whole grains and vegetables. These foods are believed to produce calmness and nobility, or what is known as an "increase in one's magnetism."

There is also a religious element. "Hindus believe that for true service to God, purity of food is necessary to maintain the desirable state of mind that leads to enlightenment. Food is consumed not only to survive but also to stay healthy and maintain mind/body equilibrium. By eating a purer quality food, such as a Sattvic diet, and regulating food consumption, one can ensure a pure heart, long life, cheerful spirit, strength, health, happiness and delight."

Indian food is widely perceived as being predominantly vegetarian but in fact less than half of the Indian population is vegetarian. Vegetarianism has indeed been a major influence in the evolution of Indian cuisine, however, the abstinence from meat eating has often been an economic consideration because many people could not afford meat. As India improves economically, the consumption of meat grows.

The socio-economic class structure has also had a considerable effect on the development of the cuisine. The overly rich, costly and exotic food that was enjoyed exclusively by the Mughal emperors is now being enjoyed at wedding buffets by middle-class Indians.

Western-style food was only enjoyed by the wealthiest of Indians but now other classes devour pizza, pasta, hamburgers, cheese, chocolate and coffee. This has caused the elites to focus on traditional regional cuisines so more regional-style dishes are finding their way onto restaurant menus.

Large global food corporations are trying to entice Indian to swap their traditional daal and roti for pizza; lassi for fizzy sodas, and local bazaars for supermarkets. In the cities they have had some success but like many things in India, the old refuses to fade away so the new is just incorporated as an additional option.

Indians believe that a proper meal should contain six flavours: bitter, sweet, pungent, sour, salty and astringent. It is also important to balance flavours and textures so soft items like rice are partnered with crunchy ones like *papad*.

There are some common dishes to many Indian meals. *Roti* is the everyday bread made from an unleavened flour and water dough. It is rolled into circular flat sheets and cooked in an iron pan. *Naan* is a somewhat similar leavened or unleavened, oven-baked flatbread. *Daal*, the genetic term for legumes is made from several different pods, water and spices. Green leafy vegetables cooked in various ways are eaten every day.

Indian cuisine is varied in taste and type. While it is difficult to describe Indian cuisine without linking it to the geographic regions, it is true to say the Indian food is generally spicy. It is made from rice, wheat flour, a variety of legumes, vegetables, fruits, and spices.

Although no dish with the name curry exists in traditional Indian cuisine, what the West calls curries are a combination of stir-fried ingredients: mainly onions, garlic, ginger, and tomatoes mixed together with spices and seasonings with added poultry, meat, fish or just vegetables. They are cooked in ghee, peanut oil, mustard oil, coconut oil or gingili oil, depending on the region.

Within the Golden Triangle area, there are some differences in cuisine. Let's start with **Delhi**.

Everyday food in early Delhi comprised unleavened wheat bread eaten with stews of daal and vegetables; rice cooked with daal and flavourings; seasonal fruit; honey; butter, curd and milk; and roasted meats. Around 500BC many high-class Hindus stopped eating meat, possibly because of the growing popularity of the doctrine of protection of all life being preached by Jains and the Buddha.

Seventeen hundred years later, India was being ruled by Muslims and records indicate that dishes served at the royal feasts of the rulers included whole sheep; rice cooked in ghee served with chicken; pastries stuffed with minced meat, almonds and other nuts; and an array of sweets made from sugar, ghee, nuts and dried fruit.

During Mughal times, the imperial kitchen became a melange of cooks from across the Empire. The royal cooks were encouraged to devise ever more elaborate dishes. Roasted meat, poultry and game stuffed and stewed and adorned with finely beaten sheets or silver and gold together with elaborate spice mixes became the nucleus of a meal. Vegetables often cooked in a well-spiced, nut-enriched sauce were a mere side attraction.

The influence of Mughal food on the cuisine of India is extensive and it percolated down into the general population over time. Religious and cultural affinity, however, meant that it is more evident in the cuisine of India's Muslim community.

Before India's partition, Delhi was predominantly a Muslim city. Many moved to newly-created Pakistan so after a few years Delhi became a large Hindu city made up largely of people from the western Punjab which was now in Pakistan.

With so many Punjabis in Delhi, the demand for their local food was strong. Some individuals set up roadside stalls selling fried snacks and simple Punjabi dishes and some of these stalls evolved into restaurants. Naturally, Punjabi cuisine dominated the menus. One such example is *Moti Mahal* which developed from a stall serving Tandoori chicken.

This is the origin of chicken *tikka* which is on the menu of most Western Indian restaurants. Butter chicken was also developed here. Today there are *Moti Mahal* restaurants throughout Delhi, across India, and in several other countries.

If you want to experience *tandoori* food at its best in modern Delhi, Bukhara at the ITC Maurya is sometimes called the 'best Indian restaurant in the world'. This style of cooking requires great expertise on the part of the chefs, since the meat is not accompanied by any sauce or gravy, but is only pre-marinated and cooked before serving.

If you go here you must try the world renowned *Daal Bukhara*, a combination of whole black lentils, tomatoes, ginger and garlic, which is cooked and simmered over slow coal fires of the tandoor for 18 hours.

Although it may not have originated here, *Chaat* is something worth trying while in Delhi. The word comes from the Hindi word 'to lick' and it is applied to a range of snacks or light meals. Many *chaats* are made of a crisp fried item, with some sweet and sour tamarind/mango chutney, and are crowned with various garnishes and sprinkles of *chaat masala*. There is no end of options for eating *chaat* in Delhi and the varieties are almost endless.

**Uttar Pradesh** is a state south of Delhi. It houses some of the oldest and holiest places of Hinduism including Mathura and Vrindavan which are covered in this book. It also houses Agra, capital of Sikandar Lodi, Delhi's reigning sultan from 1503 and then from the mid-sixteenth century when Akbar moved the Mughal capital from Delhi to Agra.

The area between Delhi and Agra is a green and gold patchwork of fields that have been productively worked for centuries. The state is a major producer of wheat, rice and sugar cane, vegetables, various daals, livestock, dairy products, and fruit. These foods have been and remain a mainstay of local food.

A typical meal in Uttar Pradesh comprises wheat *rotis* or rice, a daal, a dry vegetable dish, and a gravy-based vegetable dish accompanied by curd, pickles and chutney. Common spices are turmeric, red chilli, cumin and mustard. Half the population of Uttar Pradesh is vegetarian but the other half would include a meat-based dish.

Most of the extended Golden Triangle is in the state of **Rajasthan**. The state was formed from 22 feudal kingdoms once founded by Rajputs, a Hindu warrior caste. When the Mughals arrived they allowed the Rajputs to rule their kingdoms, provided they paid taxes and tribute into imperial coffers. When Emperor Akbar married a Rajput princess it paved the way for closer co-operation and Mughal influences extended into Rajput royal domains.

Eventually, their cooking took on the hallmarks of Mughal cuisine. In modern Rajasthan, Rajputs play a significant role in the tourism industry because they own the forts and palaces that have been so successfully turned into hotels. You will find that you are likely to encounter Rajput-style cuisine in mid to high scale restaurants and hotels right throughout the Golden Triangle region of the state.

There are two distinct cuisines in Rajasthan, however; that of the Rajputs and that of the rest. Much of Rajasthan is desert and lack of water is a huge problem. Much of the population still lives in villages growing crops where possible and raising livestock. Milk from these animals plays an important role in Rajasthani cooking where fresh milk and buttermilk is used to replace water. A glass of buttermilk is often had with meals and *daal* is often cooked with buttermilk to make *kadhi*.

Onions, garlic and red chillies are the most commonly used ingredients in Rajasthani cooking and for poor villages these might be the only flavourings that they can afford. The state is a major producer of chickpeas and a flour ground from dried chickpeas (*besan*) is used to produce a wide range of foods, including *gatte*, and *pittor*, a thick cooked paste scooped up with *roti*.

*Papad*, a crunchy accompaniment to meals, is another item made from *besan* and these are often cooked in a simple sauce of onion, garlic, chilli and coriander.

A typical breakfast for a Rajasthani villager would be *roti* with pickles or chutney, buttermilk and/or milky tea. In the bigger towns *poha* (flattened rice) is popular and this is usually bought from a street vendor. Lunch and dinner are similar with a vegetable dish, plain curd and a sweet item added. Sometimes a meat dish would also be added.

Many grand palaces offer spectacular royal Rajasthani feasts at equally spectacular prices. While these can be quite an experience, I have had equal enjoyment from a *thali*, an Indian meal made up of a selection of various dishes served in small bowls, which are placed on a round tray. Typical dishes include rice, *daal*, vegetables, *roti*, *papad*, curd, chutney or pickles and a sweet dish to top it off. Restaurants typically offer a choice of vegetarian or meat-based *thalis*.

# 12 ACCOMMODATION

The Golden Triangle region has accommodation costing from Rs2,700,000 (no this is not a misprint) to Rs80 per night. Naturally, the quality and experience vary widely.

India has some of the best and most expensive hotel rooms in the world and the facilities and service are virtually unmatched anywhere. A standard room in a five-star hotel in the major cities will cost anywhere from US$250 to US$750 a night. Breakfast may be included. Executive rooms and suites go up from here.

Many visitors choose a four or four and a half star hotel instead because rates come down dramatically and service and facilities can be almost as good. Here you will pay from US$75 to US$150.

Three-star hotels are found everywhere and some are in excellent locations. These tend to be older properties but facilities are generally satisfactory and rates of US$40 to US$80 are attractive. There are some B&Bs in this category which provide an even more personal experience.

Delhi and some other places are seeing the rise of modern budget properties catering for middle-class Indian travellers and budget international visitors. Rooms are generally small but facilities are OK and rooms can be had for US$20.

Below these are a multitude of budget hotels, hostels, B&Bs and other accommodation. Some are satisfactory while others are generally not suitable for non-Indian travellers. Prices vary but at the bottom of the market you only pay a few dollars for a bed. You need to inspect rooms before you decide to stay.

The following is by no means comprehensive and is a personal selection but all are safe and comfortable. The stars shown are approximate only.

**Delhi**

**The Leela Palace** ***** Chanakyapuri, Diplomatic Enclave, New Delhi; +91 (0)11 3933 1234; www.theleela.com

You enter via its stunning porte cochere. You're greeted at the door with garlands and escorted directly to your room for check-in. Rooms are designed with typical North Indian aesthetics, softened by jaali screens and handmade rugs. This brilliant hotel even has suites with private pools and the rooftop infinity pool is fabulous. Well-heeled locals frequent the French and Japanese restaurants Le Cirque and Megu, because of their reputation. A terrific bar provides a fantastic selection of wines.

**The Claridges Hotel** ***** 12 Aurangzeb Road, New Delhi; +91 (0)11 3955 5000; http://www.claridges.com/the-claridges-newdelhi/overview.asp

This perfect blend of old world elegance and contemporary luxury is just 3 km from the city centre. It has a temperature-controlled outdoor swimming pool, with music, ambient lighting, sun decks, cabanas, loungers and a bar. There are 7 dining options and an Ayurvedic spa. Mediterranean cuisine is served at Sevilla, while Dhaba offers North Indian fare and Jade serves Chinese food.

Traditionalists will appreciate these three classic New Delhi hotels: The Oberoi, Taj Mahal Hotel, and The Imperial.

**The Oberoi** ***** Dr. Zakir Hussain Marg, New Delhi; +91 (0)11 2436 3030; www.oberoihotels.com

This epitomizes classic sophistication, and its services are rated among the best in the world -- each room has a dedicated butler and staff are uniformly friendly and helpful. Business travellers love it here because it has all the facilities they need. Although the building is not modern, the rooms and public areas have been kept up to date. There are three restaurants serving international, Indian, Italian and Chinese cuisine and a wonderful patisserie and delicatessen. It was temporarily closed in January 2017 for a major refurbishment.

**Imperial Hotel** ***** Janpath, New Delhi; +91 (0)11 2334 1234; http://www.theimperialindia.com/

This is an art deco jewel in a wonderful central location. It was ranked as the Best Hotel in Delhi by Travel + Leisure World's Best Awards 2014. Its grand white columns and rococo interiors remind guests of India's colonial era. Rooms have every imaginable luxury including Fragonard and Bvlgari toiletries but few have views.

The breakfast (and the breakfast location), and the gardens and pool area are all excellent. English afternoon tea is offered at The Atrium while Italian specialities can be enjoyed at San Gimignano. The ultimate in New Delhi hospitality is the all-white Royal Imperial Suite at approximately US$4,000 per night.

**The Taj Mahal Hotel** ***** 1 Mansingh Road, New Delhi; +91 (0)11 2302 6162; http://www.tajhotels.com/luxury/city-hotels/the-taj-mahal-hotel-new-delhi/overview.html

This is a hotel in Mughal tradition. The 294 rooms are beautiful and elegant, clean and well maintained. There is a thirty metre heated outdoor pool and lovely grounds. Machan is a lively 24-hour cafe. The House of Ming was the first Chinese restaurant in New Delhi. Varq and the Grill Room are two other alternatives. Ricks Bar has been a mainstay in Delhi's nightlife for years. The wonderful but prohibitively priced Japanese restaurant Wasabi by Morimoto is a choice that never disappoints.

**The Lodhi** ***** Lodhi Road, 110003 New Delhi; +91 (0)12 4465 3333; http://www.thelodhi.com/index.php

This modern 40 room boutique property has a salon, fitness centre, spa and massage centre, steam and sauna room, a library, a cigar lounge and a business centre. Each indulgent air-conditioned room features space and fine furnishings and there is a private balcony and plunge pool as well as a seating area. Elan Restaurant & Bar serves pan-Indian, Mediterranean and South East Asian cuisines. Anidra is a popular supper club and night club.

**Trident Gurgaon** ***** 443 Udyog Vihar, Phase V, Gurgaon; +91 (0)12 4245 1234; http://www.tridenthotels.com/hotels-in-gurgaon

This is 32 km outside the city centre in the bustling financial and industrial city of Gurgaon. The 136-room business hotel is low-rise and spread over seven acres. It is easy to find Moroccan, Mughal and Rajasthani styles in its architecture. There are gardens, courtyards and reflection pools, a spa, swimming pool, palm courtyard, and good restaurants.

**Oberoi Gurgaon** ***** 443 Udyog Vihar, Phase V, Gurgaon, Haryana; +91 (0)12 4245 1234; www.oberoihotels.com

This seductive and exclusive all glass and metal hotel hides behind immense foliage in Delhi's satellite town and business centre. Rooms are the most spacious of any in Delhi business hotels. The hotel also has a larger-than-Olympic-size heated swimming pool, 24-hour spa and what it claims is India's only cigar lounge.

**Shangri-La's - Eros Hotel, New Delhi** **** 19 Ashoka Road, Connaught Place; +91 (0)11 4119 1919; http://www.shangri-la.com/newdelhi/erosshangrila/

This is a high-rise hotel with a good central location. Rooms have free Wi-Fi, digital newspapers and magazines, flat-screen cable TV, desk, electronic safe, and tea and coffee making facilities. International and local dishes are served all day at Cafe Uno. The 25 metre swimming pool, Jacuzzi and surroundings are very enjoyable and quiet. The 24/7 gym has an extensive range of equipment as well as a Jacuzzi and sauna. The spa has a complete range of services.

**Svelte** **** A-3, District Centre, Select Citywalk, Saket; +91 (0)11 4051 2000; http://www.svelte.in/

The hotel sits atop the city's most popular mall, Select Citywalk, in the Saket area. Svelte has 82 well-designed suites with rain-shower cubicles, customized pillow menus, and round the clock room service. The Lounge is an all-day restaurant, and there's a rooftop pool, and a fitness centre overlooking the mall gardens.

**Wood Castle Grand** *** EA/190,Tagore Garden, New Delhi; (0)11-2593 2510; http://www.woodcastlegrand.com/

I have mixed thoughts about this hotel because of its location. The building, facilities and service are all excellent but some visitors will not like the suburban location about five minutes walk from the Tagore Garden Metro Station and then 20 minutes to central Delhi. The hotel car will take you to the station and local restaurants. The welcome and personal touch by the owners and managers is first class and the food is excellent. The minibar is complimentary.

**Shanti Home** *** A-1/300, Janakpuri, New Delhi; +91 (0)11 4157 3366; http://www.shantihome.com/

The 17 rooms of this boutique hotel have different themes, and are clean, comfortable, and silent. The hotel offers lounges with comfortable couches, a desk with a notebook computer  centre, and daily housekeeping. There is 24-hour restaurant service and a small in-house spa with steam and ayurvedic massage services.

**Bloomrooms@ New Delhi Railway Station** *** 8591 Arakashan Road; +91 (0)11 4122 5666; http://www.bloomrooms.com/

This cool new hotel is in a crowded but very convenient location near the New Delhi railway station. It has clean, modern styling and an Italian cafe. Rooms are small but the price is reasonable and they come with free Wi-Fi, free water and tea and coffee. Some are noisy from honking trains so chose carefully.

**Amax Inn** ** 8145/6, Arakashan Rd, Multani Dhanda; 11 2354 3813

This is located just 550 yards from New Dehli Railway Station in an area some people may not like. The hotel, however, offers good accommodation with private bathroom facilities, and free Wi-Fi in public areas. It also has a rooftop restaurant. Staff are very welcoming and helpful.

**Udaipur**

**Taj Lake Palace** ***** Lake Pichola, Udaipur: +91 (0)294 242 8800; http://www.tajhotels.com/luxury/grand-palaces-and-iconic-hotels/taj-lake-palace-udaipur/

This is really an outstanding property. The hotel and mid-lake location are awesome. The staff are very attentive from the moment you arrive at the dock to take the boat to the hotel. You will enjoy the welcome as you are showered with rose petals. The pool, bar, lobby, and other common areas of the hotel are fantastic and feel very much like a palace.

Rooms vary from tight to palatial and all are furnished brilliantly. There are four exquisite restaurants serving Asian, Indian, contemporary Western, and Italian dishes by the lily pond, poolside or on the rooftop. You will not want to leave.

**Oberoi Udaivilas** ***** +91 (0)294 243 3300; http://www.oberoihotels.com/hotels-in-udaipur/

Grand modern architecture with pavilions and domes inspired by the palaces of Rajasthan and great service are the highlights of this property. It is located on the banks of Lake Pichola a little away from the town. There are three restaurants, two heated outdoor pools and a luxurious spa. Suryamahal is a daytime dining space under a blue dome while Udaimahal is a candle-lit evening dining space. The Bar has an almost labyrinthine layout between domes and through arches.

**Devi Garh** \*\*\*\*\* Delwara, NH8, Near Eklingji Udaipur: +91 (0)295 328 9211; http://www.lebua.com/devi-garh

Set high in the Aravalli Hills 30 km north of Udaipur, Devi Garh is a hill-top fort-palace that exquisitely brings together the best of old India with the new. It was the royal residence of the rulers of Delwara principality, from the middle of the 18th century until the mid-20th century. Its soaring exteriors contrast dramatically with the refined white and metallic contemporary design of its 39 suites and public areas. Sleek, polished simplicity creates an atmosphere of absolute calm while the use of local stone and marble adds richness.

**Shiv Niwas Palace Hotel** \*\*\*\* The City Palace, Udaipur; +91 (0)294 252 8016; http://www.hrhhotels.com/Grand_Heritage/Shiv_Niwas_Palace/

The crescent-shaped palace was built in the early 20th century and was reserved exclusively for visiting dignitaries. The 17 individually decorated suites contain portraits and furniture that were selected for the royal family while ceilings and walls are delicately hand-painted with traditional Indian motifs.

Panghat — the spa and salon welcomes you to the world of luxury and pampering. Paantya, the multi-cuisine restaurant, is adorned with original paintings of the Mewar School, gold latticework and antique chandeliers. Panera bar, with its authentic décor of glass inlay work, huge chandeliers and ornate mirrors, offers a wide selection of snacks and drinks.

**Jaiwana Haveli** \*\*\* 14, Lalghat, Udaipur; +91 (0)294 241 1103; http://www.jaiwanahaveli.com/

The twenty-four room Jaiwana Haveli hotel is located on the eastern bank of Lake Pichola just a stone's throw from the City Palace and the old bazaars. All rooms are equipped with air-conditioners, LCD's and attached bathrooms with 24 hours hot water. The roof top restaurant with its panoramic views has become a popular venue for visitors. An excellent choice of Indian, Mewari and continental cuisine is available.

**Bhanwar Vilas Guest House** ** 74, Gangor Ghat, Udaipur; http://www.bhanwarvilasudaipur.com/

This is a good guest house with clean AC and non-AC rooms, helpful staff and management, hot showers, TV and free wifi. The roof top is a great place to have dinner. The City Palace and other attractions are nearby. There are four floors and no elevator so some guests will like the lower floor rooms.

**Hari Niwas Guest House Udaipur** ** 117 Battiyani Chohatta; http://www.hariniwasudaipur.com/

The house was an old indian haveli that has been restored keeping its heritage structure. All six rooms have a private bath and there is a nice view of the City Palace from the terrace.

## Jodhpur

**Umaid Bhawan Palace** ***** Palace Road, Jodhpur; +91 (0)291 251 0101; http://www.tajhotels.com/luxury/grand-palaces-and-iconic-hotels/umaid-bhawan-palace-jodhpur/

Built between 1928 and 1943, this 394 room grand yellow sandstone palace is surrounded by over 26 acres of gardens. Sixty four of these rooms are now part of a luxury hotel featuring Art Deco and Renaissance design, with two swimming pools and pampering treatments at Jiva Spa.

Rooms and suites are equipped with a flat-screen TV, DVD player and spa baths. For the health conscious, a yoga studio, gym and tennis courts are provided. Risala serves Continental and Indian fusion cuisine, while Pillars serves Rajasthani meals.

**RAAS Jodhpur** ***** Tunwarji ka Jhalra Makrana Mohalla, Jodhpur; +91 (0)291 263 6455; http://raasjodhpur.com/

The centrally located hotel featuring intricately carved Haveli-style architecture, houses a spa, an outdoor pool, and 2 dining options. The 39 understated contemporary air-conditioned rooms have balconies and a flat-screen TV with satellite channels, a wardrobe and a seating area, and make the most of Jodhpur's pink sandstone, stunning black terrazzo, with splashes of 'Jodhpur blue'. There is a covered dining room and an al fresco café, both serving international and Indian food.

**Ratan Vilas** *** Near Bhaskar Circle, Loco shed Road, Jodhpur; +91 (0)291 261 4418; http://www.ratanvilas.com/

Built in 1920, this small palace has 20 modern, elegant and air-conditioned rooms with satellite TV, seating area, mini-bar and old-world charm. It remains the home of one of Jodhpur's royals. There is an outdoor swimming pool, a garden marquee for breakfast, a candle-lit courtyard, and an indoor restaurant that serves Indian and continental specialities. The staff are friendly and helpful.

**Vivanta by Taj Hari Mahal** **** 5, Residency Road, Jodhpur; +91 (0)291 243 9700; http://www.vivantabytaj.com/hari-mahal-jodhpur/

Spread over 6 acres of landscaped gardens, the luxurious hotel is built to resemble a 14th-century royal fort. Pampering spa treatments, a large outdoor pool and a 24-hour fitness centre are available. Large air-conditioned rooms feature original wall paintings, large windows and a work space and have a flat-screen TV and free tea/coffee making facilities. Bathrooms have massage showers and a bathtub.

There is also a library, beauty salon and a 24-hour business centre. Modern Rajasthani and Continental dishes can be enjoyed at Latitude while authentic Cantonese and Szechuan cuisines are served at The Good Earth.

**Devi Bhawan** **** Ratanada Circle, Defence Lab Road, Jodhpur; +91 (0)291 251 2215; http://devibhawan.com/

Housed in an eighty-year-old residence, the 20 room Devi Bhawan has an outdoor swimming pool and offers spacious rooms with beautiful garden views. The air-conditioned rooms have tiled flooring and antique furnishings and are equipped with a desk, and a TV. En suite bathrooms come with hot shower and free bath amenities. The in-house restaurant serves Indian, Rajasthani and Continental dishes. Free Wi-Fi access is available in its public areas.

**Mandore Guest House** *** Dadawari Lane, near Mandore Garden, Jodhpur; +91 (0)982 914 7470; http://www.mandore.com/

Just 2 minutes' walk from the Mandore Gardens and ten kilometres from central Jodhpur, Mandore Guest House has its own flower garden with ample sitting and dining areas. This family-owned property has a vegetarian restaurant with home-cooked meals. The 16 air-conditioned rooms are decorated with local art, and come with a sofa and a private bathroom with a hot shower.

**Thaveli Inn Pal** *** Near Clock Tower, Opp. Lake Gulab Saga; http://www.haveliinnpal.com/

The heritage Haveli has been converted into a cosy Inn. Those wanting the feel of a traditional Rajput home, would be right at home here. There is a pleasant rooftop terrace and a small cafe.

**Govind Hotel** ** In Front Of Main GPO, Station Road, Jodhpur; +91 (0)291 262 2758; http://www.govindhotel.com/

The location within a five minute walk of the railway station is good for restaurants and sightseeing. The fanned rooms are clean and comfortable but are up two flights of steep stairs so anyone with walking problems will find it a challenge. The rooftop restaurant is a nice place to relax although mosquitoes can be a problem at times. The food is good and they have 'real' coffee. The best part of the hotel is the family that runs it.


**Pushkar**

**The Westin Pushkar Resort & Spa** ***** Village Surajkund, Motisar Road, Pushkar; http://www.starwoodhotels.com/westin/property/overview/index.html?propertyID=4379&language=en_US

This newly opened resort is some way from the town but the rooms and facilities are absolutely first-class. Some of the 98 spacious guest rooms and suites have private pools. All have Satellite TV Channels and DVD Player. It is perfect for those who want relaxation, but there are also many activities like cycling, village excursions, gym, cricket, badminton, table tennis and swimming.

**Bhanwar Singh Palace** **** Village Hokra, Pushkar; +91 (0)145 277 2278; http://bhanwarsinghpalace.com/

The sprawling hotel in garden surroundings is located six kilometres from Pushkar Lake and the Brahma Temple so you need a vehicle. Free Wi-Fi access, an outdoor swimming pool, a fitness centre and a spa and wellness centre are available. The tastefully decorated air-conditioned rooms have flat-screen cable TV, an electric kettle and seating area. There is an all–day dining restaurant and a multi-cuisine restaurant serving Indian, Chinese, Eastern, and Continental cuisines

**Orchard Pushkar****** Chawandia Road Ganahera Village, Pushkar; +91 93 5140 7672; http://www.orchard.in/

This provides unique tent accommodation with air conditioning and electric blankets for winter in an orchard location not far from the town.

Each air-conditioned tent is equipped with a seating area and private bathroom with a shower. Toiletries and slippers are included. Golghar restaurant offers local and international dishes.

**Hotel Prem Villas Pushkar** \*\*Punch Kund Road, Pushkar; +91-(0)145-277 2505; http://www.premvillaspushkar.com/

This is on the edge of town but the lake and other attractions are walkable in the daylight. There is a 24-hour front desk and free Wi-Fi in public areas. Rooms are fitted with a TV and a telephone. Both air conditioning and a fan are provided and each room comes with a seating area. Athithi Devo Bhavh restaurant serves a selection of Indian, Chinese, and European dishes.

**Atithi Guest House** \*\* Near Sin Boys High Secondary School Choti Basti; +91 (0)145 277 2503; http://www.atithiguesthouse.com/

The ten rooms have a sofa, fan, and private bathroom with a shower, and free toiletries. Rooftop Rusta Café serves Indian, Chinese, Continental, and Italian specialities, has free Wi-Fi, and there is a small library.

**Hotel Everest** \*\* Kalo ka Mohalla, Badi Basti, Pushkar; +91 (0)145 277 3417; http://www.pushkarhoteleverest.com/ ,

Situated along a quiet lane, Hotel Everest is only 100 metres from Pushkar Lake. It features a rooftop restaurant, a 24-hour front desk, complimentary Wi-Fi access and free parking. The 15 comfortable rooms are simply furnished with a fan and seating area and a few are air-conditioned. Each room comes with an attached bathroom containing a hot shower. The roof-top terrace serves a selection of tasty Indian dishes accompanied by muted lighting and gentle music.


**Ajmer**

**Neelkamal Hotel** \*\*\* opposite St. Johns Church, Ajmer; +91 (0)145-262

7533;

This offers a spa and wellness centre with massage, a restaurant, free Wi-Fi access, car rental facilities and a 24-hour front desk. Rooms have a flat-screen TV with satellite channels, a desk, fan and a seating area. Private bathrooms come with a shower.

**Hotel Royal Palace** ** Near Dargah Sharif, Ajmer; +91 (0)960 238 6437; http://www.ajmerhotelroyalpalace.com/

The air-conditioned rooms all come with a TV, desk and wardrobe. The en suite bathrooms are equipped with free toiletries and a shower. It has a 24-hour front desk, restaurant and free Wi-Fi access in all areas of the hotel. Guests can enjoy Indian cuisine and local dishes at the Royal Restaurant.

**Jaipur**

**Rambagh Palace** ***** Bhawani Singh Road, Jaipur; +91 (0)141 238 5700; https://taj.tajhotels.com/en-in/taj-rambagh-palace-jaipur/

The luxurious Rambagh Palace was the former residence of the Maharaja of Jaipur. Now a luxurious hotel, it features an indoor and outdoor pool, full spa services, manicured gardens and beautiful Indian architecture. The 79 spacious air-conditioned rooms and suites are decorated with elegant carpets and hand-painted wall motifs and contain luxury furniture and fittings.

Breakfast and light meals are served at the informal Rajput Room while The Verandah features traditional afternoon tea, champagne and pre-dinner cocktails. Other dining options include Indian cuisine at grand Suvarna Mahal adorned with gilded mirrors and Florentine frescoes, and outdoor casual drinking and dining at Steam.

**The Raj Palace** ***** Jorawer Singh Gate, Amer Road, Jaipur; +91 (0)141 263 4077: http://www.rajpalace.com/index.php

The Raj Palace is a Heritage Grand hotel and a member of Small Luxury Hotels of the World. There is the option of selecting accommodation starting from Heritage rooms to the most expensive suite in the world, the Shahi Mahal Suite. You can enjoy the Swapna Mahal multi-cuisine restaurant, a bar, coffee shop, live barbeque, outdoor swimming pool, croquet, gym, spa, Jacuzzi, multimedia theatre, business centre, and folk dances.

**Taj Jai Mahal Palace** \*\*\*\*\* Jacob Road, Civil Lines, Jaipur; +91 (0)141 660 1111; https://www.tajhotels.com/en-in/our-hotels/hotels-in-jaipur/

Spread across 18 acres of beautiful Mughal gardens, this heritage property dates back to 1745. There is a range of rooms featuring modern and classic Indian-style décor. Rooms are both opulent and comfortable and luxurious bathrooms with a bathtub are standard in all rooms. Concierge services and a business centre are available. The property offers 4 restaurants with a wide variety of Western, Asian and Rajasthani specialities. It has an outdoor pool, spa and fitness facilities, and tennis.

**The Oberoi Rajvilas Jaipur** \*\*\*\*\* Goner Road, 302031 Jaipur; + 91 141 268 0101; http://www.oberoihotels.com/hotels-in-jaipur/

Set amidst beautiful greenery, this luxurious property has a pool, gym, spa, salon and three dining options. The stylish rooms are equipped with a sofa seating area, flat-screen TV, and bathroom with a bathtub. Available for all-day dining, Surya Mahal & Courtyard serves international dishes and fine wines. Rajmahal restaurant offers Indian specialities for dinner.

**Samode Haveli** \*\*\*\* Gangapole, Jaipur; +91 141-263 2407; http://www.samode.com/

This was built over 175 years ago as the royal family manor. Today the boutique hotel in the Old Quarter has 39 rooms and suites, a spectacular restaurant, an outdoor swimming pool and a spa and wellness centre. The air-conditioned rooms come with antique couches, a flat-screen cable TV and a bathroom with a bathtub, shower and hairdryer. Guests can enjoy a puppet show or a Rajasthani music and dance performance in the evening.

**Royal Heritage Haveli** *** Khatipura, 302012 Jaipur; +91 (0)141 408 2121; http://www.royalheritagehaveli.com/

This restored 18th-century building is surrounded by courtyard lawns. Rooms and suites have patterned flooring, a seating area and a flat-screen TV. Guests can exercise in the gym or de-stress with a yoga session. The spa and some rooms are currently undergoing renovation but you can ask for an in-room Swedish or Kerala massage. Other facilities include a restaurant, business centre and a tour desk.

**Jas Vilas** *** C-9-A, Sawai Jai Singh Highway, Bani Park, Jaipur; http://www.jasvilas.com/

This is a lovely small hotel with an old world feel. The rooms are clean, large and pretty. The staff are caring, and helpful. It provides a quiet and cosy environment. There is a great swimming pool and excellent food.

**Bhola Bhawan Bed and Breakfast** ** 21 Sangram Colony C Scheme, Jaipur; http://www.bholabhawanbedandbreakfast.com/

The air conditioned and heated rooms come with a wardrobe and an en suite bathroom with a hot and cold shower. Some rooms also have cable TV and a private balcony. Guests can relax in the common living and dining rooms. Homemade vegetarian and non-vegetarian dishes are served while guests can also use the property's kitchen to prepare their own meals. Free Wi-Fi, tea and coffee, and parking are provided.

**Alila Fort Bishangarh** ***** Bishangarh Village, Jaipur; http://www.alilahotels.com/fortbishangarh

Just an hour's drive from Jaipur, this is a heritage fortress restored & transformed into a 59-suite luxury resort. The fort has a commanding presence and overlooks stunning Rajasthani landscape. There is an all-day dining restaurant, an alfresco venue with spectacular views, a bar, cigar room and wine cellar, and a champagne bar, coffee and tea lounge.

## Agra

**The Oberoi Amarvilas Agra** ***** Taj East Gate Road, Agra; +91 (0)11 2390 4472; http://www.oberoihotels.com/hotels-in-agra/index.aspx

This delightful property is the only hotel in the city to offer uninterrupted views of the Taj Mahal from each of its rooms. Beautiful rooms come with stylish modern interiors and large windows and all are equipped with a sofa, personal safe and private bathroom. Guests can visit the opulent Oberoi Spa for a body massage, swim, or exercise at the gym. Bellevue restaurant serves international dishes and local favourites, while Esphahan offers traditional Indian specialities.

**ITC Mughal, Agra** ***** Taj Ganj, Agra; +91 (0)562 402 1700; http://www.itchotels.in/Hotels/itcmughal.aspx

The 233 opulent rooms and suites have recreated a paradise for the contemporary guest in the Mughal tradition. I stayed here in December 2014 and was blown away by the service and facilities. Rustic Eshawri has an award-winning menu of delicacies cooked in the clay tandoor while Taj Bano is the all day fine dining multi-cuisine restaurant.

The Royal Spa is the largest spa in India and offers therapy based on ancient customs. The huge property also has cycling and jogging tracks, a mini-golfing green, and a stunning swimming pool.

**Radisson Blu Agra Taj East Gate** ***** Taj East Gate Road, Agra; +91 (0)562 405 5555; http://www.radissonblu.com/hotel-agra

Air-conditioned rooms come with free Wi-Fi and a flat-screen TV, a mini-bar, tea/coffee-making facilities and en suite bathroom. Guests can work-out at the fitness centre, which overlooks the swimming pool and features a steam room and hot tub. A range of therapies and beautifying treatments are available at the spa.

Dawat-e-Nawab serves Indian specialities while The Latitude is a 24-hour coffee shop. The poolside bar or the Tea Lounge provide other options and 24-hour room service is available.

**Howard Plaza Agra** *** Fatehabad Road,Agra; +91 (0)562 404 8600 http://www.howardplazaagra.com/

All the 86 well-appointed rooms have safety lockers, in-room mini-bar, and LCD televisions. The location is relatively near the Taj Mahal and a good view is obtained from the roof top Terrace Restaurant. There is a swimming pool and spa, with sauna, steam bath and Jacuzzi. Rendezvous provides all day dining.

**The Coral Tree** ** 4 Amarlok Colony, Opp Jalma Hospital, near East Gate Taj Mahal, Agra; +91 (0)562 223 0765; http://thecoraltreehomestay.com/

The four rooms in this convenient home stay are attractive, and hot water, good beds and free Wi-Fi are available. It is a three minute walk to the Taj Mahal ticket office. Every room has a separate outside sitting area and there is a wonderful garden with a nicely decorated terrace. The family/hosts are helpful and friendly.

**Zostel Agra** ** opposite 132 KV Sub Plant, near Shilpgram, Taj East Gate Road, Agra; +91 011 3958 9005; http://www.zostel.com/zostel/Agra/

Zostel is India's first chain of branded backpacker's hostels. The staff here are helpful and very friendly. The common room is great and there is a rooftop terrace to hang out on. The rooms and beds are clean and comfortable, though the six-bedded one is a bit small. There are also 4-bedded mixed and female only dorms and a 2-bedded room. The communal kitchen is huge and very well equipped.

If you have enjoyed this book, please give us a brief review on the Amazon web site https://www.amazon.com/dp/1983793221 so that others will be encouraged to also enjoy it.

This was the eighth book in the **Experience** series. There are now a further eight.

We hope you also enjoy the other books in the series:

Experience Thailand e-book;
https://www.amazon.com/dp/B078GDR17N

Experience Thailand paperback;
https://www.amazon.com/dp/1983718718

Experience Norway e-book; https://www.amazon.com/dp/B078GL6T29

Experience Norway paperback;
https://www.amazon.com/dp/1983757179

Experience Northern Italy e-book;
https://www.amazon.com/dp/B078GRH3HW

Experience Northern Italy paperback;
https://www.amazon.com/dp/1983688924

Experience Ireland e-book; https://www.amazon.com/dp/B078GJW7JK

Experience Ireland paperback;
https://www.amazon.com/dp/1983762016

Experience Myanmar (Burma) e-book;

https://www.amazon.com/dp/B078GTRF3T

Experience Myanmar (Burma) paperback;
https://www.amazon.com/dp/1983787590

Experience Singapore e-book;
https://www.amazon.com/dp/B078H3WTF2

Experience Singapore paperback;
https://www.amazon.com/dp/1983788686

Experience India's Golden Triangle ebook;
https://www.amazon.com/dp/B078H9VPJB

Experience Istanbul ebook; https://www.amazon.com/dp/B078RKX7BX

Experience Istanbul paperback;
https://www.amazon.com/dp/1983827649

Experience Melbourne ebook;
https://www.amazon.com/dp/B078R1CZMF

Experience Melbourne paperback;
https://www.amazon.com/dp/1983494038

We welcome comments from readers. Please send them by email to len_rutledge@bigpond.com

# Index

# ABOUT THE AUTHOR

Len Rutledge has been travel writing for 40 years. During that time he has written thousands of newspaper articles, numerous magazine pieces, more than a thousand web reviews and around 45 travel guide books. He has worked with Pelican Publishing, Viking Penguin, Berlitz, the Rough Guide and the Nile Guide amongst others.

Along the way, he has started a newspaper, a travel magazine, a Visitor and TV guide, and completed a PhD in tourism. His travels have taken him to more than 100 countries and his writings have collected a PATA award, an ASEAN award, an IgoUgo Hall of Fame award, and other recognition.

You can see more details on the author's website: www.LenRutledge.com

# ABOUT THE PHOTOGRAPHER

Phensri Rutledge was born in Thailand but has lived in Australia for many years. For 30 years her photographs have appeared in a range of guidebooks and in newspapers and magazines in Europe, North America, Asia, and Australia. Her travels have taken her to all continents except Antarctica through over 80 countries.

She contributes to several travel websites and has a number of popular social media sites including a Google+ site with over 5 million views and thousands of followers. See http://google.com/+PhensriRutledge

You can follow her Facebook page **World Travel Photography** and as **pensri_focus** on Instagram.

Printed in Great
Britain
by Amazon